W9-BQA-510

For Amy Cohen, Janet Halligan and Amy Raider

CONTENTS

Foreword by Sam Rosen

100 RANGER *Greats*

SUPERSTARS, UNSUNG HEROES AND COLORFUL CHARACTERS

RUSS COHEN • JOHN HALLIGAN • ADAM RAIDER

WILEY

John Wiley & Sons Canada, Ltd.

Copyright © 2009 Russ Cohen, John Halligan and Adam Raider

All rights reserved. No part of this work covered by the copyright
herein may be reproduced or used in any form or by any means—
graphic, electronic or mechanical without the prior written permission
of the publisher. Any request for photocopying, recording, taping or
information storage and retrieval systems of any part of this book shall
be directed in writing to The Canadian Copyright Licensing Agency
(Access Copyright). For an Access Copyright license, visit www.ac-
cesscopyright.ca or call toll free 1-800-893-5777.

All photographs courtesy of the authors or the New York Rangers
unless otherwise noted.

Library and Archives Canada Cataloguing in Publication
Cohen, Russ
    100 Ranger greats : superstars, unsung heroes and colorful
characters / Russ Cohen, John Halligan, Adam Raider.

Includes index.
ISBN 978-0-470-73619-7

    1. New York Rangers (Hockey team)—Biography. 2. Hockey
players—New York (State)—New York—Biography. 3. New York
Rangers (Hockey team)—History. I. Halligan, John, 1941- II. Raider,
Adam III. Title. IV. Title: One hundred Ranger greats.

GV848.N43C64 2009   796.962092'27471   C2009-902925-1

Production Credits
Cover design, interior design and typesetting: Adrian So
Printer: Friesens

John Wiley & Sons Canada, Ltd.
6045 Freemont Blvd.
Mississauga, Ontario
L5R 4J3

Printed in Canada
1 2 3 4 5 FR 13 12 11 10 09

The Canadian Press (Todd Plitt)

CONTENTS

FOREWORD By Sam Rosen

I can't remember exactly when I began to love the New York Rangers. It was sometime in the late 1950s when I started to go to games on Sunday nights at the old Madison Square Garden. I had read about them in the sports pages of New York's many newspapers, so I knew all about Andy Bathgate and Gump Worsley, Camille Henry and Andy Hebenton, Harry Howell and Lou Fontinato. But it wasn't until I started making the mad dash up the steps to the MSG balcony, to get seats in the first two rows so I could see the entire ice without standing up for the whole game, that I truly got to know and love my heroes. They certainly weren't the best team in the league, but they didn't lack heart, and some of them, like Bathgate, Worsley and Howell, were among the best players in the game, eventually winding up in the Hall of Fame.

Of course, as all Rangers fans know, once you love the Blueshirts, there's no turning away. There were heroes aplenty. When Bathgate, Henry and Hebenton were gone, along came Rod Gilbert, Jean Ratelle and Vic Hadfield. Brad Park followed Harry Howell, and a few years after the Gumper went to Montreal, in stepped Eddie Giacomin.

The '70s began with the Rangers as serious Stanley Cup contenders and ended with an improbable run at the Cup in 1979 that came up just three wins short. Phil Esposito had come from Boston and went from hated Bruin to loved Ranger. The chants of "JAY-DEE! JAY-DEE!" filled the Garden, and Don Murdoch, Ron Duguay, Ron Greschner and the Maloney brothers, Dave and Don, were the new young stars.

That time brought a new appreciation of the Rangers for me. In 1973, I went to work for United Press International's Audio Network, and part of my time was spent covering hockey at Madison Square Garden reporting on not only the Rangers but also all the teams they played against. In 1978 came one of my most exciting, career-changing moments when I was assigned to fill in for Marv Albert on a Rangers radio broadcast. Working alongside legendary analyst and Hall of Fame broadcaster Sal "Red Light" Messina, I proceeded to spill coffee all over our notes and statistics but didn't flub the call as the Rangers played the Atlanta Flames. One of my many career dreams had come true. I was calling games for the team I had grown up with, cheered for and—win or lose—loved.

The 1980s saw the "Smurfs," led by Olympic hero Mark Pavelich, bring an exciting style of hockey to the Garden. In 1984, along came the Beezer, John Vanbiesbrouck, and Rangers fans had another star goalie to chant for. That year was also a special time for me because in September, I was chosen to be the TV play-by-play voice of the New York Rangers. What an honor! What a thrill! And I was working alongside one of the greatest players to ever play the game, Phil Esposito. When Espo moved up to the front office as general manager in 1986, another great thing happened to me: John Davidson came back to New York from Canada to be the Rangers' TV analyst. Thus began a 20-year run in the booth for me and J.D.

Also in 1986, the Rangers made what I think was their best draft pick ever when they chose Brian Leetch with the ninth pick in the first round. He joined the team after the 1988 Olympics and began a career that would see him become one of the greatest Rangers ever.

Soon after Leetch came to New York, Mike Richter followed to begin a career that would make him the best Rangers goalie of all time. In 1991 Adam Graves became a Ranger, and the heart of the team grew. Then, just after the start of the 1991–92 season, the Rangers acquired the man who would lead them to the Promised Land: the Captain, Mark Messier. He was the ultimate team leader, the best in Rangers history. That foursome was the nucleus of the team that would finally end the Stanley Cup drought in New York.

What a thrill it was for me to watch so many great players and get to know so many great people who wore the Rangers blue and created so many memorable moments. They came from all over the world and left their mark. From Sweden there was Anders Hedberg followed by Tomas Sandstrom and Jan Erixon; Reijo Ruotsalainen and Esa Tikkanen from Finland; the Russians, Sergei Nemchinov, Alex Kovalev and Sergei Zubov; Petr Nedved and Jaromir Jagr from the Czech Republic. There were all-time greats like Mike Gartner and, the greatest of them all, Wayne Gretzky. They are among the many who have made the New York Rangers so special.

This book will rekindle the memories of why we became Rangers fans and what it was about these players that made us love them. For me, that started when I was a kid and, like so many other parents, I passed that love down to my kids and now to their kids. I can't remember when it started, but I know it will last a lifetime.

Sam Rosen is one of the most respected play-by-play announcers in all of hockey. He also works as a play-by-play announcer for FOX's coverage of the National Football League.

INTRODUCTION

For over 80 years, the New York Rangers have maintained some pretty strong ties to the people of New York City, the outlying suburbs and beyond. That has never been more evident than on the evening of June 14, 1994, when captain Mark Messier passed the glistening Stanley Cup into Madison Square Garden's roaring and very appreciative crowd for the fans to touch.

It was the culmination of a truly magical season for this long-suffering "Original Six" team. In fact, it wouldn't be a stretch to call it the greatest season the Rangers have ever known.

But, and this may be hard for some fans to accept, it was just *one* season—one chapter in a much longer story that began in 1926 when boxing promoter George (Tex) Rickard was awarded an expansion team to compete against the Garden's other tenants, the New York Americans. The Rangers' clean and efficient play promptly earned them a reputation as "the classiest team in hockey," and by 1940 they had won three Stanley Cups, giving their growing legion of supporters no reason to doubt that many more championships were to come.

That one of the proudest and most storied franchises in North American team sports had to wait more than a half-century to win again is a fact that can't be sugarcoated or glossed over. But in shining a light so brightly on the feats of Messier and his merry band of dragon slayers, one risks obscuring other Rangers heroes in the glare—men like Ron Greschner, Rod Gilbert and Andy Bathgate, whose supporting casts were never quite good enough to break that so-called curse. And let's be careful not to dismiss as ancient history the accomplishments of Depression-era stars like Frank Boucher, Ivan (Ching) Johnson and Bill Cook just because they didn't model designer suits in last month's issue of *GQ*.

It was this train of thought that prompted three Ranger experts to join forces and set the record straight. Which brings us to the main objective of this book: to identify, celebrate and rank the 100 most influential players from the team's first eight decades, regardless of what they may have accomplished before or after their time in New York.

Players, many of whom were interviewed for this book, were graded according to their contributions to the overall success of the teams on which they played, plus individual achievements such as points scored, awards won, popularity and length of service.

So exhaustive is our top 100 list that it includes 26 Hall-of-Famers (and counting), 20 career Rangers, a dozen goaltenders, nine members of the 1994 Stanley Cup team, four Dons, three pairs of siblings, two Finns, a Civil War buff and even a "Polish Prince."

Our list does *not* include names like Guy Lafleur, Bernie (Boom Boom) Geoffrion, Tim Horton, Terry Sawchuk, Doug Harvey or Pat LaFontaine. They are all Hall of Fame legends, to be sure, but their Ranger careers were simply too brief to warrant consideration for this compendium. As well, we were forced to omit the likes of Johnny Bower, Rick Middleton, Eddie Shack, Marc Savard and Doug Weight—all superb players who began their NHL careers in New York, but rose to stardom elsewhere.

The jury's still out on Ryan Callahan, Chris Drury, Marc Staal and some other current Rangers, though we expect some or all will muscle their way onto the list in a future edition (sequel, anyone?).

Looking back, however enjoyable it may have been for the three of us, deciding which players to include and where to rank them was hardly an easy task, and far from an exact science. The process was one that we agonized over at considerable length, particularly when we got to the top ten.

Then again, books of this type are, by their very nature, designed to spark friendly debates and arguments.

We've had our fun. Now it's your turn.

Let the debates begin.

Russ Cohen, Glassboro, NJ
John Halligan, Franklin Lakes, NJ
Adam Raider, West Hartford, CT
May, 2009

100

NICK FOTIU

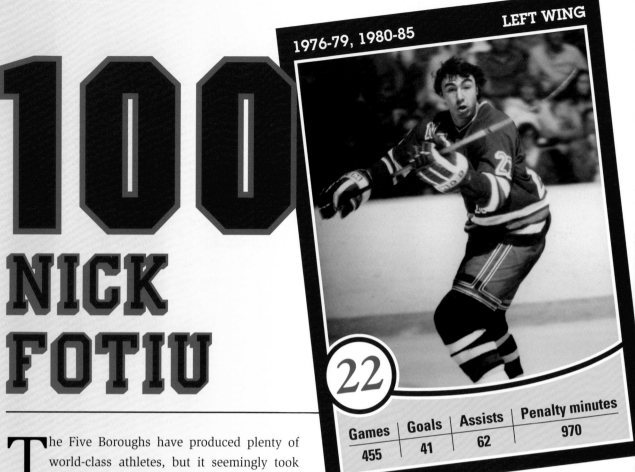

1976-79, 1980-85

LEFT WING

22

Games	Goals	Assists	Penalty minutes
455	41	62	970

T he Five Boroughs have produced plenty of world-class athletes, but it seemingly took forever for the first native New Yorker to suit up for the Rangers. Nicholas Evlampios Fotiu made the most of the opportunity, compensating for a dearth of natural ability with grit and desire.

It was hockey's ultimate Cinderella story ... if Cinderella was six-foot-two, weighed 210 pounds and had hands big enough to catch pop flies in Yankee Stadium without the aid of a glove.

Fotiu (pronounced "Foe-TEE-you") grew up on Staten Island in the blue-collar Dongon Hills-South Beach section where he was raised by his Italian mother and Greek father. A huge Rangers fan, he didn't learn to skate until he was 15 and would travel for nearly three hours (Staten Island Ferry to the subway to the Long Island Railroad) to find ice at Skateland, the Rangers' old practice rink in New Hyde Park.

"I carried a small hatchet in my bag," he recalled, "since I always traveled alone at three, four, five in the morning."

By then, Nick was already telling anyone who would listen—his folks, buddies from the neighborhood, and even Rangers' assistant trainer Jimmy Young—that one day, he'd be the first fan to come down from Madison Square Garden's old "blue seats" (being the least expensive and farthest from the action) to play for the Rangers. Of course, nobody believed him.

But by adopting a rugged style and remembering a few tips he'd picked up at Rod Gilbert's summer hockey camp, Fotiu found success playing in the Metropolitan Junior Hockey League, an amateur league started by former Ranger coach and general manager Emile Francis in the mid 1960s. From there the brawny left wing literally fought his way onto the Cape Cod Cubs of the North American League and then the World Hockey Association's New England Whalers.

In a roundabout way, Atlanta Flames winger Curt Bennett is responsible for getting Fotiu to the NHL. On March 7, 1976, Bennett blindsided Ranger defenseman Dave Maloney and when no other Rangers came

to his rescue, an infuriated GM John Ferguson decided the club needed to add some muscle. Fotiu, then in his second season with the Whalers, was at the top of Fergy's wish list.

In exchange for Fotiu's negotiation rights, Ferguson agreed to have the Rangers play three exhibition games in Hartford over the next three years.

"Nicky Boy" was Broadway-bound and would stay for a total of eight seasons in two tours with the Blueshirts, combining modest offensive production and surprising quickness with a deserved reputation as one of the game's top enforcers—one who could go toe-to-toe with Dave (The Hammer) Schultz, Paul Holmgren and other tough guys of the day.

How good a fighter was Fotiu? Good enough to win a Police Athletic League crown. His agent, the late Larry Rauch, even wanted Nicky to pursue "the sweet science" as a full-time profession.

"I thought he had a much better future in the ring than on the ice," Rauch said. "But the kid was so obsessed with making it in hockey that I gave up."

Enforcers come and go but what really set Fotiu apart from the garden-variety goon was his special bond with the fans. It's common these days for players to gently toss souvenir pucks over the glass at the Garden, but Nick's habit of throwing pucks all the way to the blue seats after pregame warm-ups endeared him to the crowd while greatly disturbing his coaches, who feared a shoulder injury, as well as Garden lawyers and security folks who feared for someone falling out of the balcony.

It was not lost on Fotiu, who got into scouting and coaching after his retirement in 1990, that his popularity was a big factor in his being named the

A huge Rangers fan, he didn't learn to skate until he was 15.

100th greatest Ranger. "I don't mind being near the bottom of the list at all," he said. "Hell, if the fans voted, I'd be number one."

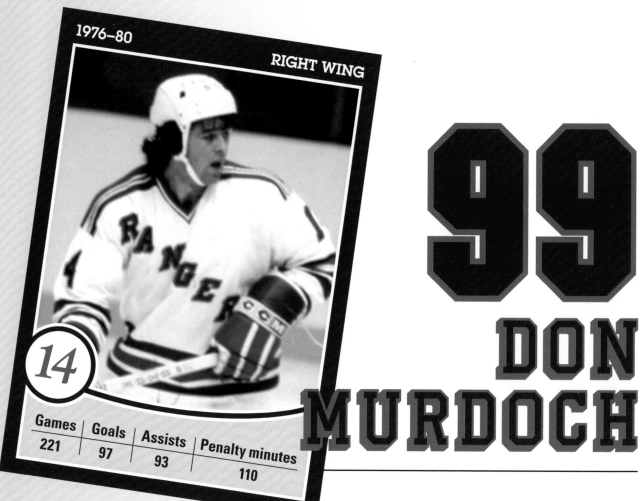

1976–80

RIGHT WING

14

Games	Goals	Assists	Penalty minutes
221	97	93	110

99
DON MURDOCH

A h, to be a young celebrity in New York City. Don Murdoch was on the fast track to stardom, but in an era of excess, a career that began with so much promise was derailed by substance abuse.

Ranger scouts first fell in love with Murdoch after he posted back-to-back 80-goal seasons with Medicine Hat of the Western Canadian Junior Hockey League. Many in the organization viewed him as perhaps the best young player in all of Western Canada and were stunned when he was still available when the Rangers picked sixth overall at the 1976 draft.

One of Murdoch's greatest assets was his deceptive stride. Appearing heavier than his 180 pounds, he didn't look especially quick or agile but he knew how to fake an opposing player into over-committing himself. Gaining speed, he'd glide around flat-footed veterans who, out of sheer frustration, might reach out and grab him or dive into his skates—anything to prevent him from getting off a shot.

Murdoch often found himself a marked man in juniors, too. Once, he jumped off the bench to rescue his team's goaltender who had just been attacked by some players on the New Westminster Bruins. Three Bruins beat Murdoch unconscious but his heroics earned the respect of GM John Ferguson, himself a former enforcer, and greatly improved the young winger's chances of making the Rangers straight out of juniors instead of being assigned to the minor leagues.

Replacing veteran Bill Fairbairn in the lineup, Murdoch was put on a line with Walt Tkaczuk and Greg Polis and scored twice in his first pro game. On October 12, 1976, he scored five goals against Gary Smith of the Minnesota North Stars—a club record he still shares with Mark Pavelich.

"Donnie," observed former roommate and team captain Dave Maloney, "was one of the top three natural goal scorers I ever played with."

Injuries limited Murdoch to 32 goals in a season that saw him finish runner-up to Atlanta's Willi Plett for the 1977 Calder Trophy as rookie of the year. His

second season was hampered by a shoulder injury but he still collected 27 goals.

The future still looked bright for the hotshot teammates nicknamed "Murder," even though his idea of conditioning was 20 push-ups before the pregame skate, occasionally followed by tearful apologies to his mates ("I'm sorry guys, I'll do better, I promise"). It was impossible not to love Murdoch. He was like an adult teddy bear.

But Murdoch's is a cautionary tale of how a young celebrity can succumb to the temptations of stardom. A regular at the city's hottest nightspots, he was by no means the lone sinner on a team of saints, but his wild behavior began to affect his job.

In August 1977, Murdoch was caught at the Toronto airport with almost five grams of cocaine. Years later, he admitted that the strain of his newfound fame had turned a drinking habit into a drug addiction. After pleading guilty to the charge, Murdoch was suspended 40 games for the 1978–79 season.

He returned in time to take part in the 1979 playoff run and had some success playing on the "Godfather Line" with Phil Esposito and Don Maloney, but Murdoch had already done irreparable damage to his image in the eyes of Rangers brass. It was clear that his days in New York were numbered.

The next year Murdoch was traded to Edmonton where he played on a line with Dave Semenko and a young Mark Messier. He had a last shot with the Detroit Red Wings before ending his career in the minors.

"Donnie was a great talent, an unbelievable goal scorer and just an absolutely great guy in the room," said Mike McEwen, who teamed with Murdoch for three seasons. "He was one of the funniest guys around, telling stories. If he had taken better care of himself, he would have had a great career. He just burned the candle at both ends."

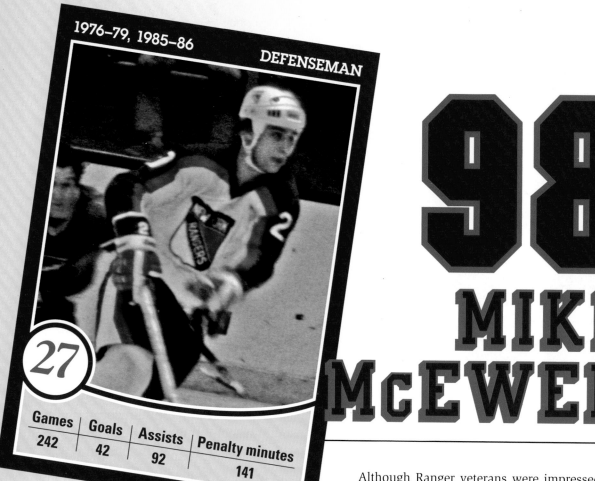

1976–79, 1985–86

DEFENSEMAN

27

Games	Goals	Assists	Penalty minutes
242	42	92	141

98
MIKE McEWEN

One of many in the long line of converted baseball players, Mike McEwen was a talented offensive defenseman who played over 700 NHL games in the 1970s and 1980s.

McEwen, who had been a star pitcher in his teens, was chosen 42nd overall by the Rangers in the 1976 draft after a stellar junior career with the Toronto Marlboros, with whom he won a Memorial Cup the prior season.

During his rookie campaign of 1976–77, "Q" was paired up with veteran Carol Vadnais and made a nice first impression with 14 goals and 43 points.

"But I drove coaches crazy because I was weak defensively," McEwen said. "I don't think I ever played on a penalty-killing unit my whole time in the NHL. But I could move the puck, get back and beat a forecheck, get the rush going in neutral ice and create opportunities for the forwards or myself."

Although Ranger veterans were impressed with McEwen's obvious skill, he found it difficult to find allies in the dressing room.

"I don't know if I had a bit of an attitude," he said, "but I was a hard worker and really driven. I didn't do things the wrong way but I just pissed everybody off because anytime they tried to help me I'd say, 'I know, I know' and I wasn't open to suggestions from my teammates, which I should have been."

Former teammate Pat Hickey saw something of himself in the stubborn-minded defenseman, and the two became good friends.

"Q was like me when I came in," Hickey said. "He was just a young, cocky kid who needed a friend. A lot of guys sort of jumped on his back. He was as talented as Ron Greschner, but different. You never knew what he was going to do. He had breakaway speed and man, he could turn a nothing play into something really quick with a good pass or good legs or a good shot. He was that type of player."

In 1978–79, McEwen scored a career-best 20 goals, led all Rangers defensemen with 58 points and helped the Blueshirts reach the Stanley Cup Final. Although the Rangers didn't win it all, he called that playoff run the highlight of his career.

"I won in a few other places," he said, "but it was nothing like New York. When we beat the Islanders in the sixth game of the semifinals at the Garden, I guess there were 10,000 people outside and they shut off Eighth Avenue to Seventh Avenue. On 33rd Street, we had to be escorted out by the cops for about a block because the fans were crazy and everybody was celebrating. I had my family with me from Toronto and they had four mounted police officers on each side of us. There we were, walking between these four horses through this crowd of crazies who were all happy, yelling and screaming."

The next year, McEwen was part of the package sent to the Colorado Rockies for star blueliner Barry Beck.

McEwen eventually ended up back in New York but on the other side of the East River. Joining a defense corps with Denis Potvin and Ken Morrow, McEwen was part of three straight Stanley Cup winners on Long Island.

Six years later, the Rangers got McEwen back from Detroit in exchange for Steve Richmond but they lost him again in 1986 when he was traded to Hartford for Bob Crawford. McEwen's career also included stints with the Washington Capitals and Los Angeles Kings.

He later joined the pro coaching ranks with the Central Hockey League's Oklahoma City Blazers and became active in the city's youth hockey programs.

1932–35   GOALTENDER

1

Games	Record	Shutouts	GAA
106	47-43-16	11	2.35

97 ANDY AITKENHEAD

Precious little is known about the blond, blue-eyed man described in a 1933 *TIME* magazine article as the Rangers' "youthful, mop-haired, talkative goaltender."

We do know that Andy Aitkenhead (as in "an achin' head") had one of the great names for a player whose idea of skull protection was a tweed cap and that his acrobatic style was a hit with fans. We also know that he led the 1932–33 Rangers to the Stanley Cup, their second in only seven years of operation.

Nicknamed "The Glasgow Gobbler" because he was born in Glasgow, Scotland, and, presumably, because he gobbled up pucks like a hungry octopus, Aitkenhead played ten years in various minor leagues out west before a twist of fate led to him getting his big chance in the NHL.

In October 1932, the Detroit Falcons—precursors to the Red Wings—purchased John Ross Roach from the Rangers in a cash deal that saw one of the best goalies of the day switch cities.

The Rangers were $11,000 richer but now had a gaping hole on their roster. Enter Aitkenhead, whose fortunes brought him to New York a year earlier for a job stopping rubber with the Can-Am League's Bronx Tigers. He immediately became the leading candidate to succeed Roach, but the Rangers stayed on the lookout for a more experienced goalie … just in case.

Since a better substitute never materialized, Aitkenhead was in net on November 10, 1932, when the Rangers opened the season on the road against the Montreal Maroons. Making some spectacular saves that even coaxed applause from the locals, the new acquisition backstopped the Blueshirts to a 4–2 victory and kicked off a magical year for himself and the hockey club.

Accustomed to playing before sparse crowds at the old Bronx Coliseum near Webster Avenue, Aitkenhead was soon the darling of 15,000 fans at Madison Square Garden.

He posted a 23-17-8 record and was equally marvelous in eight playoff appearances, winning six and recording two shutouts en route to a four-game victory over Toronto in the championship series. At only

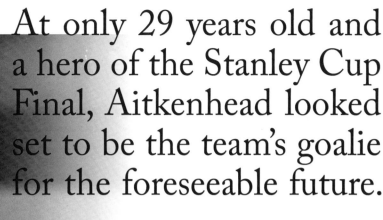

At only 29 years old and a hero of the Stanley Cup Final, Aitkenhead looked set to be the team's goalie for the foreseeable future.

29 years old and a hero of the Stanley Cup Final, Aitkenhead looked set to be the team's goalie for the foreseeable future.

But then, the following March, it was revealed that the goalie had suffered what was termed a "nervous breakdown." The true nature of Aitkenhead's malady is unclear, but it was severe enough to prompt manager Lester Patrick to ask permission to borrow Ottawa goalie Alex Connell for the 1934 playoffs if his own netminder was unable to perform.

That contingency plan was abandoned when Aitkenhead returned to close out the regular season and prepare for another run at the Stanley Cup. His play was sharp but the Rangers were upset by the Maroons in a best-of-three quarterfinal series.

Patrick's confidence in Aitkenhead didn't waver until the goalie dropped seven of his first ten starts the following season. A shake-up was required and as swiftly as his Ranger career began, the Gobbler lost his job to veteran Davey Kerr.

Professionally speaking, it was a terrible break for a goalie trying to make his way in what was then a nine-team league (the NHL didn't become a six-team circuit until 1942). Since clubs did not carry backups, only the nine best goalies in the game were ever assured employment.

Aitkenhead's first shot at the big time would be his last and he spent the next six seasons back in the minor pros before retiring in 1941.

1954–61

DEFENSEMAN

Imperial Oil-Turofsky/Hockey Hall of Fame

8

Games	Goals	Assists	Penalty minutes
418	22	57	939

96 LOU FONTINATO

The Rangers have a long, proud history of tough defensemen, most of whom also had catchy nicknames. Ivan (Ching) Johnson and Clarence (Taffy) Abel started the trend in the 1920s. Murray (Muzz) Patrick, Walter (Babe) Pratt and Art (The Trapper) Coulter picked up the mantle in the late 1930s and early 1940s. But the 1950s belonged to only one man: "Leapin' Lou" Fontinato.

Fontinato was a one-of-a-kind rearguard. His rhinoceros-like rushes up and down the ice made him a fan favorite, the "People's Choice" in fact, in an era that was as colorful as any in Rangers history. Fontinato was the most colorful player on those teams, exceeded only, at times, by his flamboyant coach, Phil Watson, and by goaltender Lorne (Gump) Worsley.

Part of his color, his appeal to the fans, came from the nickname "Leapin' Lou," which had two sources. His crisp, clean body checks were often preceded by

a leap from his skates. Another leap, this one straight up in the air, often followed to protest the many penalties he drew.

Make no mistake—Fontinato was a solid defenseman, a fearsome body checker, and well skilled at getting the puck out of the Rangers' defensive zone. But it was his fighting, brawling really, that brought him fame. He took on all comers, big and small alike, won most all of his bouts and seemed to enjoy it heartily, smiling widely before and after many of his altercations.

"Some day, I'm gonna get licked," he said at the time. "It happens to everybody. But they gotta beat me to make me believe it." The beating he'd been expecting came in spades on February 1, 1959, during an afternoon game with the Detroit Red Wings at Madison Square Garden. Those who were there will never forget it.

Gordie Howe, Detroit's nonpareil right wing and probably the strongest man in the NHL at the time, was having his way in a fight with Fontinato's teammate, left wing Eddie Shack. "Leapin' Lou" barreled

halfway across the rink and took on Howe, landing several robust punches.

Howe responded with a single punch—a short right hand—that shattered Fontinato's nose and left it pointing south while the rest of Louie's face pointed east. It was a bloody knockout, even though Fontinato never went down. Fontinato's face was such that even officials Glen Skov and Frank Udvari couldn't look as he was escorted off the ice.

A photo of Louie, by ace New York *Daily News* lensman Charlie Hoff, made the wire services and ran in newspapers across North America. Observed one sportswriter: "It [Fontinato's nose] looked like an afterthought, like it was stuck on his weather-beaten face by a careless sculptor."

Ever the battler, Fontinato claimed for years afterward that he didn't really lose the fight by as wide a margin as that picture made it seem. At times, he's been reluctant to call it a loss at all. "It was no worse than a draw," he said more than 40 years after the historic clash. "I'm sure I must have thrown a few punches to go that far." The most important detail about that night is the one most often forgotten: the Rangers won the game, 5–4.

Fontinato came to New York in 1954 following a solid junior career with the Guelph Biltmores, who were Memorial Cup champions in 1952, and some pro experience with Vancouver and Saskatoon of the Western Hockey League. He stayed for seven years and 418 games, amassing 939 penalty minutes. He led the NHL with 202 minutes in 1955–56 and with 152 minutes in 1957–58.

Fontinato was dealt to the Montreal Canadiens in exchange for perennial All-Star Doug Harvey on June 13, 1961. His playing career would end tragically when he suffered a broken neck in a game against the Rangers at the Montreal Forum on March 9, 1963. Ironically, the man Fontinato was trying to check at the time was the Rangers' new fan favorite and captain-to-be, Vic Hadfield.

Today, Lou operates a cattle farm in Campbellville, Ontario.

95

LORNE CHABOT

Turofsky/Hockey Hall of Fame

GOALTENDER

1926–28

1

Games	Record	Shutouts	GAA
80	41-25-14	21	1.61

A World War I veteran and former Royal Canadian Mountie, Lorne Chabot first rose to prominence as the best amateur goalie in the Dominion after backstopping the Port Arthur Bearcats to consecutive Allan Cup triumphs in 1925 and 1926. Following the second of these, Conn Smythe signed Chabot to play for a new National Hockey League club about to open play in New York City: the Rangers.

Two months into the Rangers' inaugural 1926–27 season, Smythe was fired by team president Col. John S. Hammond and Chabot took the starting job away from Hal Winkler.

Early on, Lorne received an introduction to bush-league marketing techniques.

Someone in the Rangers front office, probably publicity man Johnny Bruno, decided that the team needed a more ethnic flavor to attract the city's rapidly growing immigrant population. So Lorne Chabot, a French Canadian out of Montreal, became the deliberately Semitic-sounding "Lorne Chabotsky" in press releases and box scores. He

was not pleased, and neither was general manager-coach Lester Patrick.

Chabot and the team soon put that botched publicity stunt behind them, but the nickname stuck with him for years.

At six-foot-one and weighing 185 pounds, the bushy-haired rookie was an exceptionally large player by the standards of the era, but he had terrific mobility and focus. And he was *good*, posting a 22-9-5 record with ten shutouts.

He earned a reputation for honesty, too, reportedly turning down a sizeable bribe to throw a game and immediately reporting the incident to Patrick.

The following season, Chabot played all 44 regular-season games and blanked the opposition 11 times while helping New York reach the Stanley Cup Final. But as fate would have it, the young goalie was about to play an unfortunate role in one of the most remarkable episodes in the history of the sport.

In the second game of the championship series against the Montreal Maroons, Chabot was badly hurt when Montreal winger Nels Stewart unleashed a shot that struck the Ranger goalie in his left eye. Blood gushed from the wound, and Chabot had to be helped off the ice. A severe hemorrhage developed, and he was taken to the Royal Victoria Hospital where doctors initially feared he might lose his eye.

The Rangers, however, still had a game to finish.

Teams didn't carry backup goalies, and the Maroons refused to let the Rangers use Ottawa goalie Alex Connell, in attendance that evening as a specta- tor. So Patrick, the 44-year-old coach who'd retired as a defenseman six years earlier, was forced to make an emergency appearance between the pipes. The inspired (and somewhat desperate) Blueshirts ral- lied around old Lester and went on to win that game in overtime. Joe Miller, on loan from the New York Americans, started in place of Chabot for the remain- der of the series, helping the Rangers win their first Stanley Cup. Released from the hospital a week after his injury, Chabot sat in the stands during the Cup- clinching game wearing a black eye patch.

Chabot eventually made a full recovery but he lost the confidence of Patrick, who seemed to fear that the events of the previous spring might leave the netminder a bit puck shy. So in October of 1928, the Rangers traded Chabot to the Toronto Maple Leafs with $10,000 for John Ross Roach and Butch Keeling.

Over the next seven years Chabot remained one of the league's elite goaltenders, adding a second Stanley Cup to his résumé in 1932 and a Vezina Trophy in 1935. If Lorne was puck shy, he had an odd way of showing it.

But only ten years after playing his final game, Chabot passed away in Montreal at the age of 46 from nephritis, a chronic kidney disease.

His career record of 201 wins against 148 losses (and 72 shutouts) compares favorably to those of many Hall of Fame goalies, but induction to that shrine still eludes the man once known as "Chabotsky."

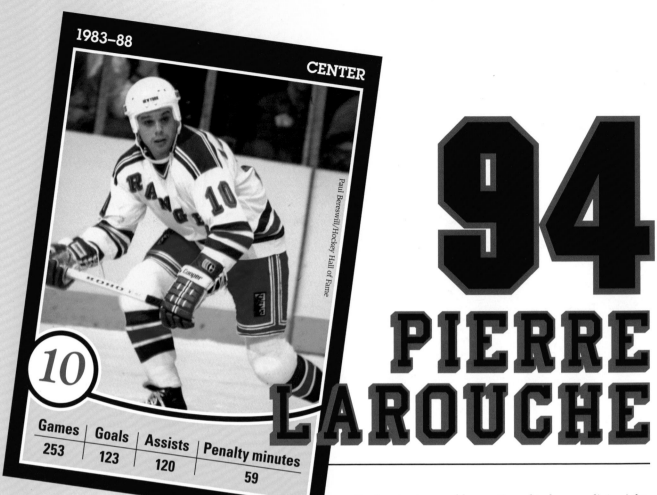

1983–88

CENTER

Paul Bereswill/Hockey Hall of Fame

10

Games	Goals	Assists	Penalty minutes
253	123	120	59

94
PIERRE LAROUCHE

Skill and charisma made "Lucky Pierre" Larouche a fan favorite everywhere he played, and New York was no exception.

His nickname was misleading since much of the success Larouche enjoyed as a goal scorer came not from luck, but from stealth and cunning. At his most dangerous when drifting unnoticed through the offensive zone, Larouche would emerge from a cluster of players at the goaltender's doorstep, poised to convert a pass for an effortless tap-in goal.

"Tubby [another of Larouche's nicknames] was one of my favorite people of all time in the game," said former line mate Kelly Kisio. "He was a card—so loose. And he was so talented. He played the game so well that you kind of shook your head sometimes at some of the stuff he could do with the puck. He was a great guy and it was fun to play with him."

As a youth, the free-spirited French Canadian had been one of the greatest scorers in the history of the

Quebec juniors and he continued to be a goalie's nightmare as a rookie on the Pittsburgh Penguins. In 1976, he became the youngest 50-goal scorer in NHL history (a record since broken by Wayne Gretzky) when he achieved the feat five months after his 20th birthday.

But Larouche was somewhat undisciplined in his early years—there were occasional suspensions for lateness to practice and missing curfew—and he struggled to find consistency. It was a stigma that he carried with him from city to city.

Signed as a free agent by the Rangers in 1983 after wearing out his welcome in Montreal (where he won a pair of Stanley Cups) and Hartford, Larouche strived to shake a reputation for immaturity and earn a job centering one of New York's top lines.

In his first Rangers season, Larouche led the team with 48 goals and joined teammate Don Maloney at the 1984 All-Star Game. In terms of style, the two couldn't have been more different.

Where Maloney oozed grit, Larouche was the essence of finesse. Herb Brooks, that master of the one-liners, once said that asking Larouche to dig in the corners was "like asking Picasso to paint a garage," but there were no complaints. The Rangers were happy to have a pure goal scorer who could bring fans out of their seats with miraculous moves, and Larouche was excited to get a fresh start with a new team.

But Pierre never scored more than 28 goals in his next three seasons, and the unpredictability that vexed Montreal's Scotty Bowman and other coaches also caused friction between Larouche and Brooks's replacement, Ted Sator, who interpreted the center man's bubbly personality as a lack of seriousness about the game.

Others suspected that Larouche just wanted to feel appreciated and was tired of having to prove himself year after year in order to earn performance bonuses … and respect.

"If you treat a guy like a maverick," former agent Bob Ingraham said, "he'll be one."

Sator wasn't buying it and in his first season behind the Blueshirts' bench, he banished Larouche to the Flyers' farm team in Hershey—a move officially announced as compensation for the Rangers having signed Sator away from the Philadelphia organization—but had to bring the veteran back in the final weeks of the 1985–86 season to rescue a team desperate for goals.

Larouche had such a hot hand during the '86 playoffs that around the locker room, he became known as "the fire starter." The Rangers made it to the Conference Finals in a campaign that looked lost before the return of Lucky Pierre, who ended up being one of the few players in the history of hockey to score 20 goals in two different leagues in the same year.

There's no telling how wide the rift with Sator might have grown had it not been for a pinched nerve in Larouche's lower back, an injury that eventually ended his career when he decided to retire during training camp in 1988.

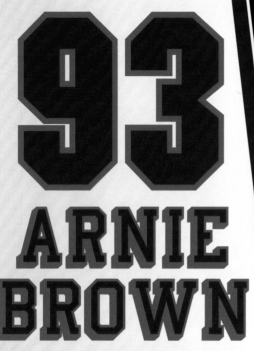

93
ARNIE BROWN

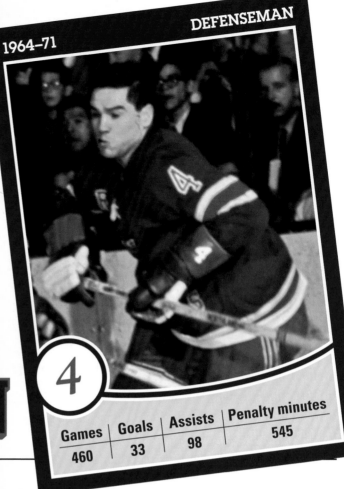

1964–71

DEFENSEMAN

4

Games	Goals	Assists	Penalty minutes
460	33	98	545

The blockbuster trade that brought Arnie Brown to New York on February 22, 1964, was the biggest in Rangers' history at the time. It shocked almost everyone—players and fans alike. No one, however, was more shocked than Brown himself, a robust 22-year-old defenseman who quite literally had been raised in the organization of the Toronto Maple Leafs.

As a junior, Brown came up through the legendary St. Mike's Majors program, even winning Canada's junior hockey championship, the Memorial Cup, in 1961 under coaching icon Father David Bauer. The Leafs, loaded with defensemen at the time, looked at Brown for a handful of NHL games, signed him to a pro contract and sent him to their top farm club, the Rochester Americans of the American Hockey League.

Then the trade, "the Bathgate Trade" as it became known, happened. The Rangers shipped their captain, superstar right wing Andy Bathgate, north with center Don (Slip) McKenney. Coming to New York were Brown, highly touted defenseman Rod Seiling and veterans Bob Nevin, Dick Duff and Billy Collins.

If there was any extra pressure on Brown, having been traded for such a luminary as Bathgate, it never showed. He spent 11 games in the minors with the AHL's Baltimore Clippers at the end of the 1963–64 season, and then the five-foot-eleven, 180-pounder cracked the Ranger lineup for good. He stayed for seven years and 460 games.

Brown's first two years in New York were boisterous, physical ones. He led the Rangers with 145 penalty minutes in 1964–65 and following that with 106 minutes the next year. "Arnie was like a bowling ball those first two years, knocking guys all over the place," recalled teammate Vic Hadfield. "He had a wicked hip check that wiped people out at the blue line."

Soft-spoken, thoughtful and articulate, Brown became somewhat of a media favorite. Veteran hockey writer Mel Woody of *The Newark News* called him "the

best interview on the team, and one of the easiest guys I've ever covered. He doesn't talk in platitudes, and is as comfortable discussing red wine or Broadway shows as he is discussing Bobby Hull or Jean Béliveau."

Despite his dyed-in-the-wool Maple Leafs pedigree, Brown quickly grew to appreciate New York and its pleasures. "Don't get me wrong, when the trade happened, I felt a little betrayed," he said. "I really resented being traded and couldn't understand why. I felt like I was being sent to the dark depths. I had never even been to New York.

"In retrospect, though, the trade was the best thing that ever happened to me. If it hadn't happened, I might still be a mediocre, unhappy player in Toronto."

About midway into his time in New York, under the tutelage of veteran Harry Howell, his longtime defensive partner, Brown discarded his aggressive style, lost a little weight and became, of all things, a scorer! After scoring only five goals in his first four seasons as

a Blueshirt, he tallied 10 times in 1968–69, and added 15 more the next year, the most ever by a Ranger defenseman at the time.

Just past midseason of 1970–71, the Rangers were heavy on defensemen. Brad Park was at his prime, the great Tim Horton had been acquired from Toronto and veterans Dale Rolfe, Jim Neilson and Ron Harris were also aboard.

General manager and coach Emile Francis thought the team was ready for a run at the Stanley Cup, but he needed a right wing for his third line. He traded Brown, plus Mike Robitaille and Tom Miller, to Detroit for right wing Bruce MacGregor and defenseman Larry Brown (no relation to Arnie).

Arnie Brown played just a season and a half for the Red Wings, and wound down his NHL career with the New York Islanders and the Atlanta Flames. He also served briefly as an assistant coach of the Vancouver Canucks.

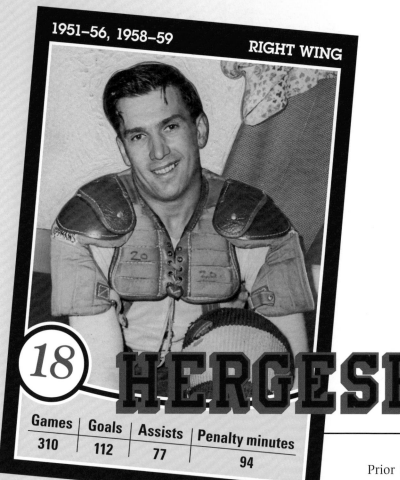

1951–56, 1958–59

RIGHT WING

18

92 WALLY HERGESHEIMER

Games	Goals	Assists	Penalty minutes
310	112	77	94

They called diminutive right wing Wally Hergesheimer a "garbage collector" because of his habit of shoveling short shots, "gimmees" some would say, past goaltenders from just outside the crease, much like Steve Vickers and Phil Esposito would do decades later.

Hergesheimer was one of many smallish forwards the Rangers seemed to sign in the early 1950s. His size certainly proved no hindrance, and he quickly became a hit on Broadway by leading the team in goals scored his first three seasons in the league. He had 26 goals as a rookie in 1951–52, a career-high 30 the next season, and 27 in 1953–54.

"When I made it to the National Hockey League, it was something I never really expected," he recalled. "It was always 'little Wally' this and 'little Wally' that. But I just kept going, and everything seemed to fall into place."

Prior to joining the Rangers, Hergesheimer had a knockout season in 1950–51 with the Cleveland Barons of the American Hockey League. They called him "The Mighty Mite" that single season in Cleveland, but the little guy won the Dudley (Red) Garrett Award as AHL rookie of the year. With Hergesheimer leading the way, the Barons won the Calder Cup playoff championship.

Cleveland coach Bun Cook had long been telling his brother Bill, then the Rangers' coach, that Wally was ready for the big time. General manager Frank Boucher concurred, and Wally was on his way to New York.

That Walter Edgar Hergesheimer should make the NHL at all was remarkable in itself. The five-foot-eight, 155-pounder from Winnipeg had lost two fingers, the index finger and the middle finger, on his right hand as the result of an industrial accident in 1944.

Hergesheimer's first line mates were Paul Ronty at center and left wing Herb Dickenson. Sportswriters

called them "The Light Brigade," since they were all little guys. "It was a heckuva line, but only for a short time," recalled ace sportswriter Herb Goren of the *New York Sun*. "They kinda played second fiddle to other guys like Don Raleigh, Edgar Laprade, Charlie Rayner and Allan Stanley. 'Hergie' was something special, though. He wasn't a great skater and he didn't really have a hard shot, but boy could he score goals."

One of Hergesheimer's most dramatic performances came on March 12, 1952. He scored three goals in 7:30 against goalie Harry Lumley of the Chicago Blackhawks, and the Rangers scored seven times in the final 13:10 of the game to win, 10–2, the first time the team had scored in double digits since January 25, 1942.

"Hergie" played in two NHL All-Star Games, 1953 and 1956. He scored two goals in the first 5:25 of the 1953 game, a record that stood for 40 years until Mike Gartner of the Wales Conference—and the Rangers—scored two in 3:37 in 1993.

The low point of Hergesheimer's career in New York occurred when he broke his left leg, not once but twice, in calendar year 1954, limiting him to a career-low 14 games played—and a mere six points—in 1954–55.

Traded to Chicago in exchange for Red Sullivan on June 19, 1956, Hergesheimer proved ineffective with the Blackhawks, scoring only two goals and eight assists in 41 games. He spent 1957–58 in the minors with the Buffalo Bisons of the AHL, but had a brief return with the Rangers, scoring just three goals in 22 games in 1958–59. That left him with 112 goals and 77 assists for 189 points in 310 games on Broadway.

Minor-league stops with Buffalo, plus the Calgary Stampeders and the Los Angeles Blades of the Western Hockey League, followed before his retirement in 1962.

Imperial Oil-Turofsky/Hockey Hall of Fame

1954–60

CENTER

Turofsky/Hockey Hall of Fame

19

Games	Goals	Assists	Penalty minutes
402	75	127	150

91 LARRY POPEIN

Q uiet, taciturn and mostly unsmiling, Larry Popein the coach more or less mirrored the style of Larry Popein the player.

At five-foot-ten and 165 pounds, the Yorkton, Saskatchewan, native was a smallish center who, starting in 1954–55, got a plum of an assignment, at least within the organization of the New York Rangers. General manager Muzz Patrick and coach Phil Watson put Popein on the Rangers' number-one line with superstar Andy Bathgate on his right and Dean Prentice on his left. Bathgate would go on to win a scoring title and the Hart Trophy as the league's most valuable player. Prentice, as solid a digger as the team has ever had, is arguably the best player not to be selected for the Hockey Hall of Fame.

"They [the fans] always remember Andy and Deano," Popein has often mused, "but never the scoreless pivot between them." Popein wasn't exactly scoreless, but with a mere 75 goals in 402 games

over six-plus seasons in New York, he was hardly going to garner the fan affection that Bathgate and Prentice were getting.

"I probably had the worst shot in hockey, especially by today's standards," Popein joked. "There were times when I had the puck with an empty net in front of me, but the goalie got back to his position before I even got the shot off. That happened a lot."

With their big line, and the redoubtable Lorne (Gump) Worsley in goal, the Rangers made the Stanley Cup playoffs three times during Popein's time, but never advanced past the first round and achieved no overwhelming success.

Early in the 1960–61 season, Popein was shipped to their Vancouver farm team in the WHL, where he would spend the next eight years in a city that would become his permanent home.

Popein had a brief 47-game sojourn with the expansion Oakland Seals of the NHL in 1967–68 and two more seasons as player-coach with the Omaha Knights of the Central League. After this the

New Ranger coach Larry Popein (right) is interviewed by football great turned sportscaster Frank Gifford in June, 1973.

Rangers decided on a coaching career for Popein. Emile Francis, the club's general manager, prepped Popein with further minor-league bench stints with the Seattle Totems of the Western League and the Providence Reds of the American League.

Then, on June 4, 1973, Francis made Popein the 13th head coach in Rangers' history. That began one of the shortest—and strangest—coaching runs in team history, a run that lasted just 41 games and resulted in Popein being fired despite a respectable 18-14-9 record.

"I always considered myself a disciplinarian," Popein said at his inaugural press conference, "but I try to be honest and fair." One day that discipline and fairness went horribly awry, at least in the minds of all his players.

At the time, the Rangers took chartered flights home after Saturday night road games to be ready for Sunday night home games at Madison Square Garden.

The plane would customarily land at LaGuardia's Marine Air Terminal, and the players would bus into Manhattan for a night's sleep.

The bus would drop Rod Gilbert on First Avenue, where he would hop a cab to his Second Avenue apartment. On the way to the hotel, Popein inexplicably changed the time of the pregame meeting the next day from 12:30 p.m. to 12:00 noon.

No one, not Popein nor any of the players, thought to phone Gilbert, and he showed up the next day half an hour late. Popein, the disciplinarian, rashly suspended Gilbert for that night's game.

The players, to a man, were in an uproar, and threatened not to play the game. Only an emergency meeting between Francis, team captain Vic Hadfield and the rest of the club quelled the unrest. The game was played, but Popein had lost the confidence of the team, and Francis had to fire him 12 days later, on January 11, 1974.

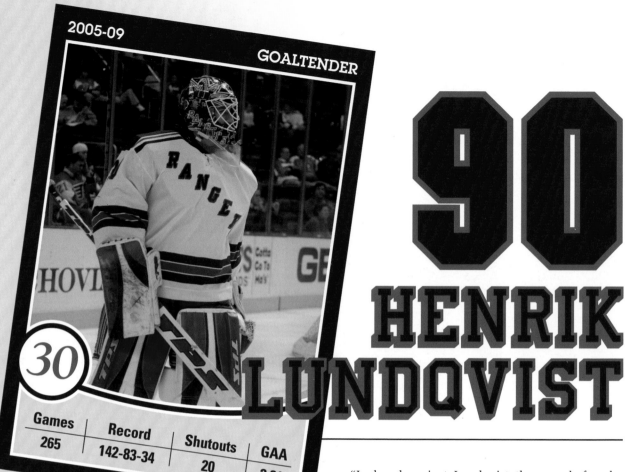

2005-09		GOALTENDER	
Games 265	Record 142-83-34	Shutouts 20	GAA 2.31

90
HENRIK
LUNDQVIST

T hat infamous *Chicago Tribune* headline blaring "Dewey Defeats Truman" illustrates the importance of getting all the facts in before rushing to judgment.

At the risk of committing a similar journalistic snafu, the authors of this book are confident that Henrik Lundqvist's early success on the biggest, brightest stage in sports is no fluke and that his assault on the Rangers' record book has only just begun.

The 205th overall pick in the 2000 draft, Lundqvist was another great late-round find by European scout Christer Rockstrom, the man who discovered Alexei Kovalev, Fedor Tyutin and Sergei Zubov, among others. The attributes that first caught Rockstrom's eye—world-class skills and a competitive fire that burns white-hot—are the same ones that have endeared Henrik to the Rangers faithful.

"I played against Lundqvist the year before he came over to the NHL," said former Swedish Elite League goalie Mike Valley, "and he pretty much kicked butt. He loves being in the spotlight, and I think a lot of his old teammates would say he can handle it."

As a rookie in 2005–06, Lundqvist was in the spotlight early and often. With lightning-quick reflexes, a great glove hand and all the poise of a ten-year veteran, he wrestled the starting job from Kevin Weekes, went on to set a franchise record for victories by a rookie (30), helped the Rangers earn their first postseason berth since 1997 and was named a finalist for the Vezina Trophy. Along the way, he found time to win a gold medal for Sweden at the Olympic Winter Games in Torino, Italy.

Fans spoiled by a decade of watching Mike Richter had a new masked marvel to support, and they voiced their approval virtually every home game with chants of "HEN-RIK! HEN-RIK!"

"The Rangers certainly felt Lundqvist was good enough to be an NHL player," said MSG Network

play-by-play man Sam Rosen, "but I don't think anyone had the idea or could have predicted that he would come so far so fast."

The club has had its share of fantastic freshmen over the years, dating back to the days of Kilby MacDonald and Edgar Laprade and more recently Brian Leetch and Steve Vickers. But what made Lundqvist's Broadway debut so special was that it came on the heels of a bitter work stoppage and helped bring hope back to the Garden at a time when enthusiasm for hockey—for Rangers hockey—had waned in some quarters.

Since then, his star has continued to rise. In 2007–08, he was named a Vezina Trophy finalist for the third consecutive year, led the league with 10 shutouts and won 37 games. In 2008–09, he won 38 games, becoming the first goalie in league history to post 30 victories in each of his first four seasons.

But everything that has transpired so far may have been just a warm-up for the man teammates call "Hank" but whom fans have crowned "King Henrik." He's acutely aware of the expectations that come with his job, though it's hard not to be in a building where reminders of the Rangers' last championship are never far from view.

"It's a great challenge to make the playoffs and then go all the way, especially here in New York," Lundqvist said. "You really understand how big it was, 1994, when you're here in the locker rooms and you see all the pictures and talk to people that were here. That is definitely something I want to try to experience during my career here."

To the fan who held up that now-famous sign declaring "Now I can die in peace" when the Rangers won their last Stanley Cup, we offer these few words of advice:

Stick around. The best may be yet to come.

89
BRIAN MULLEN

1987–91

RIGHT WING

19

Games	Goals	Assists	Penalty minutes
307	100	148	188

The true story of Brian Patrick Mullen, the Irish kid from Hell's Kitchen who got to play for his hometown New York Rangers, is more engaging than any fairy tale Hollywood could manufacture.

One of four brothers, Mullen grew up playing roller hockey in a schoolyard across the street from his family's apartment on 49th Street.

"My dad worked at MSG for 40 years," Mullen recalled, "and he was at the old Garden when it was on Eighth Avenue. Once in a while we got to skate at the Garden and he'd come home with all of the busted-up sticks from the Ranger game the night before. We would tape them up and use them to play roller hockey. I was the youngest and got what was left after my brothers got their choice."

At 15, Mullen landed a job as stick boy for the Rangers, putting him closer than ever to his favorite team. But a chance encounter with former coach Emile Francis really helped his hockey dreams take off.

"The schoolyard across from my apartment building was sunken in and about one story down," said Mullen. "When you walked by it, you could only see the tops of people's heads. Emile Francis was walking past the schoolyard one day, before a Rangers game, and he went over to the fence and peeked his head in and saw all of these kids playing roller hockey. He watched for a while and thought there must be a way to get these kids on the ice. He had started the Metropolitan Junior Hockey League, and that's where me and all of my brothers played their ice hockey."

Mullen parlayed his experience in the Met League into a hockey scholarship at the University of Wisconsin. Drafted in 1980 by the Winnipeg Jets, he established himself as a smallish but crafty NHLer with good offensive instincts and a willingness to skate through traffic. And, like any good New Yorker, he took the hits as good as he gave them.

In June 1987, Rangers GM Phil Esposito called to tell Mullen that he'd be coming back to the Garden, but this time he wouldn't be hauling sticks. Mullen had been traded to the Rangers for draft picks; his childhood dream was about to come true.

Tentative at first because he didn't want to embarrass himself in front of friends and family, Mullen eventually rediscovered the moxie that got him to the NHL in the first place. He went on to score 25 or more goals in three of his four seasons on Broadway, with some of his best moments occurring while playing on a line with Kelly Kisio and John Ogrodnick.

The year 1989 was a special one for the Mullen clan as Brian represented the Rangers in his first All-Star Game while older brother Joey, a member of the Calgary Flames, also made his first All-Star appearance. Of course, proud parents Tom and Marion made the long trip to Calgary to watch.

But when the NHL expanded into San Jose for the 1991–92 season, Mullen was left unprotected and was claimed by the Sharks. After one season in teal, he was traded to the Islanders.

Mullen's career was interrupted in 1993 when he suffered a small stroke. He appeared to be on the road to recovery, but a subsequent seizure ended any notions of a comeback and he was forced to retire the following year.

After his retirement, Mullen worked for the NHL front office before joining MSG Network for two years as a radio analyst alongside play-by-play man Kenny Albert.

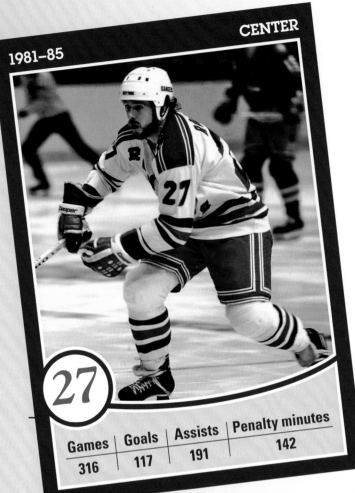

Games	Goals	Assists	Penalty minutes
316	117	191	142

88
MIKE ROGERS

Pat Hickey had his turn. So did Mark Pavelich, Anders Hedberg and countless other wingers lucky enough to call Mike (Buck) Rogers their linemate during the four-plus seasons he spent as a New York Ranger.

"If you have Mike Rogers for your center," Hickey said, "there's just no excuse for not scoring goals."

Like so many of the highly skilled but undersized skaters on Rangers teams of the early 1980s, Rogers and his fellow "Smurfs" faced the challenge of having to prove themselves in a league that often valued brawn over brains.

The five-foot-eight, 170-pound pivot had the misfortune of turning pro in an era when the Broad Street Bullies and the Big Bad Bruins were bludgeoning opponents into submission, and teams were looking for big, tough players of their own just to keep up.

With the market for slick, small scorers so limited, Rogers was drawn to the WHA by the promise of immediate ice time. Rogers played for the New England Whalers alongside Gordie Howe and son Mark Howe, and his speed, agility and stickhandling skills helped make him one of the rebel league's highest scorers.

In 1979, the Whalers joined the NHL, and Rogers continued to be an important piece of their offense. He found himself dangled as trade bait, however, when the Whalers went shopping for defensemen. In October 1981, the bearded Calgarian was sent packing to the Rangers for blueliners Chris Kotsopoulos and Gerry McDonald and forward Doug Sulliman.

Coming off back-to-back 105-point seasons for Hartford, Rogers was shocked by the trade. He had been the Whalers' captain and just moved into a new house in Connecticut where he planned to spend the rest of his career with his wife and daughter.

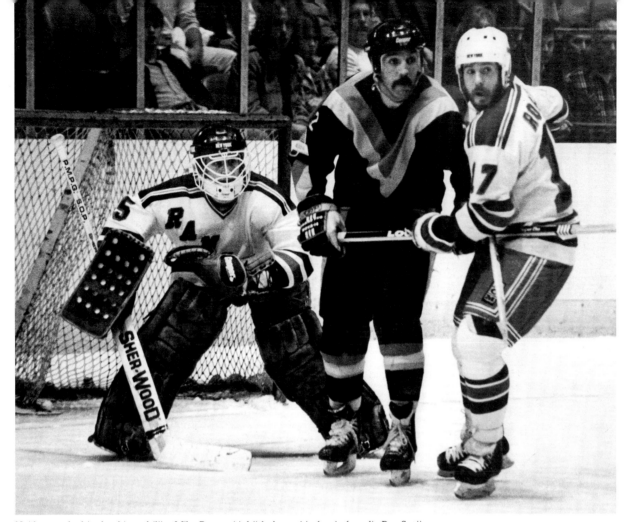
Not known for his checking ability, Mike Rogers (right) helps out in front of goalie Ron Scott.

"Buying the house was the kiss of death," he quipped. "But then I really looked at it and analyzed what a great opportunity it was for me to go to a much better hockey club. And to play in New York for an Original Six team was a huge thrill. The Rangers were sending a jet for me. And I said to myself, 'I can't ever see the Hartford Whalers doing that if I had gotten traded there.'"

Herb Brooks, coach of the Rangers at the time, injected his European-style game into the NHL years before it became the standard, and Rogers was among those who benefited most. After a slow start to the 1981–82 campaign, he went on to become just the third Ranger to top the 100-point mark on 38 goals and 65 assists. Incredibly, he did it in a season that saw almost nightly changes to his linemates.

"When you haven't won a Cup," Rogers said, "you cling to the personal achievements, and that was definitely a real highlight of my Ranger career. I'll bet you I didn't play with the same wingers more

than two games in a row. Herb came up to me not once but numerous times during the year, almost apologizing, saying 'Look, I hope you don't mind…' because I guess he felt that I could play with anyone. I went through anybody and everybody and I enjoyed it."

Off the ice, Rogers displayed the same leadership qualities that had earned him the captaincy in Hartford. Even if he never wore the "C" as a Ranger, he relished being a go-between for the younger players and some of the established veterans.

But when Rogers's offensive game sputtered in the early weeks of the 1985–86 season, new coach Ted Sator wasted no time demoting the 31-year-old playmaker to the Rangers' AHL affiliate in New Haven. A short time later he was traded to Edmonton, which turned out to be his last stop in the NHL.

After his retirement from the playing ranks, Rogers returned to his native Alberta and worked as a radio commentator for the Calgary Flames.

87 TOM LAIDLAW

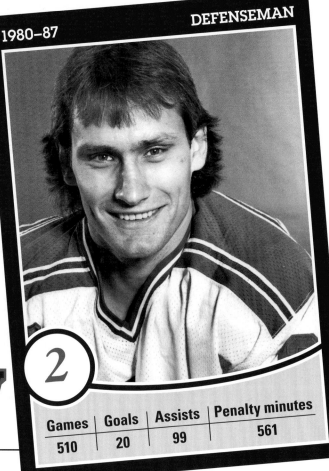

1980–87

DEFENSEMAN

2

Games	Goals	Assists	Penalty minutes
510	20	99	561

There's a bus company called Laidlaw and, like the brawny, no-frills vehicles bearing that moniker, Tom Laidlaw filled the role of brawny, no-frills defenseman for seven seasons as a New York Ranger.

Laidlaw's job was simple but could easily be overlooked by fans of run-and-gun hockey. Strong on his skates and tough as nails, he was essentially an insurance policy for the Rangers' cadre of small, skilled players who had neither the aptitude nor inclination to play defense.

Truth be told, no other role would have suited Laidlaw, a point hammered home early in his NHL career.

"When Herb Brooks came in my second year," Laidlaw recalled, "he pulled everybody to center ice one day after practice at Playland. He was giving one of his preseason speeches, telling each player what his role was. When he came to me, right in front of the whole team, he said, 'Laidlaw, if you get the puck, give it to somebody else. You're not supposed to have it.' The guys got a chuckle out of that. It was kind of harsh but he was sending a message in a funny way that I didn't have a whole lot of offensive skill. At the same time, Herbie also gave me a heck of a lot of confidence because he treated me very well and gave me a big role on that team."

A native of Brampton, Ontario, Laidlaw played on Northern Michigan's first Division I hockey team in 1976–77. It's become part of hockey lore that he celebrated his first college goal by breaking a stick over his bare head. New York papers hyped up the story after he was drafted 93rd overall by the Rangers in 1978, in part to show that the Philadelphia Flyers with their Broad Street Bully image didn't have a monopoly on toughness.

Years later, Laidlaw is still answering questions about his collegiate antics. "It's funny," he said, "because I coach some youth hockey now and every time I coach a team, kids look me up on the Internet and that's what they end up finding out."

Defenseman Tom Laidlaw (2) heads for the corner while Tomas Sandstrom (28) and Barry Beck (5) help secure the Rangers net.

The steady blueliner exhibited poise and grit while playing all 80 games as a rookie in 1980–81. Over time, he became a leader by example on the ice and was a natural choice to serve as interim captain during the 1984–85 season while Barry Beck was out with an injury.

"I really enjoyed being captain," Laidlaw said. "It was a real honor. It probably means more to me now when I look back on it. I remember that Herb Brooks went to Anders Hedberg in particular and said he felt that Anders should be captain. But Anders told Herb, 'You know what, I don't really think it should be me. I think Tom should be captain.' I was honored that it happened that way."

In 1987, the Rangers traded Laidlaw along with Bobby Carpenter to Los Angeles for Jeff Crossman and Marcel Dionne. Although he would miss playing in New York, Laidlaw didn't realize how much his former arena meant to him until the first time he came back as a member of the Kings.

"I guess I didn't realize when I was playing there how great it was," he said. "Not just the city, but the Garden in particular. There is no other building like it in the world. It's the atmosphere, even for a preseason game. It's the lighting, the sound, the history, the banners. Yeah, it's a special place."

Laidlaw became a prominent agent after his playing days, counting former Rangers like Bryan Berard and Rem Murray among his list of clients.

8

Games	Goals	Assists	Penalty minutes
325	122	133	183

86
DARREN TURCOTTE

Aquick shot and even quicker feet helped earn Darren Turcotte a full-time job on the successful Rangers teams of the early 1990s.

Born in Boston but raised in Ontario, Turcotte had been a junior star for the Ontario Hockey League's North Bay Centennials and was taken 114th overall by the Rangers in the 1986 draft. When he continued to victimize goaltenders in the International League, Turcotte made it impossible for the Rangers to keep him in the minors.

"The first game I ever played for the Rangers," he said, "was opening night in 1988 at the old Chicago Stadium. It was an extremely loud place and I still remember standing on the bench, listening to the national anthem. Scoring my first goal in New York against Sean Burke of the Devils was another big moment. Every game at the Garden was something I'll always remember. The fans of New York were unbelievable. I always tried to be exciting or dynamic and do things to get the crowd into the game. As much as they fed off of what I was doing on the ice, I fed off of what they were doing in the stands."

As a rookie, Turcotte drew the choice assignment of playing with two legends, Marcel Dionne and Guy Lafleur, but was later tabbed by coach Roger Neilson to supply the spice on a meat-and-potatoes line between checkers Kris King and Paul Broten. Because his wingers were so reliable defensively, Turcotte could take more chances offensively.

He went on to record four straight 20-goal seasons in New York, starting with a career-high 32 goals in 1989–90. In 1991–92, he scored 30 goals while helping the club finish at the top of the regular-season standings.

It was easy to understand why Turcotte, with his obvious skill, youth and affordability, had become an attractive asset to other teams. With GM

Doug MacLellan/Hockey Hall of Fame

Neil Smith on the prowl for veterans to help snap New York's Stanley Cup jinx, and a new taskmaster coach in Mike Keenan, who favored grit over finesse, it seemed inevitable that Turcotte would soon end up in another team's uniform.

The slick centerman held out hope he still fit into the Rangers' plans.

"I always had to prove people wrong, going back to when I was told I was too small to play junior hockey," he said. "Then I was too small to be drafted or too small to play in the NHL. When Mike came in, I took that same attitude. I didn't care if he liked me or not, or if he liked the way I played—I was going to do whatever I could to prove him wrong. If I had to adapt or change my style, I'd do it because I loved playing for the Rangers and would do whatever I could to stay."

His efforts proved futile, however. On November 2, 1993, a three-team deal saw Turcotte and defenseman James Patrick dealt to the Hartford Whalers while Steve Larmer came to Manhattan from Chicago.

"It was probably one of the most devastating times in my career," Turcotte said of leaving the Rangers. "But that's hockey."

In all, Darren played for six teams but injuries prevented him from ever matching the success he enjoyed in New York. He retired in 2000 with 195 goals and 411 points in 635 NHL games.

Now coaching junior hockey back in North Bay, Turcotte has gotten over the trade that effectively killed his best shot at winning a Stanley Cup. His one regret: "I lived in New York for five years but I'm going to have to take a vacation there to do some sightseeing. That's something I kick myself for sometimes."

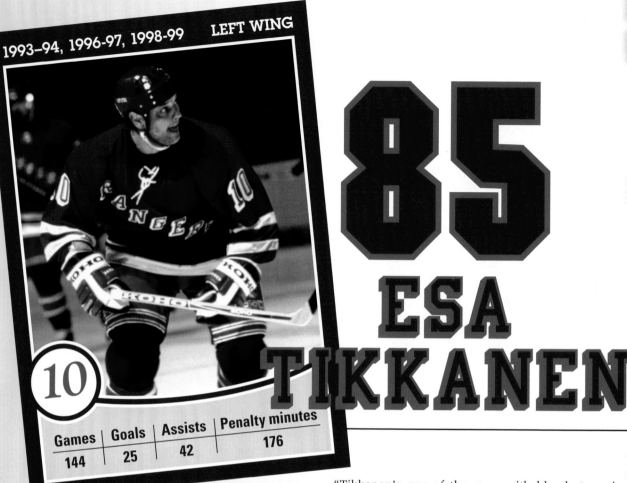

1993–94, 1996-97, 1998-99   LEFT WING

Games	Goals	Assists	Penalty minutes
144	25	42	176

85 ESA TIKKANEN

It was St. Patrick's Day, 1993, and Esa Tikkanen, the Edmonton Oilers' resident 200-pound gnat, had already taken the morning skate and chowed down with teammates at the pregame meal when he learned he'd been dealt to the Rangers.

As luck would have it, the Oilers were visiting Madison Square Garden that evening, and it took the newest Ranger all of ten seconds to draw a penalty against his former mates.

Tikkanen was a reliable two-way player with decent speed, scoring ability and the versatility to play any forward position. But it was his prowess as a battler and super-pest that most attracted the Rangers, who so coveted Tikkanen's grinding, irritating style that they were willing to part with 22-year-old center Doug Weight to get him.

"When you look down the bench at the end of the night," noted former Ranger coach Colin Campbell, "Tikkanen's one of the guys with blood streaming down his face."

In Tikkanen, the Blueshirts landed one of the best shadow men in the history of the game—a persistent bugger who delighted in holding, hooking, bumping and otherwise harassing whomever he was assigned to cover.

An ardent trash-talker, Esa spewed forth insults in an almost unintelligible mishmash of Finnish and English known as "Tikkanese." It didn't matter that neither friend nor foe understood what he was saying—he'd just yap away, his verbal barrage accentuated by a ghoulish, gap-toothed grin.

Tikkanen was not born a maker of mischief. He was barely old enough to shave when scouts from the Western Junior Hockey League invited him to play in Saskatchewan for the Regina Pats. With a little encouragement from his pop, a former boxer, Tikkanen left his home in Helsinki at age 15 to pursue a hockey career in North America.

In Regina, where fighting was often the norm, he quickly developed a taste for playing a chippy, in-your-face brand of hockey.

Those skills came in handy during New York's 1994 playoff run when Tikkanen not only got under the skin of opponents—planting a kiss on the nose of Capitals tough guy Keith Jones during the semifinals took gamesmanship to a new level—but also showed how relaxed he could be under the greatest pressure imaginable.

Mark Messier, who won a total of five Stanley Cups with Tikkanen (four in Edmonton, one in New York), absolutely adored Esa's ability to raise his game when it mattered most. "The bigger the game," Messier said, "the better he plays."

Traded to St. Louis in 1995, the feisty Finn was back on Broadway two years later, just in time for the 1997 playoffs. Facing ex-Ranger John Vanbiesbrouck and the Florida Panthers in the division semis, Tikk showed he still had a flair for scoring clutch goals.

With 3:31 remaining in overtime of Game Three, Tikkanen's hard slap shot ricocheted off a tiny camera inside the Florida net and caromed out, forcing several minutes of review. Meanwhile, Tikkanen stood confidently, his arm around goalie Mike Richter, awaiting the goal judge's review. The shot was ruled a goal, and the Rangers took a 2–1 series lead.

He had the overtime touch again in Game Five, delivering the game and series-clinching goal as New York eliminated the defending Eastern Conference champions. In all, Tikkanen's nine postseason goals were second only to Wayne Gretzky's ten.

Esa's third tour of duty with the Rangers, in 1998–99, turned out to be his last and, ultimately, least memorable. He spent the following two seasons playing in Europe before calling it quits ... or so he thought.

In 2004, Tikkanen signed a contract with the Seoul, South Korea-based Halla Winia club, which he originally believed was a deal to coach but also included a commitment to play. So, at age 40, he strapped on his skates one more time to become the most annoying player in the Asian Ice Hockey League.

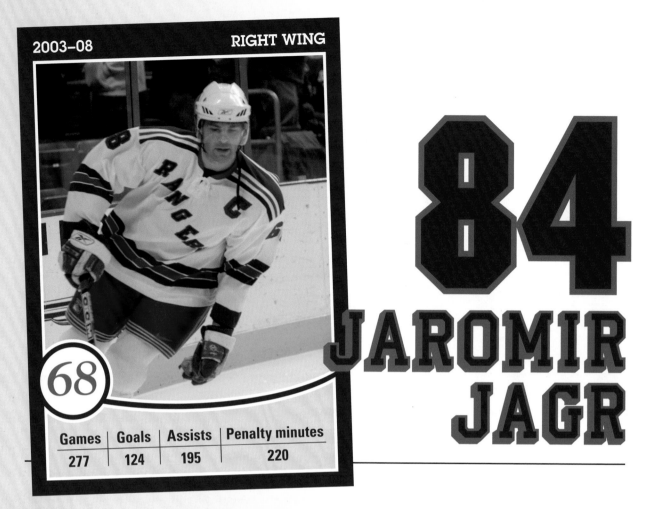

68

Games	Goals	Assists	Penalty minutes
277	124	195	220

84
JAROMIR JAGR

The New York Rangers Media Guide lists Jaromir Jagr as the team's 24th captain. More dauntingly, he was the first captain of the post-Mark Messier era, which is a little like going on stage *after* Bruce Springsteen.

But the Rangers weren't expecting a captain in the mold of Messier when they asked Jagr to wear the "C." What they wanted, and what Jagr delivered, was a superstar who would put himself at the forefront of a Ranger renaissance.

Born behind the Iron Curtain when the Soviet Union still held an iron grip over the former Czechoslovakia, Jagr first achieved fame as a mulletted teenager playing alongside Mario Lemieux on the Pittsburgh Penguins. Sometimes, it was hard to tell them apart. Both men were huge but graceful specimens with extraordinary hand skills and the strength to brush off most defenders. A Pittsburgh scribe pointed out that even the name "Jaromir" could be rearranged to spell "Mario Jr."

Eleven seasons, two Stanley Cups and five scoring titles later, Jagr found himself on a talent-thin Washington Capitals team going nowhere fast. The Rangers had pursued him unsuccessfully for years, but it wasn't until January 23, 2004, that they finally got their man. The trade—a future Hall-of-Famer straight up for Anson Carter—was almost laughably lopsided, even more so when one considers that Washington agreed to pick up a hefty chunk of Jagr's salary.

The Rangers were getting a proven franchise player but, along with him, some uncertainties.

Would he be happy in New York? And if not, would he make everyone else miserable? The six-foot-two, 240-pound right wing had a reputation for being moody, and given their recent history, the last thing the Rangers needed was an expensive malcontent poisoning their locker room.

But somewhere between Virginia's Reagan National Airport and 8 Pennsylvania Plaza, Jagr lost his baggage. Not the Samsonite variety. We're talking about *emotional* baggage—the kind that brands some-one a coach-killer, erodes team morale and feeds the jackals at the local tabloids.

Instead of poison, Jagr turned out to be just the tonic the team needed. Pumped to have a fresh start in the Big Apple and surrounded by fellow Czechs Michal Rozsival, Martin Straka and others, No. 68 felt so at home in Ranger blue that he delivered a training-camp guarantee that the team would finally break its playoff jinx in 2006.

Coach Tom Renney called Jagr's proclamation "a bold statement by a bold man who can back it up."

He backed it up, all right, going on an offensive rampage that saw him pass Jari Kurri as the highest-scoring European in NHL history, set franchise marks for most goals (54) and points (123) in a season and win his third Lester B. Pearson Award, a trophy giv-en annually to the league's best player as judged by members of the NHL Players' Association.

"Everybody was questioning whether or not he had the heart or the desire to play, up until that year," Anson Carter said. "I think he proved to us that when he's focused, and he wants to play, he's one of the best players of all time."

A freak shoulder injury in Game One of the 2006 quarterfinals derailed Jagr's record-breaking season, and without their biggest weapon, the Rangers went on to lose four straight to the Devils. It was a bizarre finish to a year that began with so much promise, but the bar had clearly been raised. Thanks in large measure to Jagr, the Rangers were back on the map and in the coming seasons continued to make strides toward becoming a Stanley Cup contender.

In 2008, the team decided that Jagr no longer fit into its long-term plans, prompting him to accept a lucrative offer to continue his career in Russia.

"When Jaromir Jagr came to the Rangers," said MSG Network's Sam Rosen, "there were doubters but he really took to New York because he understands the big stage and has the ability to play at a high level on it. I think when all is said and done, his stay in New York will be remembered as a very good one."

1981-86

CENTER

83

MARK PAVELICH

16

Games	Goals	Assists	Penalty minutes
341	133	185	326

A clever playmaker immortalized for his Olympic Gold Medal performance at Lake Placid in 1980, Mark Pavelich is also remembered 290 miles south for the five high-scoring seasons he devoted to the New York Rangers.

"I can't think of anybody who was more consistent or more valuable to us than Pav," his former coach Herb Brooks said. "He gave us a great effort, both offensively and defensively, every shift."

Of all the U.S. Olympians who jumped to the NHL immediately following the "Miracle on Ice," Pavelich was among the most successful because he adapted easily to the pro game. It helped that the Rangers, with whom he signed as a free agent in June 1981, played a wide-open style and were run by a pair of familiar faces: Brooks, coach of the 1980 Olympic team, and Herbie's former assistant Craig Patrick, who had just been hired as the youngest general manager in Rangers history.

They knew better than anyone what Pavelich could do and in New York, he finally put to rest any concerns that he might be too small (five-foot-eight, 170 pounds) to handle the NHL grind.

"I didn't try for the NHL originally because I didn't think I'd get a fair shot," he said. "Even the teams that wanted me to come to their training camps warned me that my size would be against me."

But by using his quickness and anticipation to beat bigger players, Pavelich could dodge hits in open ice by ducking or darting around opponents. And if he ran out of room, he was tough enough to absorb a stiff body check to make a play. The rough stuff didn't faze Pav. In fact, he seemed to enjoy it.

His first three Ranger seasons were offensively prolific. Often playing alongside Ron Duguay, Dave Silk or another former Olympian, Rob McClanahan, Pavelich scored at close to a point-per-game clip during the regular season and playoffs. On February 24, 1983, he tied a club record by scoring five goals—from

five different angles—against Greg Millen in an 11–3 rout of the Whalers.

A magician on the ice, Pavelich was quiet and shy out of uniform and very much a product of his rural Minnesota upbringing. A disheveled appearance only enhanced his image as the displaced outdoorsman who would rather be fishing or strumming his guitar than accompanying teammates to Manhattan's trendy nightclubs.

"Pav had one pair of jeans and a fishing pole," joked Dave Maloney, in his youth a sometimes hot-headed defenseman whose dressing-room stall neighbored Mark's. "I remember at one point saying to him, 'I really wish I had your demeanor one day a week,' and Pav said, 'Dave, I really wish I had *your* demeanor one day a week.'"

Nothing, it seemed, could ruffle Pav's feathers.

That would change in 1985 when the Rangers replaced Brooks with Ted Sator, who introduced a new dump-and-chase style of hockey that Pavelich and other stars found stifling. But it was more than just a difference of ideologies that divided the men. Pavelich viewed Sator as a mean-spirited bully who criticized his every move, and it didn't take long for the little center to become disenchanted with his NHL experience.

So he quit. At only 28, Pavelich was willing to give up the game rather than compromise his style. There were no long goodbyes or tear-filled press conferences. This was, after all, a guy who declined dinner at the White House after the 1980 Winter Games to go ice fishing.

Pav's "retirement" was short-lived, however, as the Rangers traded him to the Minnesota North Stars in 1986. He played there only briefly before heading overseas to continue his career. A comeback attempt in 1991 with the expansion San Jose Sharks lasted only two games before he quit for good.

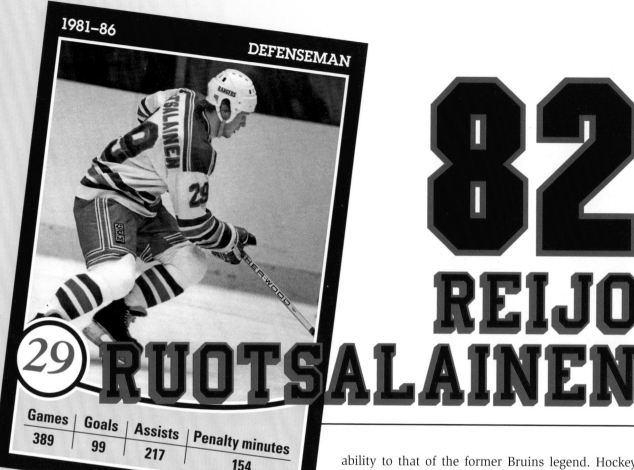

1981–86

DEFENSEMAN

82
REIJO
RUOTSALAINEN

29

Games	Goals	Assists	Penalty minutes
389	99	217	154

The first time Ron Greschner saw Reijo Ruotsalainen in action was in 1981 during an exhibition game in Sweden against the Washington Capitals.

As the tiny Finn made a 360-degree turn to actually skate backward while carrying the puck past a helpless defender, Greschner shook his head and wondered aloud what might happen to a less agile player who tried to pull off moves that deft.

"If I twisted my legs like that," he deadpanned, "I'd be dead."

"Rexi" was the original Finnish Flash, a five-foot-seven, 165-pound elf who came to the Rangers as a virtual unknown but soon emerged as one of the club's most important players.

Teammates old enough to have played with and against Bobby Orr compared Ruotsalainen's skating

ability to that of the former Bruins legend. Hockey compliments simply don't get any better than that.

"I hated him," former defense partner Tom Laidlaw recalled with mock disdain. "He was such a good skater. Herb Brooks had this drill where you had to go around the rink three times in 45 seconds. It was embarrassing for us with Reijo there because he would skate past us laughing. That meant three laughs going around because he was so much faster than us. I had never seen a skater like that. He was a great athlete."

"Ruotsalainen," said Finnish hockey authority Risto Pakarinen, "was just phenomenal. He would cross over from the left face-off circle to the right, turn backwards just below the red line, take a pass, turn forward again, go around the defenseman, then take a shot from the top of the circles. What balance, and his eyes were always on the play. He was just fantastic."

He was also accustomed to being underestimated. Ruotsalainen's lack of size when he was a youngster relegated him to the one position on the ice where

he couldn't exploit his burgeoning speed: goaltender. Even after rising to stardom in his country as an offensive defenseman, scouts insisted he would never make it to the NHL.

The Rangers took a chance on Ruotsalainen anyway, selecting him 119th overall in the 1980 draft. It turned out to be a steal.

Throughout the first half of the decade, Ruotsalainen provided the Rangers with as dangerous an offensive weapon as they have ever possessed and he created scoring chances almost every time he stepped on the ice. His speed was obvious but he also had one of the hardest slap shots around and was particularly effective when shooting off the pass.

"A lot of guys at that time really hadn't mastered the art of the one-timer," Laidlaw said. "Rexi was one of the first guys that not only could do it but do it all of the time, like it was easy for him. That's one of the reasons why we hated him so much—because we couldn't do it."

Moved to the wing during the 1984–85 season to spice up the Rangers' offense, he led the team in scoring and set career highs with 28 goals and 73 points.

After five exciting seasons on Broadway, however, Ruotsalainen decided to return to Europe in 1986 because he had no desire to continue playing for new coach Ted Sator—a recurring Ranger theme, as the reader may have noticed.

Even after rising to stardom in his country as an offensive defenseman, scouts insisted he would never make it to the NHL.

Rexi returned for brief stints with the Edmonton Oilers, with whom he won a pair of Stanley Cups, and New Jersey Devils before leaving the NHL for good in 1990.

He was later named head coach of Mikkelin Jukurit, a team in the Finnish Mestis league.

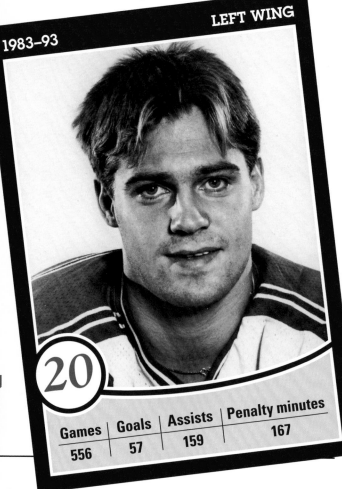

1983–93

81
JAN ERIXON

20

Games	Goals	Assists	Penalty minutes
556	57	159	167

Pictorially, it is the most vivid of images, perhaps even the most graphic one ever of a Ranger. Some can hardly bear to look at it at all. It is a black-and-white picture of left wing Jan Erixon recovering from a puck-to-the-eye accident in the early 1990s.

The photo shows Erixon's right eye and upper cheek, grotesquely swollen, heavily bandaged and no doubt heavily medicated as well. In a way, that photo symbolizes Erixon's career with the Rangers: ten years, but none of them complete due to a wide array of injuries.

Drafted 30th overall in the second round of the 1981 draft, Erixon didn't make his NHL debut until two years later due to military commitments back home. At age 21, he came to New York and appeared in 75 games with the Rangers, scoring five goals and 25 assists. That ended up being a career-high point total for the former Swedish Elite League star.

As evidenced by his preference to chase the puck rather than shoot it, Erixon didn't play for personal acclaim. For nearly a decade this six-foot, 195-pound import was one of the premier defensive forwards in the league and routinely matched against other teams' top scorers. A finalist for the Selke Trophy in 1988, Erixon had a style that made him a genuine favorite with the fans, reminiscent of Blueshirt predecessors Walt Tkaczuk, Bruce MacGregor, Andy Hebenton, Dutch Hiller and Clint (Snuffy) Smith.

"Jan was a checking Swede before they had checking Swedes," said Kelly Kisio, the former Ranger center. "He was a great guy to play with who did a lot of dirty work for you if you happened to be on a line with him. He was so strong from the waist down, so strong with the puck and a great penalty killer."

Erixon's proficiency as a checker and his fine hockey sense made him an ideal complement to offensive stars like Anders Hedberg, Pierre Larouche and Mike Gartner. In the high-flying, freewheeling 80s when it seemed like *anyone* could be a 50-goal scorer, Erixon was content to fill a support role.

Although he only had Erixon for about a season and a half, coach Herb Brooks called him "one of the most coachable players I ever handled. He and Pav [center Mark Pavelich] listened to everything I said. Plus, neither of them ever said a word. What more could a coach ask for?"

"Jan was quiet," concurred Dave Maloney, "and his skills on the ice were probably just as quiet. But he was bright and a very effective player who might've gotten lost in the crowd because of the solitude of his personality."

Then again, Erixon's "Nordic silence," as Maloney termed it, may have had more to do with culture shock than anything else. A young man in an unfamiliar place surrounded by strangers speaking a foreign tongue isn't likely to fill up reporters' notebooks.

By the early 1990s, however, Erixon was among the longest-tenured and most respected Rangers. It was a measure of his resilience that he played as long as he did.

The injuries were too numerous to list for the gritty winger—injuries to his neck, his leg, his knee, his face and his back, the latter eventually requiring surgery prior to the 1990–91 season and no doubt hastening his NHL retirement after the 1992–93 campaign.

"Jan was a checking Swede before they had checking Swedes."

He finished with 57 goals and 216 points in 556 regular-season games—not the kind of output that lands one's likeness on a box of Wheaties. But an even greater measure of Erixon's contributions to the Rangers' cause was that the team made the playoffs eight times in his ten years with the team.

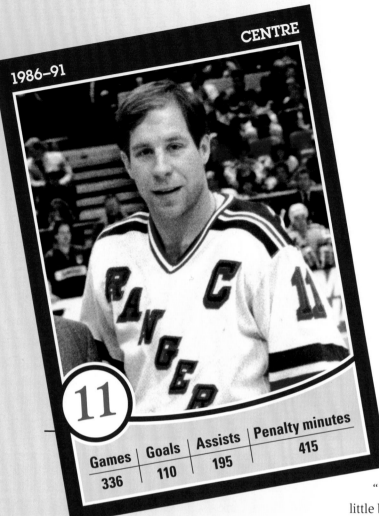

1986–91

11

Games	Goals	Assists	Penalty minutes
336	110	195	415

80

KELLY KISIO

With speed, exceptional hockey sense and a heart so big it barely fit in his five-foot-nine, 170-pound body, Kelly Kisio was a team leader, playmaker, checker, penalty killer and power play specialist.

Being a jack-of-all-trades was more than just a source of pride for the former Ranger captain—it was a matter of professional survival.

"If you're versatile," he said, "you're gonna be used in different situations. It's not a lot of fun sitting on the bench watching other guys play. For me to be successful in the NHL, I had to be solid in all areas of the game … and I thought I was."

Although he had been a dynamic scorer in juniors, registering back-to-back 60-goal seasons in the Western Hockey League, Kisio was never drafted because scouts were scared off by his lack of size.

"I wasn't overly surprised," he said, "but I was a little bitter. It was the time of the Broad Street Bullies. I understood it. I knew what teams were looking for but at the end of the day, you still have to put the puck in the net to win hockey games. I used my stick as much as anybody when I played and hooked and held and cheated as much as I could just to stick around the game."

Determined to make the big leagues, Kisio entered pro hockey as a free agent in 1980–81 with the AHL's Adirondack Red Wings. Patience and hard work paid off and within a few years, he was playing in the NHL for Detroit.

After three seasons in Motown, Kisio was the centerpiece of a multi-player deal with the Rangers in 1986. Longtime Rangers scout Lou Jankowski declared: "The only real hockey player in this deal is Kelly Kisio. The others are just window dressing." Jankowski would be proven right. Kisio would play five seasons and 336 games for the Rangers, while

Captain Kelly Kisio celebrates a goal against Boston's Reggie Lemelin.

defenseman Jim Leavins would play only four and right wing Lane Lambert would play 18.

Topping the 20-goal mark four times as a Ranger, Kisio chalked much of his success up to playing on some good lines.

"For a while," he said, "I had Donnie Maloney and Pierre Larouche on my wings and I also had Johnny Ogrodnick and Brian Mullen. Both of those lines were fun to play with. Pierre was so skilled and Donnie worked his butt off all the time and did a lot of dirty work for us. With Brian and Johnny and myself, we just clicked."

It took the native of Wetaskiwin, Alberta, no time at all to realize that playing in New York is unlike playing in any other town.

"The newspapers and the fans are so keen," he said. "If one reporter got on you or didn't like you or if you had a bad game, you could get run out of town pretty quick. That drove me quite a bit, too. I read the papers. Guys lied if they told you they didn't."

Kisio had no reason to hide from local reporters. He delivered a solid performance every season, even if his team did not. In his five years with the Rangers, the club missed the playoffs twice and suffered two first-round sweeps.

Kisio's efforts at leading were decidedly low-key, usually delivered *sotto voce* in the locker room, and always with a sly grin. Once he said to Ron Greschner, then married to leggy supermodel Carol Alt, "Hey, Gresch, do you mind if I come home with you and just watch? No wonder you've got a bad back." All Gresch could do was throw a balled-up pair of socks at him.

Claimed by the Minnesota North Stars and then traded to San Jose in the 1991 expansion draft, Kisio brought the same wit and moxie to the Sharks that he did to the Rangers. He ended his playing career with the Calgary Flames in 1995.

Three years later, Kisio began a long and highly successful turn as general manager of the WHL's Calgary Hitmen.

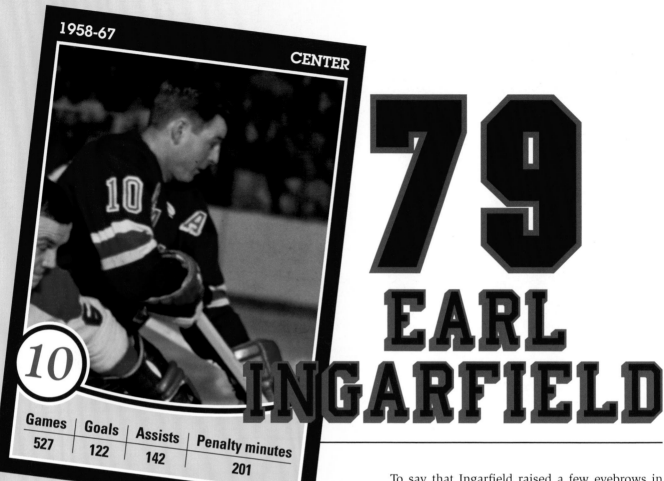

1958-67

CENTER

10

Games	Goals	Assists	Penalty minutes
527	122	142	201

79 EARL INGARFIELD

When Larry Popein was farmed out to the Vancouver Canucks of the Western Hockey League four games into the 1960–61 season, it opened up a prime position in the lineup of the New York Rangers.

The coveted position was center ice between superstar Andy Bathgate at right wing and slick left wing Dean Prentice, an enviable assignment indeed that fell to 26-year-old Earl Ingarfield, who had been with the team for two seasons, but mostly in a utility role as a checking forward.

The year before Ingarfield's ascension to the top line, the five-foot-eleven 185-pounder from Lethbridge, Alberta, knew he needed more ice time than he was getting, and he said so. General manager Muzz Patrick agreed, and was able to option Earl to the Cleveland Barons of the American Hockey League midway through the 1959–60 campaign.

To say that Ingarfield raised a few eyebrows in Cleveland would be a gross understatement. All the crafty centerman did was score 25 goals and 40 assists for 65 points in 40 games, prompting Barons' owner Jim Hendy to say that Ingarfield was "the best center Cleveland has ever had," no small statement since Cleveland had been in the AHL since 1937.

Ingarfield was summarily brought back to the Rangers for the 1960–61 season, and he never played another game in the minors. The next season, with Bathgate and Prentice, was Ingarfield's best: 26 goals and 31 assists for 57 points.

"The time in Cleveland was crucial," Ingarfield recalled. "That's what I needed—ice time. I always thought I was a pretty fair playmaker. I know I had pretty good hockey skills and my skating was all right." Modest to a fault, Ingarfield would also say of his time in Cleveland: "It didn't hurt that my right wing was Freddie Glover, who won the AHL scoring championship that year."

With help from a sliding Vic Hadfield, center Earl Ingarfield (10) breaks free in a game against Toronto.

The trade of Prentice to Boston for Don McKenney on February 4, 1963, ended Ingarfield's dream assignment with Prentice and Bathgate, but he remained an effective Blueshirt for four more seasons, mostly on a line with left wing Val Fonteyne and right wing Donnie Marshall, uniting three of that era's premier checking forwards.

"I loved playing with Andy and Dean, don't get me wrong," Ingarfield said at the time, "but whether you're on the first line or the third line, your main focus is to help the team." That he did in spades, notching 62 goals over the next four years.

"We had a very close-knit bunch in New York," Ingarfield recalled. "Harry (Howell), Camille (Henry), Gump (Worsley), Red (Sullivan) and Vic (Hadfield) were all terrific friends. We had some pretty good teams, too."

Ingarfield's Ranger days ended rather abruptly after parts of nine seasons (and 527 games) when the Pittsburgh Penguins grabbed him in the expansion draft on June 5, 1967.

After a season and a half in Pittsburgh, where he was briefly reunited with Bathgate, Ingarfield was traded to the Oakland Seals in January of 1969, and his playing career ended on the West Coast when he retired following the 1970–71 season.

After a brief stint coaching the junior Regina Pats of the Western Canadian Hockey League, Ingarfield would return to New York and was a longtime scout for the New York Islanders, and even coached the team for 30 games (6-22-2) in their inaugural NHL season of 1972–73. The Islanders wanted Ingarfield to be their head coach in 1973–74, but he preferred to stay in scouting, where he was instrumental in drafting future Hall-of-Famer Bryan Trottier in 1974.

> " ... but whether you're on the first line or the third line, your main focus is to help the team. "

Earl Ingarfield, Jr., like his father a left-handed shooting center, was born in New York City and also played briefly in the NHL with Atlanta, Calgary and Detroit.

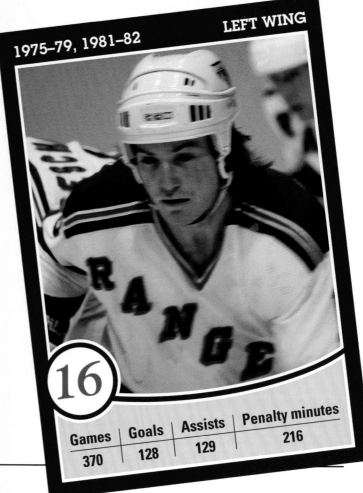

LEFT WING

1975–79, 1981–82

16

Games	Goals	Assists	Penalty minutes
370	128	129	216

78
PAT
HICKEY

Spending his teen years hauling heavy bundles of turf on a sod farm in his native Ontario, Pat Hickey developed the unusually broad forearms that would one day power his lethal wrist shot.

"I'm still an advocate of simulating that in real life instead of going to the gym," Hickey said. "Putting in a good day's physical work makes you sleep at night. Plus, I got paid and had a little bit of a loan at the bank for the car that I wanted to drive, as everybody does as a teenager."

In two tours as a Ranger (1975–79 and again in 1981–82), "Hitch" was a solid and versatile left wing who also played a bit of right wing and center. His toughness was exceeded only by his speed. Hickey was unquestionably one of the fastest skaters in the NHL.

Drafted 30th overall in 1973 by the Rangers, Hickey opted instead to join the WHA's Toronto Toros since they offered the prospects of big-league play (and a fat signing bonus) while the Rangers only offered him a chance to toil in the minors.

During his two seasons in the WHA, Hickey matured into an excellent two-way player. Such development didn't go unnoticed by the Rangers, who still held his NHL rights. They were willing to pay Hickey more money than the impoverished Toros could afford. But to help get Hickey's signature on a Ranger contract, GM Emile Francis went out and signed Pat's younger brother, Greg. The move worked, and Pat signed, although Greg would play only a single game in New York in 1977–78.

Hickey made his debut on Broadway in 1975–76 playing on a line with Walt Tkaczuk and Bill Fairbairn. He was eventually placed alongside Anders Hedberg and Ulf Nilsson and the trio was dubbed "Swede 16" (Hickey was identified only by his uniform number).

"That line," Hickey recalled, "had to be the most fun because it was the biggest challenge dished to me at the time. Our coach, Fred Shero, was asked at the beginning of the year who was going to play with

Hickey's enduring fondness for the Rangers and New York City was evident.

the two Swedes. So Shero put me on that line which was great because I was a bit of a spontaneous player anyway. We just went where we wanted.

"When reporters asked, 'Why Hickey?' Shero said, 'I'll tell you at the end of the year.' The season went on and Ulf broke his ankle and we went to the finals. Then one of the reporters asked again, 'Fred, you said you would tell us at the end of the year why Hickey's on a line with the Swedes.' He said, 'Because Hickey is the only guy on the team that wouldn't try to change them.'"

Hickey was part of the huge trade that brought defenseman Barry Beck to New York from the Colorado Rockies in November 1979. Hitch would play only 24 games in Colorado before being dealt again, this time to Toronto—his third team of the season—four days after Christmas.

In 1981, the Maple Leafs dealt Hickey back to the Rangers for a brief, 53-game return, but he was quickly traded yet again, this time to the Quebec Nordiques. He closed out his career with the St. Louis Blues.

Although he wore several sweaters in his 10 NHL seasons, Hickey's enduring fondness for the Rangers and New York City was evident. In 1986, he helped start New York's hugely popular Ice Hockey in Harlem program, helping inner-city kids learn the game.

Hickey, who studied economics at McMaster University while playing junior hockey in Hamilton, returned to Canada after his years as a minor-league executive and became a financial consultant.

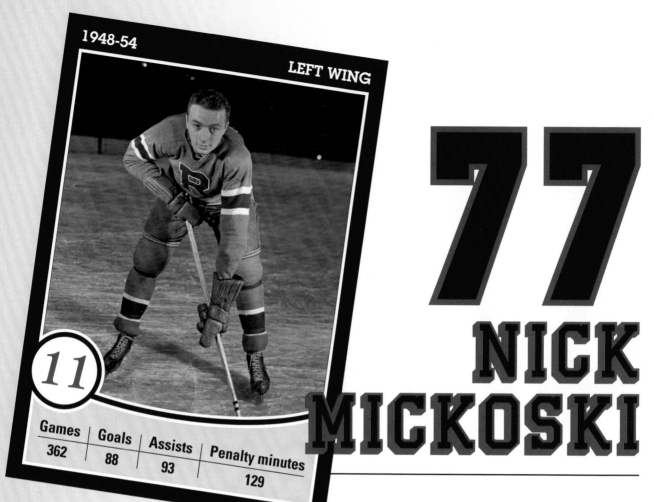

1948-54

LEFT WING

11

Games	Goals	Assists	Penalty minutes
362	88	93	129

77
NICK MICKOSKI

O h, but for the matter of an inch or so, Nick Mickoski could have been the hero for the Rangers, who ever-so-unexpectedly came within an eyelash of winning the Stanley Cup in 1950.

That was the year the underdog New Yorkers surprised the Montreal Canadiens, four games to one, in the semifinals, and then were matched against the powerful Detroit Red Wings with the Cup on the line.

Outdistanced by the Wings by 21 points during the regular season, the Rangers were given little chance of survival in the finals. The odds were further stacked against them by the circus, which had once again taken over Madison Square Garden and forced the Blueshirts to play their two "home" games at Maple Leaf Gardens in Toronto. The balance of the series would be played at the Olympia in Detroit.

Tied at three games apiece, the Rangers entered Game Seven with a real chance to win it all. The game went to double overtime and Mickoski, a rangy left wing in only his second NHL campaign, barreled in on Detroit goalie Harry Lumley in the second OT.

Mickoski's shot was a good one, and it had Lumley beat, before ringing harmlessly off the goal post. Minutes later, at 8:19, utility forward Pete Babando won the game—and the Cup—for the Red Wings. The Rangers wouldn't make the finals again for 22 years.

Goalie Chuck Rayner remembered the moment only too well: "You could hear the clank of puck on metal all the way down at my end of the ice. That wasn't a good sound."

In 1947–48, after two seasons with the semipro New York Rovers and one with the pro New Haven Ramblers of the American Hockey League, Mickoski got the call to New York for a pair of playoff games against the Red Wings. He was only 20 years old but played like a veteran, notching a single assist. More important, he firmly established himself in the eyes of general manager Frank Boucher and coach Lynn Patrick.

Nick was full-time with the Rangers the next season and for seven seasons total. Wearing number 11 throughout his career, and playing mostly on a line with center Don Raleigh and right wing Ed Slowinski, Mickoski appeared in 362 games and scored 88 goals and 93 assists for 181 points.

At six-foot-one, 190 pounds, Mickoski was the tallest player on the Rangers at the time. They called him "Broadway Nick," even though he and fellow Winnipeg native Wally Hergesheimer were the only players of their era to live in Brooklyn (Brooklyn Heights, to be precise). They shared an apartment that had views of Lower New York Bay and the Statue of Liberty, and they took the subway to work.

Mickoski also became quite a favorite with the Rangers' faithful. As was the custom at the time, his last name was prominently plastered on a banner—more like a bedsheet, really—that hung along with several others from the end and side promenades at the Garden.

The highlight of Mickoski's career in New York came on Christmas Eve, 1950, when he became only the second Ranger (Raleigh was the first) to score four goals in a game. He got them against his old nemesis and future Hall-of-Famer Lumley, the very guy who stoned him in the finals a year earlier and had since been traded to the Chicago Blackhawks. The Rangers won, 6–1, at the Garden. That season, Mickoski's career-high 20 goals led the team.

Traded to Chicago on November 23, 1954, Mickoski would play four seasons with the Hawks, two with the Red Wings and one with the Boston Bruins, before winding down with five years in the Western Hockey League.

Mickoski's athletic career didn't end with his retirement from hockey. He became one of the top amateur golfers in Canada and played competitively well into his 60s.

He died in 2002 at the age of 74.

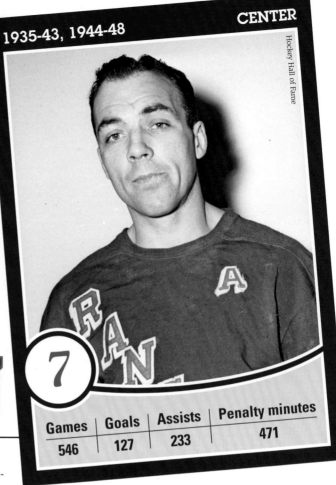

Hockey Hall of Fame

CENTER

1935-43, 1944-48

⑦

Games	Goals	Assists	Penalty minutes
546	127	233	471

76
PHIL WATSON

If there existed a list of the most colorful characters in the long history of the New York Rangers, the name of Philipe Henri Watson, "Fiery Phil" they called him, would be at the very top.

For 12 seasons as a player and four as a coach, Watson bled Ranger blue. He won a Stanley Cup with the 1939–40 team, assisting on Bryan Hextall's Cup-winning goal.

A native of Montreal (although he was half-Scottish), Watson was a pepperpot center on the "Powerhouse Line" with Lynn Patrick at left wing and Hextall on the right side, one of the most formidable trios the Rangers have ever had. That Watson, Patrick and Hextall would be the number-two line in 1939–40 was testament to the strength of that club, which coach Frank Boucher often called "the best team I had ever seen."

Watson was the second Ranger to wear uniform number 7, succeeding Boucher and preceding such luminaries as Don Raleigh, Red Sullivan and Rod Gilbert.

Following a solid junior career in his native Montreal, Watson arrived in New York at the start of the 1935–36 season unable to speak a word of English. "All I knew how to say was ham and eggs and steak, so that was all I ate," he recalled. Teammate and roommate Murray (Muzz) Patrick soon took Watson under his wing, beginning a lifelong friendship.

Never was that friendship more apparent than during the 1939 playoffs, with the Rangers facing the rival Boston Bruins in the semifinals. Boston's Eddie Shore, the NHL's resident tough guy, was working Watson over particularly hard one night at the Garden. Patrick came to his rescue, pummeling Shore mercilessly and leaving him with a bloodied face and a busted nose. It was the worst beating Shore had ever endured, and his battered mug made the cover of *LIFE* magazine.

Watson never scored a lot of goals with the Rangers—in his best season he had only 17—but

he did lead the NHL in assists with 37 in 1941–42. He possessed, according to Patrick, a great knack for needling opponents and throwing them off their games. "Nobody, *nobody*, did that better than Phil," said Patrick. "That was invaluable."

Hollywood, for a time, even beckoned Watson, who had Gallic good looks. Metro-Goldwyn-Mayer was planning a hockey movie called *The Great Canadian*, starring Clark Gable and Myrna Loy. Location shots were done at the Garden, and Watson was picked as Gable's skating double. Phil even grew a pencil-thin mustache for the shoot. The movie was eventually canceled, cheating Watson out of a screen debut. "I looked like Gable, I really did," Watson lamented. "He was a hell of a guy, but he sure couldn't skate."

Turning to coaching after his playing days, Watson was tabbed by then general manager Patrick to lead the Rangers in 1955–56. He lasted four-plus seasons, making the playoffs three times, but always failing in the first round. Watson's coaching tenure was marked by controversy. There were frequent battles with players, particularly goalie Gump Worsley, who Watson often thought was out of shape.

Watson's zaniest act occurred on February 15, 1959, following a 5–1 loss to the Montreal Canadiens at the Garden. Phil ordered the entire team, save for Worsley, back on the ice for a grueling, post-game practice that consisted just of stops and starts, skating drills and no pucks. That practice, many players said, killed the Rangers physically and psychologically. The team missed the playoffs on the final night of the season.

How much did Phil Watson love the Rangers? In May of 1979, the Rangers were to play Montreal in the finals. Watson called friends in New York and said: "If the Rangers don't win this series, I'm coming to New York myself and kicking every player's [bleeping] [tail]."

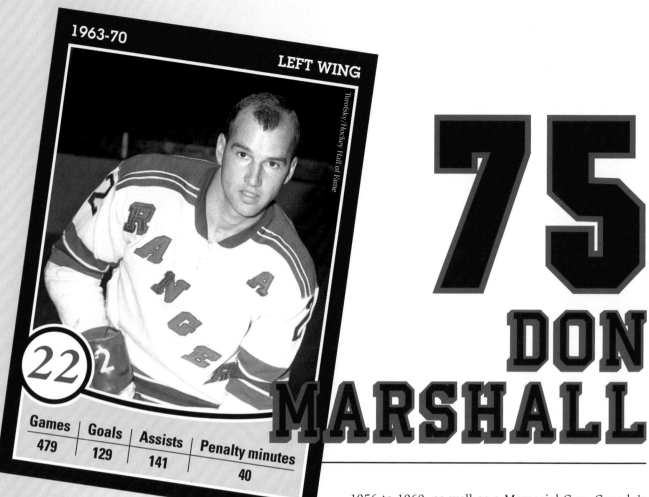

1963-70

LEFT WING

Imofsky/Hockey Hall of Fame

22

Games	Goals	Assists	Penalty minutes
479	129	141	40

75
DON MARSHALL

At first glance, the big trade that brought Donnie Marshall to New York on June 4, 1963, was really about superstar goalies Jacques Plante and Lorne (Gump) Worsley, who swapped teams in the deal.

But it was Marshall and longtime teammate Phil Goyette who eventually proved to be the most important additions to the Rangers.

Sam Pollock, the shrewd general manager of the Canadiens—"Trader Sam" they called him—knew what he was losing in Marshall: simply one of most versatile forwards in the National Hockey League. "He is the type of player every winning team has to have," Pollock said of Marshall.

In addition to his superb defensive skills, Marshall brought something else to New York, something the Rangers at the time desperately needed: a winning attitude. After all, the man had won five consecutive Stanley Cups with les Canadiens from 1956 to 1960, as well as a Memorial Cup, Canada's junior hockey championship, with the Montreal Jr. Canadiens in 1950.

Understandably enough, especially with a pedigree like that, Marshall was shocked to hear about the big trade. "I was in my car, and I heard it on the radio," he recalled. "It wasn't the nicest way to leave, but then I got a call from the Rangers, welcoming me to their team. The Canadiens called after that."

With all their vaunted offensive players—Maurice and Henri Richard, Jean Béliveau, Boom Boom Geoffrion and Dickie Moore among them—the Canadiens had used Marshall strictly as a defensive specialist and ace penalty killer. In New York, it was a different story. The shackles were off, and Marshall became a significant two-way threat, scoring 129 goals and 141 assists over seven seasons.

"At first, when I went to New York, I really thought that they didn't have a team plan," Marshall said. "Players did their own thing. In Montreal, it was much more team-oriented. I had a difficult transition

Defensive specialist Donnie Marshall (22) guards Detroit great Gordie Howe.

my first year there, trying to get acclimatized, but after that, things changed for the better."

The Rangers were in a serious rebuilding mode when Marshall arrived. Emile Francis had taken over the general manager's chair from Muzz Patrick, and Francis made the five-foot-ten, 160-pounder a big part of his overall scheme.

Francis immediately named Marshall and veteran defenseman Harry Howell assistant coaches while both men were still playing. "They were the very first assistant coaches in the history of the NHL," Francis remembered, "and they were perfect in their roles, respected veterans who knew what they were doing. They were a great help to me."

Ranger fans certainly saw a lot of Marshall. He played left wing, center and right wing, and was probably the best stickhandler on the team. His best

season was 1965–66, when he scored 26 goals and 28 assists for 54 points, and continued his always-outstanding penalty-killing duties. "Plus, Donnie was great on face-offs," Francis said. "I would use him in almost any type of situation."

Growing up in Montreal, Donald Robert Marshall had been a fine all-around athlete, excelling not only in hockey but in football and baseball as well. In 1950, he was on a team of Montreal All-Stars that played a bunch of Brooklyn Dodger rookies at Ebbets Field.

In 1970, the Buffalo Sabres snared Marshall from the Rangers in the expansion draft and he posted a respectable 20 goals and 49 points for the first-year club. His 18-year career wound down the following season with the Toronto Maple Leafs.

Today, Marshall is retired and living in Florida.

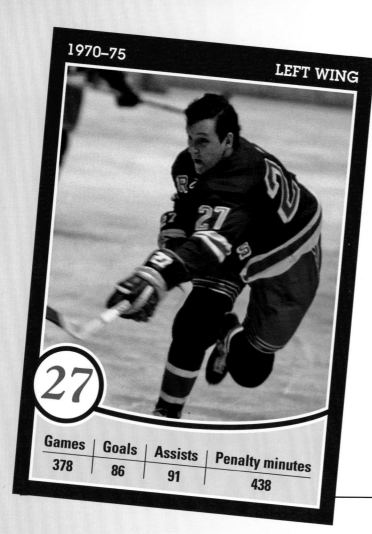

1970–75

LEFT WING

27

Games	Goals	Assists	Penalty minutes
378	86	91	438

74 TED IRVINE

This rugged left wing was among the most popular New York Rangers, and his on-ice combativeness existed in sharp contrast to his off-ice involvement with numerous charitable causes.

In that regard, you might think of Ted Amos Irvine as the original Adam Graves.

Irvine came up through the Boston Bruins minor-league system but was eventually acquired by Los Angeles in the 1967 expansion draft. Although he'd displayed a good work ethic and respectable offensive skills in three seasons with the Kings, the trade that brought Irvine to New York for Juha Widing and Réal Lemieux in February 1970 was considered anything but a blockbuster.

But GM Emile Francis knew what he was getting in this gritty Winnipeg native: a character player who would back up his play and his teammates with gutty, two-fisted ferocity. His robust style made him an instant hit with fans.

"When I got to New York," Irvine recalled, "Emile Francis had a role for me: just play on the checking line with [Pete] Stemkowski, [Bruce] MacGregor or whomever it may be. My job was to check and be physical but also score some goals. The best thing about the Rangers then was that they had a role for every player on the team and everybody respected his role. There was no jealousy. There was a real camaraderie."

Irvine and other foot soldiers were an ideal complement to stars like Ed Giacomin, Rod Gilbert, Jean Ratelle and Brad Park. Together, they faced Boston in the 1972 Stanley Cup Final.

In 10 NHL seasons, Irvine's teams never missed the playoffs.

"I took great pride in knowing I could perform at another level," he said. "My playoff record is something I'm very proud of. I scored points in the playoffs, was used in important situations and fought at the right times. I guess there was pressure but I

A dancing Ted Irvine, with stick raised high, scores against Montreal goalie Rogie Vachon.

didn't feel it. I just felt, 'Boy, this is what it's all about to be a hockey player.'"

Irvine topped the 20-goal mark twice in five and a half seasons on Broadway and although he was never named to an NHL All-Star Team, his charitable endeavors did not go unnoticed. He was recognized by numerous local groups for his activities, particularly with disabled children.

"You notice more after getting out of hockey how lending your name or going to different events can help," he said. "When I was playing, I never felt people were watching me or even knew what I was doing. I just went and did it for the right reasons. I guess it started when I was growing up. My family was the kind that had a lot of the neighborhood kids coming over for supper or sleepovers and if they were a little off-track, they were always welcome in our house."

Traded to St. Louis for John Davidson in 1975, Irvine played two seasons with the Blues before retiring. He later returned to Winnipeg to become a financial planner but still remembers his New York experience fondly.

"When you're young and playing you just float through years," he said, "but when I look back on it now, it's probably the greatest time I ever had in my life at anything I've ever done. Playing in New York in front of the media, the fans, the coaches and the other players was the epitome of what being a hockey player could be."

In the 1990s, Ted's son became a professional wrestler and musician performing under the name Chris Jericho. A frequent participant at Rangers SuperSkate events, Jericho inherited his father's toughness and charisma.

73
DUTCH HILLER

LEFT WING

Imperial Oil-Turofsky/Hockey Hall of Fame

⑧

Games	Goals	Assists	Penalty minutes
198	49	70	116

According to those who played with him, and perhaps more important, those who played against him, Dutch Hiller was the fastest skater of his era, bar none.

Was Hiller the fastest skater to ever play for the Rangers? Probably yes, but each era has a claimant to that honor, including Murray Murdoch from the 1920s, Danny Lewicki from the 1950s, Pat Hickey and Reijo Ruotsalainen from the 1980s, and more recently, Mike Gartner, Radek Dvorak and Matt Cullen.

Hiller, five-foot-eight and 170 pounds, was the left wing on the third line with Alf Pike at center and Clint (Snuffy) Smith at right wing when the Rangers won the Stanley Cup in 1940. Recalled Frank Boucher, the team's longtime coach: "They were all good skaters, but Dutch was the fastest. Nobody could keep up with Dutch. Nobody."

Wilbert Carl Hiller wasn't really Dutch at all, but German. His hometown of Kitchener, Ontario, had a strong Dutch population, which is surely the origin of his nickname. Junior and senior teams there have long been called the Kitchener Dutchmen.

The most memorable goal of Hiller's eight-year NHL career wasn't even his—it was Bryan Hextall's Cup winner for the Rangers against the Toronto Maple Leafs on April 13, 1940, in Game Six of the finals. Hiller remembered muscling the puck away from Ted Kennedy behind the Ranger net and whistling a crisp pass to Phil Watson at the first blue line.

Watson found Hextall unprotected and sent him barreling in on the great Turk Broda in goal. Hextall's sharp backhander eluded Broda's catching glove, and the Rangers were suddenly whooping and hollering, celebrating their third Stanley Cup championship. "It was the greatest moment of my career," Hiller often said.

World War II was looming, and the face of hockey was changing dramatically. Due to draft restrictions, there was considerable confusion over which players would be able to play, and who would be able to play where. The Detroit Red Wings grabbed Hiller on waivers for seven games before the Wings sold his services to the Boston Bruins, who traded him to the Montreal Canadiens on August 15, 1942.

Hiller landed back in New York for the 1943–44 season in a complicated wartime "loan agreement" that also saw Watson end up in Montreal. Although primarily a defensive player, Dutch responded with his best offensive season ever: 18 goals and 22 assists for 40 points in 50 games. Nonetheless, the Rangers returned Hiller to Montreal the next season, and he promptly won another Stanley Cup in 1946.

The most memorable goal of Hiller's eight-year NHL career wasn't even his.

Hiller chose southern California for his retirement years, but he didn't stray far from hockey. He was a longtime goal judge for the Los Angeles Kings, starting in their inaugural season of 1967–68. "His eyes were like darts," recalled Ed Fitkin, the Kings' first publicist. "He never missed a thing, a perfect goal judge."

In recent years, the National Hockey League started a magnificent campaign to have the Stanley Cup travel all over North America, visiting with former, and mostly aging, Cup winners. Dutch Hiller's turn came on Friday, September 9, 2005. Wearing a Rangers' baseball cap, Hiller proudly displayed the Cup before a gaggle of fascinated friends at a Burger King in LaCrescenta, California.

When Hiller died at the age of 90 on November 12, 2005, that left the Rangers with only two survivors from the 1940 team, and ironically enough, they were Hiller's linemates: Pike and Smith.

Hockey Hall of Fame

1992-95

DEFENSEMAN

Doug MacLellan/Hockey Hall of Fame

21

Games	Goals	Assists	Penalty minutes
165	30	126	61

72 SERGEI ZUBOV

In basketball, the best point guards make the transition from defense to offense look easy, think pass first, and can create scoring opportunities for the players around them as well as for themselves. For a scant three seasons, Sergei Zubov was the Rangers' point guard on ice: a defenseman who could control the tempo of a hockey game with his superb stickhandling skills and ability to work the puck out of his own zone before spearheading a counterattack.

Before arriving in North America, Zubov spent four years on the Central Red Army club, a team he was groomed to join from childhood. There, he played with some of the biggest names in Russian hockey including Sergei Makarov, Igor Larionov, Slava Fetisov and Vladimir Konstantinov.

"That Red Army club was great," he said. "I'd say we could easily outmatch any team on the planet—not just in the Russian league. It was just amazing to play with guys like Larionov and Fetisov. Even the guys of my generation like Sergei Fedorov, Pavel Bure and Alex Mogilny—they were all unbelievable individuals. It was hard not to learn from them. I'd just watch, listen and try to do the same thing."

But at the end of the 1991–92 season, the club failed to pay its players, triggering a mass exodus to the NHL. By then, Zubov had already been drafted by the Rangers and informed his parents that if an opportunity to play in New York presented itself, he would go.

Using buddy Sergei Nemchinov as an interpreter, Zubov met with Rangers GM Neil Smith in a Moscow hotel room and signed his first NHL contract. He and another Rangers prospect, Alexei Kovalev, were on a plane to New York a few days later.

The Russian rearguard arrived to find that the Rangers didn't have room for him, so he ended up with their AHL affiliate in Binghamton. Since players of Zubov's caliber tend not to stay in the minors very long, he soon joined the varsity on Broadway.

His all-around play—and conditioning—improved markedly under the watchful eye of coach Mike Keenan, who delivered this ultimatum to the young defenseman early in the 1993–94 campaign: shape up or go back to Binghamton ... for good.

"Zubie" responded to Keenan's threat by leading the Rangers with 77 assists and 89 points, many of those scored during the man advantage. Although his arsenal includes an accurate and powerful slap shot, Zubov prefers to thread a gorgeous pass through traffic to the open man than let one rip from the point. Together, he and Brian Leetch were probably the most potent power-play quarterbacks the Rangers have ever had.

In the playoffs, Zubov scored 19 points in 22 games before he, Nemchinov, Kovalev and defenseman Alexander Karpovtsev became the first Russians to get their names engraved on the Stanley Cup. And the triumphant Rangers, the club that introduced the first Finnish and Swedish players to the NHL, continued to be on the cutting edge of international hockey.

There was no letup in Zubov's point production during the shortened 1994–95 season when he scored 36 points in 38 games.

At only 25 and earning a modest (by NHL standards) wage, the Muscovite with the perpetual five o'clock shadow had become one of New York's most prized assets. So when the Rangers sought to add a dimension of size and toughness to their defense corps, clubs naturally demanded Zubov in return.

In August 1995, the Rangers traded Zubov with Petr Nedved to the Pittsburgh Penguins for Luc Robitaille and Ulf Samuelsson. A year later he was traded to Dallas, where he won a second Stanley Cup in 1999.

> "Mike Keenan delivered this ultimatum to the young defenseman: shape up or go back to Binghamton…for good."

Doug MacLellan/Hockey Hall of Fame

CENTER

93

Games	Goals	Assists	Penalty minutes
478	149	202	312

71 PETR NEDVED

They say that in life there are no second chances, but Petr Nedved accomplished the near impossible: erasing the memory of a disappointing debut to earn a permanent place of honor in the history of the Rangers.

At 17, Nedved left the former Czechoslovakia to play in an international midget tournament in Calgary. Because of the limited opportunities in his homeland under Communist rule, he decided to defect to Canada and sought political asylum at a Calgary police station.

Free to pursue a pro career in North America, Nedved was drafted second overall by Vancouver in the 1990 draft and played three seasons for the Canucks before moving on to St. Louis. When the Blues hired Mike Keenan away from the Rangers in the summer of 1994, New York demanded compensation and received Nedved in return as part of a trade for veterans Esa Tikkanen and Doug Lidster.

On paper, it certainly looked like a no-brainer for the Rangers, who were coming off a Stanley Cup

but showed signs of age at key positions. Now 23, Nedved was a promising young center with star potential, expected to anchor the second line behind Mark Messier. That was the plan, anyway.

But after Nedved led the league in scoring during preseason, his production trailed off and he found himself mired in a terrible slump, and also in coach Colin Campbell's doghouse.

"He'll come around," Campbell assured. "He's too good a player not to come around."

But in the lockout-shortened 1994–95 season, Nedved simply ran out of time to alter people's perception of him as a skilled but soft player who wouldn't battle through checks and put in the dirty work that is part of winning. After the season, he was traded with Sergei Zubov to the Penguins for Luc Robitaille and Ulf Samuelsson.

The parting of ways benefited Nedved more than the Rangers. Playing with Jaromir Jagr in Pittsburgh restored Petr's confidence, and he scored a career-high 99 points in 1995–96.

But a lengthy contract dispute with the Penguins led to him being traded back to New York for Alexei Kovalev in November 1998.

There was something unmistakably different about Nedved, and the Rangers noticed it immediately. The tall, lanky kid they discarded three years earlier was gone and in his place was an older, tougher competitor who no longer shied away from the physical aspects of the game and actually thrived on going head-to-head with the league's top forwards.

He got his first taste of top-line duty when Wayne Gretzky went down with an injury in February 1999, but Nedved's Ranger career really took off when Campbell's successor, John Muckler, placed him between wingers Jan Hlavac and Radek Dvorak. It was a stroke of brilliance and with their instant chemistry, the "Czechmates" became one of the hottest lines in hockey.

One of the more durable players since his return to New York, Nedved rarely missed any game action and used his accurate wrist shot to post three consecutive 20-plus goal seasons for the Blueshirts.

But one-line hockey teams are rarely successful and a roster shakeup was inevitable. During the 2003–04 season the Rangers struggled and Nedved was subsequently dealt to the Edmonton Oilers. He also played in Phoenix and Philadelphia before heading back to Europe. An unsuccessful comeback attempt with the Rangers in 2008 signaled the end of his NHL career.

Nedved's Ranger memories are bittersweet. "Playing with Gretzky on the same team was very special," he said. "I cherish the moments that I had playing with him. It was a treat. Obviously, there were times that were frustrating, especially toward the end of each season because we didn't make the playoffs. Other than that, playing in New York was a great experience."

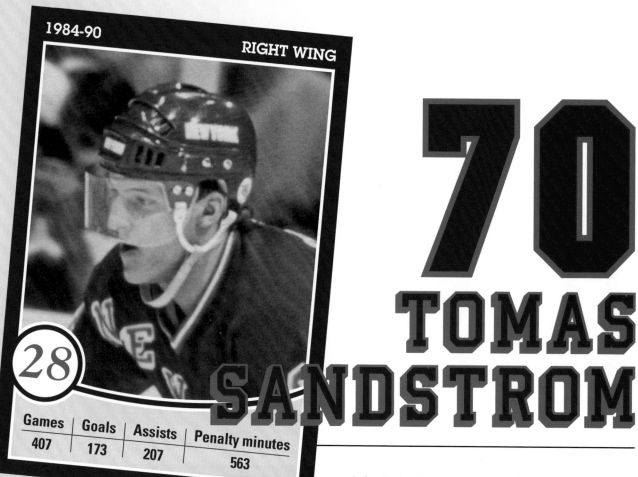

RIGHT WING

70

TOMAS SANDSTROM

28

Games	Goals	Assists	Penalty minutes
407	173	207	563

Another import who steamrolled Don Cherry's absurd stereotype of the "yellow Swede," Tomas Sandstrom combined skill with size and considerable strength to become one of the top-scoring European-born players in the history of the NHL.

The Rangers have a long tradition of looking overseas for talent. In fact, they brought the NHL's first Swedish player, Ulf Sterner, over in 1965. Sterner was an artful left wing, but a little too artful for the rigors of the NHL. He lasted only four games with the Rangers, going scoreless, and got bullied quite a bit by enforcers of the day.

Sandstrom, drafted 36th overall in 1982 by the Rangers, had no such problem. He adapted brilliantly to the North American game with its smaller rinks and more physical style because he could beat opponents with power or finesse. Barreling into the offensive zone, he could deftly slip the puck between a defender's skates, step around, reclaim it and then fire a shot on net. He was just as dangerous without the puck, splattering opposing players in open ice or crunching them up against the boards.

Because Sandstrom didn't mind being a target on the ice, he made his share of enemies. During a game against the Flyers in 1987, he speared Philadelphia's Mark Howe in the gut. Before Howe could enact revenge, Flyers tough guy Dave Brown jumped in and broke Sandstrom's jaw with a cross-check to the face.

Anders Hedberg, at one time the Rangers' senior European player, acknowledged that Sandstrom was something of a loose cannon.

"Tomas was so determined not to give an inch that he sometimes lost his cool," Hedberg said. "If he got slashed and wasn't able to slash back or retaliate, he lost his focus. The opposition could use that to their advantage. Part of my role was to tell him, 'Okay Tomas, you'll get a chance to give it back eventually but tonight we have to win the game.' He was so competitive, and absolutely fearless."

He adapted brilliantly to the North American game with its smaller rinks and more physical style because he could beat opponents with power or finesse.

Early in his career, Sandstrom's uncompromising style got him into hot water with the club's veteran netminder, Glen Hanlon.

"Back when Tomas was new to the team and his English wasn't that good," former Ranger Tom Laidlaw recalled, "he said something that came out in a way that our goalie didn't like. Glen was still steaming about it during practice. So Tomas came skating down in warm-ups and fired a hard shot that went close to Glen's head. Glen came rushing out of the net to chase Tomas down. Half of us were dying laughing because we could see this whole thing had developed because Glen just didn't understand what Tomas had said. And the rest of us were like, 'Oh my God, here's our goalie chasing Tomas Sandstrom all over the rink.' So we settled everything down and got Glen back in the net.

"Well, Tomas was such a fiery competitor and by now, he's mad too. So the warm-ups continued and as he came down to take another shot, he fired another high, hard one right at Glen's head. Again, Glen came out of the net and chased Tomas all over the ice.

"We later came to realize that Sandstrom was a great team guy and that whole episode had just been a big misunderstanding."

New York's lone representative at the 1988 All-Star Game, Sandstrom was a major part of the Rangers' offense for almost six full seasons until January 1990 when he was traded with Tony Granato to Los Angeles for Bernie Nicholls. His 15-year NHL career also included stops in Pittsburgh, Detroit and Anaheim.

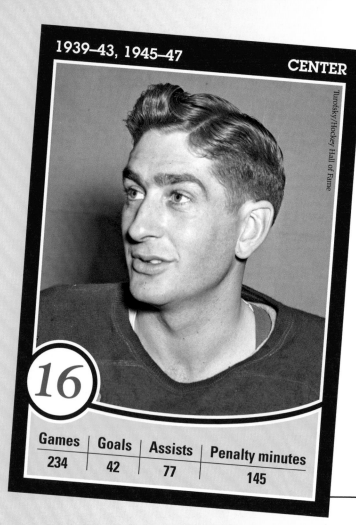

1939–43, 1945–47

CENTER

Turofsky/Hockey Hall of Fame

16

Games	Goals	Assists	Penalty minutes
234	42	77	145

69
ALF PIKE

Not that records have ever been kept on such things, but it's a pretty safe bet that Alf Pike bore the brunt of more locker room humor than any other Ranger. The reason was his nickname: "The Embalmer." The moniker was legitimate. Pike indeed had once been a licensed mortician when he wasn't playing hockey.

Alfred George Pike, a crafty center, also holds a more conventional club record. He is the youngest Ranger to win the Stanley Cup, a feat he accomplished at 22 years of age in 1940.

Pike was hardly known as a goal scorer, netting only 42, plus four more in the playoffs, during his six seasons in New York. Yet the two most important goals of his career occurred during those 1940 playoffs.

The Embalmer won Game One of the final with a goal at 15:30 of overtime, giving the Rangers a 2–1 victory at Madison Square Garden on April 2, 1940. Ironically enough, Pike could have been the goat that night instead of the hero. Earlier in the game,

he inadvertently knocked the puck into his own net behind goalie Dave Kerr. The goal was credited to Leafs center Red Heron.

Eleven days later, on April 13, Alf scored the tying goal of Game Six halfway through the third period, and neatly set the stage for Bryan Hextall's winning tally early in the first sudden-death period. The Rangers were the champions of the world for a third time, thanks in no small part to the six-foot 190-pounder from Winnipeg.

Pike, who passed away in February 2009 at age 91, vividly recalled that final game. "We were in the dressing room between the second and third periods," he said, "and just before we went out, I spit on Bryan Hextall's stick, the backhanded side. It was just for good luck. I said, 'I'll get the tying goal and you get the winner.'" That's just what happened.

Pike also remembers the incredible closeness on that

championship team. "You travel by train, 20 hours at a clip, you had better get along," he said. "We had great comradeship. We used to have a saying, 'Once a Ranger, always a Ranger.' They still use it today."

Pike was the pivot man on the third line of that great team. His line mates were Wilbert (Dutch) Hiller at left wing and Clint (Snuffy) Smith on the right side. The trio was almost interchangeable. All three players shot left-handed. Linemates forever, until recently they remained the only living members of the 1940 team, which had 14 men on its Cup roster.

As it did for so many other Ranger stars, World War II interrupted Pike's playing career. He played two seasons, 1943–44 and 1944–45, with the Winnipeg Royal Canadian Air Force team, and returned to the Rangers for two more seasons in 1945.

Despite his relatively short stay in New York (234 games total), Pike wore four different uniform numbers (16, 2, 14 and 9), one of only a handful of Rangers who can make that claim.

Pike eventually turned to coaching and led the junior Guelph Biltmores to the Memorial Cup, Canada's junior championship, in 1952. That team produced the "Guelph Gang" of Andy Bathgate, Dean Prentice, Lou Fontinato and Harry Howell, all of whom went on to play for the Rangers.

In 1959, Pike succeeded his old teammate Phil Watson as coach of the Rangers but he lasted only until the end of the 1960–61 season, winning just 36 games and losing 66, the worst record of any Ranger coach who worked more than 100 games. Said one of his players from those squads: "Alf Pike is simply too nice a guy to be a coach."

Paul Bereswill/Hockey Hall of Fame

1996-99

CENTER

99

Games	Goals	Assists	Penalty minutes
234	57	192	70

68
WAYNE GRETZKY

Professional sports is littered with burned-out stars who play a season or two longer than necessary just to pad their stats or fatten their bank accounts.

But Wayne Gretzky, the league's all-time leading scorer and holder of over five dozen NHL records, was always too proud and too competitive to go out that way. He would not have signed with the Rangers in 1996 if he didn't sincerely believe he could help bring another Stanley Cup to New York.

He also came at the urging of good buddy and fellow Oiler alum Mark Messier, who sold The Great One on the joys of playing in New York City and spoke from firsthand experience about how winning a championship there would be unlike anything Gretzky had ever experienced. Messier's presence also ensured that Gretzky would not be the focal point of the team, something the nine-time MVP found appealing.

If Phil Esposito had his way, No. 99 would have been a Ranger a decade earlier.

As the story goes, Esposito—then the Rangers' general manager—negotiated a blockbuster trade for Gretzky with Edmonton GM Glen Sather at the 1988 NHL meetings in Palm Beach, Florida. In return, the Oilers were going to get Kelly Kisio, Tomas Sandstrom, John Vanbiesbrouck, a draft pick and $15 million.

But much to Espo's dismay, Garden management refused to pony up the cash. The deal died on the spot and Gretzky was traded to Los Angeles four days later.

Whether the entire episode played out exactly as Esposito has alleged remains a matter of conjecture and was of little concern anyway to the ecstatic Rangers fans, who welcomed Gretzky into the fold with an earsplitting better-late-than-never reception at his home debut on October 6, 1996.

Pacing the club with 25 goals and 97 points in his first Ranger campaign, the biggest-drawing card in the history of hockey proved he was worth the wait. He continued to shine in the playoffs, rifling three slap shots past Vanbiesbrouck (now a Florida Panther) in Game Two of the quarterfinals, a series the Rangers won in five games.

After a five-game dismantling of the Devils in the division semis, the Rangers advanced to face Philadelphia in the Conference Finals. Playing on the wing alongside Messier, Gretzky registered his second hat trick of the postseason in Game Two to tie the series. When someone suggested that Wayne was lucky to be performing so well out of position, Messier shot back, "His luck's been good for 20 years."

But mounting injuries took their toll on the Rangers, who lost the next three games and the chance to play for the Stanley Cup.

Gretzky played two more seasons in New York, winning his fifth Lady Byng Trophy along the way, but he and the team were never again able to reach the heights achieved during that 1997 playoff run.

As the 1998–99 campaign drew to a close, the weight of 21 seasons and over 1,700 NHL games prompted Gretzky to announce that he would retire at season's end.

Prior to Gretzky's final game on April 18, 1999, NHL commissioner Gary Bettman set a precedent by declaring that the number 99 would be retired throughout the league. The announcement, which was met by a deafening Garden ovation, only confirmed what everyone already knew in their hearts: there would never be another Gretzky.

The Hall-of-Famer went on to become a managing partner and coach of the Phoenix Coyotes.

"I've said many times before that the greatest three years I had, in life and in sports, were in New York," Gretzky told an interviewer in 2006. "It's a great city with great fans and to put on a Ranger uniform was pretty special."

> "It's a great city with great fans and to put on a Ranger uniform was pretty special."

67
MIKE GARTNER

22

Games	Goals	Assists	Penalty minutes
322	173	113	231

Hockey has seen bigger stars, but few who could match the class and amazing consistency of Mike Gartner, a speedy right wing acquired by the Rangers in 1990 to give their offense some pop.

Initially, critics considered the trade that brought Gartner over from the Minnesota North Stars a risky maneuver by the Blueshirts. He was already 30 years of age, a full seven years older than the player they gave up, winger Ulf Dahlen. And while Gartner had never scored fewer than 30 goals and showed no signs of slowing down, how much longer could he keep it up?

In no time, however, it was clear the Rangers got the better end of a lopsided deal.

Over the next three seasons, Gartner continued to find the back of the net with regularity, posting goal totals of 49 (just one shy of what was then a franchise record), 40 and 45. He recorded 30 or more goals in 14 consecutive seasons, a new NHL mark. During his time in the Big Apple, he also became just the 16th player to reach the 500-goal plateau, sixth to reach 600 goals and 33rd to score 1,000 points.

Even with those gaudy numbers, it was his skating ability and stamina that really set Gartner apart from the rest of the crowd. At no level of hockey was he ever considered the best player in the league but he was always the fastest, owing in large part to a childhood of being dragged to power skating classes by his dad, Alf. At age 34, Mike won the fastest-skater competition at the NHL All-Star Game for the second time.

"I guess you never know how you'll fare against other guys around the league," he said, "but I wasn't really surprised. I didn't abuse my body. I always felt confident in my skating and my speed."

If only Gartner's employers had the same confidence in his postseason play.

It was said of Gartner that he was a hard-working and responsible pro who played winning hockey but never for teams that needed to win when it mattered most. That unfairly branded him a playoff goat in some circles, even after he set a Rangers record with six goals in one series during the 1992 semifinals against New Jersey.

Then the Rangers hired Mike Keenan, and Gartner, who had prospered under predecessor Roger Neilson, had to prove himself to one of the game's most demanding coaches.

"It was a daily mental challenge with Keenan," Gartner revealed. "Over the course of the season it created stress, anxiety and questioning."

He might have finally proven his detractors wrong had he not been dealt to the Toronto Maple Leafs for Glenn Anderson in March 1994, one of several big moves the Rangers made in preparation for a lengthy postseason run. It was the third time in his career Gartner had to pack his bags at the trade deadline but, understandably, the toughest to digest.

"I felt like we had a great team that year," he said, his voice still resonating with disappointment. "It was a special year right from the start. I was happy for the guys in New York winning the Stanley Cup but it was hard to watch."

Gartner retired in 1998 with 708 regular-season goals, fifth-best in NHL history (at the time) behind only Wayne Gretzky, Gordie Howe, Marcel Dionne and Phil Esposito. He lacked the star power of those players and never realized his dream of winning the Stanley Cup but his plaque at the Hall of Fame is acknowledgment of a career well-spent … and well-played.

"It was a daily mental challenge with Keenan."

One of the first players to represent himself in contract negotiations in the age of collective bargaining, Gartner had a good head for the business of hockey and went on to hold a number of high-profile positions with the NHL Players' Association.

1956-61

CENTER

7

Games	Goals	Assists	Penalty minutes
322	59	150	300

Turofsky/Hockey Hall of Fame

66 RED SULLIVAN

True to the color of his hair, George James (Red) Sullivan was a fiery competitor, a spark-plug center who supplied guts and character for Ranger teams that were mostly unremarkable from 1956 to 1961. What was remarkable, however, was Sullivan himself since, in New York at least, his career was almost ended before it began.

The date was January 19, 1957, the Rangers versus the Montreal Canadiens, at Madison Square Garden. Doug Harvey, the Canadiens' peerless defenseman, egregiously speared Sullivan in the stomach. The redhead suffered a ruptured spleen and was rushed to St. Clare's Hospital, where he received the last rites of the Catholic Church. He missed the final 28 games of the season, his first in New York.

Sullivan recovered nicely, never missing another game the next four seasons, and was named the Rangers' tenth captain, succeeding Harry Howell, for the 1957–58 campaign. Playing mostly on a line with

Andy Hebenton at right wing and Camille Henry on the left, the wiry five-foot-eleven 155-pounder was a defensive ace, an outstanding poke checker and sweep checker who knew how to get under the other team's skin.

"Let's face it, Red was a pest, simple as that," remembered goaltender Gump Worsley, a friend for many years.

"Gump was right," Sullivan confirmed. "I *was* a pest, that was my style."

Nonetheless, he had an outstanding offensive season in 1958–59, scoring 21 goals and 42 assists for 63 points, the latter total being second only to Andy Bathgate on the team's scoring list. He was the co-winner, with Hebenton, of the Players' Player Award that season, the first time that trophy was awarded.

Sullivan's will to win was one of his greatest assets. In 1961–62, mild-mannered Alf Pike was coaching the Blueshirts, and not too successfully. One night, after a particularly galling loss at the Garden, a voice boomed from the Rangers' shower room: "Alf Pike couldn't fire up a furnace," it said.

Sportswriters, anxious to find out who said it, combed the locker room for comment. As usual, Worsley was there to help. "I'm not sure who said it," Gump deadpanned, "but I think he had red hair." Sullivan never admitted to that, but he never denied it either.

Prior to joining the Rangers, Sullivan played for the Boston Bruins and the Chicago Blackhawks. But it was New York that captured his soul.

"I really enjoyed my time in New York," Sullivan recalled years later. "It was wonderful. The city has so much to offer. My only regret was not being able to spend more time there, but I had a growing family back in Peterborough, Ontario."

After retiring from the NHL following the 1960–61 season, Sullivan played two more years, one with the Kitchener Beavers of the Eastern Professional League and one with the Baltimore Clippers of the American League. Midway through the 1962–63 season, Sullivan got the call to coach the Rangers,

succeeding Murray (Muzz) Patrick. He coached for three seasons, winning only 38 of 196 games behind the bench.

Off the ice, during his coaching years, Sullivan and his boss, Emile Francis, became the Rangers' one-two punch in the banquet league, promoting the Blueshirts whenever they could, since the team was floundering, and not drawing well at the Garden.

"I talked to Boy Scouts, advertising executives, dentists, bartenders, even a group of undertakers," said Sullivan. "Can you believe that?"

Said Francis: "That's what we did. Grass-roots promotion. We had to sell tickets."

Sullivan became the first coach of the Pittsburgh Penguins in 1967, and recruited no fewer than 11 former Rangers to staff the Penguins' expansion effort. He also briefly guided the Washington Capitals in their inaugural season of 1974–75. He scouted for the NHL and the Philadelphia Flyers for a bit before retiring to Ontario.

65
EDDIE JOHNSTONE

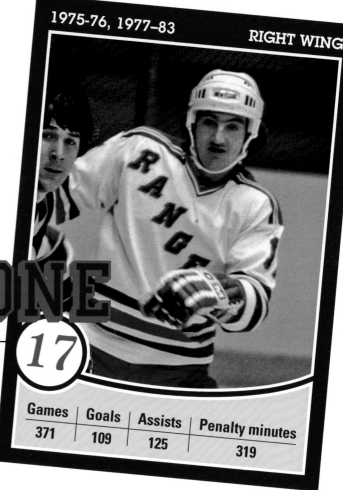

1975-76, 1977–83

RIGHT WING

17

Games	Goals	Assists	Penalty minutes
371	109	125	319

Despite the city's long-standing reputation for attracting glamorous debutantes and pampered socialites, Eddie Johnstone proved that New Yorkers really hold a special place in their hearts for the working-class "regular Joe."

That pretty much summed up the scrappy right wing whose knack for winning battles along the boards and in the corners helped make him a fan favorite at Madison Square Garden for seven seasons. Johnstone was very much a self-made star who, given his small stature, had to fight for whatever successes he enjoyed.

"Here was a guy five-foot-eight who played like a guy who was six-foot-four," said Walt Tkaczuk, another blue-collar Blueshirt. "He would always get his nose dirty. When a game was slow and lazy he would spark the energy back into it."

A proficient provocateur, Johnstone could always tell when he was getting under an opponent's skin. That's usually when a frustrated foe would resort to a surreptitious slash or utter some four-letter words.

Manitoba born but raised in Vernon, B.C., Johnstone was part of the deep Medicine Hat team (with Hall-of-Famer Lanny McDonald) that reached the Memorial Cup Final in 1973. NHL scouts loved the blend of skill and grit he brought to the arena every night, prompting the Rangers to choose him 104th overall in the 1974 draft.

Mike Rogers played with Johnstone in New York and against him in juniors and admired the rugged winger's style.

"Eddie's game was built on brute strength and toughness," Rogers said, "and for him to be able to do that against guys that were six inches taller, and 20 to 30 pounds heavier, absolutely amazed me. You'd

Usually known as a premier defensive forward, right wing Eddie Johnstone (17) eludes St. Louis defenseman Ed Kea and fires at goalie Mike Liut.

look over on your right side and see Eddie Johnstone there and know that he would go through a wall for you. If there was a puck in the corner, he would get it out for you. He was just a tremendous individual and I loved the way he played."

All of that helped make Johnstone one of the most popular Rangers of his time, and he constantly indulged in playful banter, a nonstop give-and-take really, with his teammates. His appearance was a frequent target of good-natured derision because Eddie had a prototypical hockey face, which is to say that no one mistook him for a movie star. When a fight broke out, inevitably someone on the Ranger bench would quip: "You get out there, Eddie, you've got nothin' to lose!"

That's probably why he wasn't invited to film any TV commercials for Sasson jeans with the more photogenic Don Maloney and Anders Hedberg. A product like Coca-Cola was more Johnstone's speed, anyway, and he landed a print-ad deal with the soft-drink company around the same time that Maloney and Hedberg were skating pirouettes while singing "OOohh La La Sasson."

Injuries forced Johnstone out of the lineup for much of the 1978–79 season but he returned for

the playoffs as the Rangers reached the Stanley Cup Final. He was especially handy during the quarterfinals, scoring four of his five postseason goals against the Philadelphia Flyers.

In 1980–81, he recorded his first of two consecutive 30-goal seasons and was chosen to represent the Rangers in his first and only NHL All-Star Game. Pat Quinn, coach of the Campbell Conference All-Stars, noted that Johnstone's contributions went beyond goals and assists.

"What Johnstone does," Quinn said, "doesn't always show up in the offensive statistics. He's aggressive. He's the kind of player any team would love to have."

Looking to shake themselves out of a five-year funk, the Red Wings acquired Johnstone, Ron Duguay and Eddie Mio from the Rangers in 1983 for forwards Mike Blaisdell and Mark Osborne as well as Willie Huber, the biggest defenseman in the league at the time.

Johnstone battled injuries and reduced ice time with the Red Wings before retiring in 1987 to begin a lengthy career coaching in juniors and the minor pros.

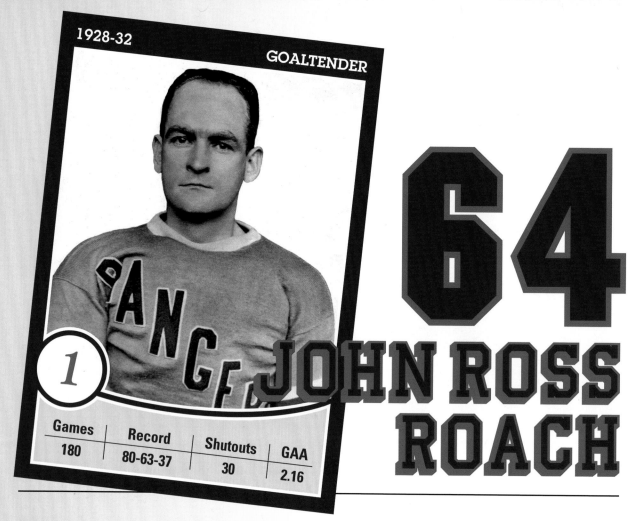

1928-32   **GOALTENDER**

1

Games	Record	Shutouts	GAA
180	80-63-37	30	2.16

64
JOHN ROSS ROACH

B rought to New York from Toronto in a 1928 trade to replace Lorne Chabot, John Ross Roach became one of the most successful goalies in team history, setting club records that still stand and backstopping the Rangers to the Stanley Cup Final twice in four years.

At five-foot-five and tipping the scales at only 130 pounds, the pride of picturesque Port Perry, Ontario, was certainly the smallest goalie ever to guard the Blueshirt cage. Appearing anxious and fidgety, Roach was known to be in almost constant motion in front of his net. Off the ice, at least one former teammate characterized him as "moody," although that's hardly a novel observation when applied to goalies.

The circumstances under which Roach became a Ranger were not without controversy.

Behind the deal, which also included a $10,000 cash payment to the Maple Leafs, was a league-wide tug-of-war over a coveted prospect named Dave Trottier. A goal-scoring winger and hero of Canada's gold medal at the 1928 Olympics, Trottier

was considered Leafs property but had yet to sign with the club. Offers for his services poured in from other teams, with the Rangers believing they had the inside track.

But when team president Col. John S. Hammond learned that Trottier *might* be headed to Boston instead, he demanded restitution from the Maple Leafs. It's unlikely Toronto manager Conn Smythe would have parted with Roach, a superstar in his day, if Hammond hadn't made such a fuss.

In addition to making the Rangers slightly better, at least on paper, the trade also gave local sportswriters a chance to fan the flames of a simmering rivalry between the Rangers and Madison Square Garden's first team, the Americans, who had just acquired future Hall-of-Famer Roy (Shrimp) Worters. Imagine—the NHL's two best goalies battling for supremacy, in New York, and under the same roof!

Although saddled with the redundant nickname "Little Napoleon," Roach covered enough of the net

to record 13 shutouts and a 1.48 goals-against average in his first Ranger season, marks that have yet to be eclipsed. He was equally stellar in the postseason, blanking the opposition three more times and posting a minuscule 0.77 goals-against average as the Blueshirts advanced to the 1929 Stanley Cup Final.

But in the first final between two U.S.-based teams, Roach was outplayed by Boston's fabulous rookie Cecil (Tiny) Thompson, earning the Bruins their first championship.

Roach started every game for the Rangers over the next three seasons and after stonewalling the Canadiens in the 1932 semifinals, he and the Blueshirts were back in the Cup round facing Toronto. After falling tantalizingly short of the silver chalice in his last finals appearance, Little Napoleon had a shot at redemption.

What followed was one of the most lopsided finals ever played. The press dubbed it "The Tennis Series" after the Maple Leafs scored six goals in every game of their three-game sweep.

That embarrassment was more than Rangers manager-coach Lester Patrick could stomach, and after the season he sold Roach to the Detroit Red Wings.

In fact, Patrick and the Rangers were so eager to get Roach out of town they were willing to rest their hopes on a relative unknown, rookie Andy Aitkenhead, to replace him. The move paid off and with Aitkenhead in goal, in 1933 the Rangers promptly won their second Stanley Cup.

Roach played a few more years in Detroit before closing out his career in the minors. On July 9, 1973, he passed away at the age of 72.

Although his time with the Rangers was short and ended somewhat ignominiously, Roach still ranks among the franchise leaders in goals-against average (2.16) and shutouts (30).

63
BILL GADSBY

1954-61   **DEFENSEMAN**

④

Games	Goals	Assists	Penalty minutes
457	58	213	413

Given what he endured when he was only 12 years old, it's no wonder that rock-steady defenseman Bill Gadsby would go on to play 20 seasons in the National Hockey League. Seven of those seasons would be with the Rangers, with whom Gadsby was a superb playmaker, robust body checker, expert shot blocker and three times a First Team All-Star.

On September 3, 1939, Gadsby was traveling with his mother aboard the North America-bound steamship *Athenia*, one of the last scheduled steamships to leave Southampton, England, at the onset of World War II. In the Irish Sea, the *Athenia* was hit and sunk by a German torpedo.

About 50 passengers, including the Gadsbys, crammed into a single lifeboat. "I was too young to realize how serious the situation was," Gadsby recalled years later. "But I saw men and women going crazy with panic. I saw up close the horror and terrible things I can never forget."

A rescue ship eventually spotted the lifeboat and returned the survivors to Southampton, where the Gadsbys boarded yet another steamship, the *Mauretania*, for a safe passage to New York and their eventual destination, Calgary, Alberta.

As a young hockey player, William Alexander Gadsby caught the eye of the Chicago Blackhawks, who signed him to a contract for $7,000 when he was just 18 years old. He played only a dozen minor league games with the Kansas City Pla-Mors of the United States Hockey League in 1946–47 before getting called to Chicago.

Once he made it to the NHL, the six-foot-one 190-pounder never looked back, playing 1,248 games without another in the minors.

In 1952, the same year he was named captain of the Blackhawks, Gadsby contracted polio and spent ten days in medical isolation. Fortunately, his symptoms eventually disappeared, and he was able to resume his hockey career.

Stalwart defenseman Bill Gadsby (left) made the NHL's first All-Star team with the Rangers three times in the late 1950s.

Traded to the Rangers on November 23, 1954, Gadsby was only 27, near the peak of his career, and with eight seasons of NHL experience under his belt. He became one of the steadiest defensemen the Rangers have ever had. In 1958–59, he set what was then a single-season record for defensemen with 46 assists, two more than Montreal's Doug Harvey had two seasons earlier.

The Rangers were a solid club during Gadsby's time in New York. He anchored a defensive corps that featured Harry Howell, Lou Fontinato and Jack (Tex) Evans. Captain Andy Bathgate led the offense and Lorne (Gump) Worsley was in goal. The Rangers made the playoffs three times, from 1955–56 to 1957–58, with Gadsby named a First Team All-Star in 1956, 1958 and 1959.

Injuries of all kinds dogged Gadsby throughout his career. He broke his nose seven times, and his left leg was broken twice. His body (mostly his face) took over 600 stitches. Nonetheless, Gadsby missed only 15 games with the Rangers. "Gads was a real trooper," recalled Murray (Muzz) Patrick, the Rangers' general manager during most of Gadsby's time in New York. "If it wasn't for Andy (Bathgate), he could have been captain."

The Rangers traded Gadsby to Detroit on June 12, 1961, in exchange for Les Hunt. It was one of the worst trades the Rangers have ever made. Hunt never played a game in the NHL, while Gadsby played five more seasons, and 323 games, for the Red Wings.

Following his playing career, Gadsby coached two seasons with the junior Edmonton Oil Kings and returned to coach the Red Wings for a single season, 1968–69, plus the first two games (both of which the Wings won!) in 1969–70.

He broke his nose seven times, and his left leg was broken twice.

Sadly, hockey's ultimate prize, the Stanley Cup, eluded Gadsby, although he made the finals in 1963, 1964 and 1966. He was elected to the Hockey Hall of Fame in 1970.

1979-86

DEFENSEMAN

62 BARRY BECK

5

Games	Goals	Assists	Penalty minutes
415	66	173	775

It was easy to mistake Barry Beck for a linebacker on skates. The big, bruising Vancouver native played middle linebacker in high school and was even offered college football scholarships. But "Bubba" abandoned the gridiron to pursue a career on ice that would eventually take a much-hyped tour through New York City.

It was with a bit of discomfort, to be sure, that Beck became a New York Ranger, coming over from the Colorado Rockies in exchange for a gaggle of players on November 2, 1979. Fortunately for the Rangers and their fans, Beck had broad shoulders. An awful lot was expected from the man they called "the big guy," and it was expected quickly.

Six months earlier, the Rangers had unexpectedly crashed the Stanley Cup Finals, before losing to the Montreal Canadiens. Beck, in some quarters at least, was immediately (and perhaps unfairly) cast in the role of a Messiah, the savior that would put the Rangers over the top.

"It was sort of common knowledge that [Montreal defenseman] Larry Robinson beat us the year before in the finals," said Pat Hickey, one of five players sent to Colorado in the big trade. "We didn't have that one extra element. Barry Beck was the guy that was out there who was like Larry Robinson."

The Rangers of Phil Esposito, John Davidson, Ron Duguay, Don Murdoch, and the Swedes, Ulf Nilsson and Anders Hedberg, quickly embraced Bubba even as top Madison Square Garden marketing officials were trying to ditch the nickname as more appropriate for a football lineman than for a sophisticated hockey player living in Manhattan.

Broadcaster Bill Chadwick called Beck a "gentle giant," and that he was. He almost reluctantly took to Manhattan and its pleasures. "In the long run," Beck later said of his Big Apple experience, "New York is the best place to play hockey. But you've got to take advantage of it, or else just sit in your apartment and go bananas. I tried to take advantage."

The city agreed with Beck as he scored 59 points in 61 games, but the club was eliminated in the second round of the 1980 playoffs. The next year he was a key factor in the Blueshirts' march to the semifinals. Beck also served as captain for parts of his seven seasons with the club.

When healthy, Beck was often a dominant presence on the Ranger defense, and his versatility enabled coaches to pair him with a variety of players. His heavy shot and willingness to join the rush allowed him to show off his offensive skills but if partnered with Reijo Ruotsalainen or Ron Greschner, he could play a simpler, stay-at-home style that maximized his strength and toughness. He seemed comfortable in either role.

Although Beck believed he played better when he was a little sore, his performance was often hindered by a host of injuries, most notably a left shoulder that never seemed to stay in place.

That can be traced to Game Four of the 1984 quarterfinals when Islanders rookie Pat Flatley hammered Beck into the boards halfway through the third period. Seconds after the hit, with the Ranger captain crumpled in the slot, the Isles took a 2–1 lead and eventually forced a fifth and deciding game. The injury that ended Beck's season doomed the Rangers as well, and they lost the series.

In 1986, dissatisfaction with coach Ted Sator prompted Beck to announce his retirement at age 29. In the process, he walked away from a $385,000 contract—a lot of money at the time—but decided to come back the following season after Sator was replaced with Michel Bergeron.

During a preseason game in September 1987, Beck reinjured his shoulder and called it quits again. Two years later, he mounted a brief comeback with the Los Angeles Kings but retired for good in March 1990 after deciding he was too slow for the NHL game.

In later years, Beck became heavily involved in teaching the game to young players and in 2007, he moved to Hong Kong to run the Hong Kong Academy of Ice Hockey.

Hockey Hall of Fame

1931-36

DEFENSEMAN

2

Games	Goals	Assists	Penalty minutes
204	27	41	338

61 EARL SEIBERT

Their names are spelled differently but that hasn't prevented considerable confusion from surrounding the stellar careers of Earl Seibert and Albert (Babe) Siebert, teammates on the Rangers for all of 56 games, but long enough to win the Stanley Cup for New York in 1933.

Both men eventually made it to the Hockey Hall of Fame—Earl in 1963 and Babe a year later—and each was considered a "goaltender's best friend." Earl, a defenseman, was particularly adept at blocking shots while Babe, a left wing, was a master of blocking out opposing forwards and keeping the crease clear of bodies.

When it came to length of service, however, Earl had Babe licked. Four and a half of his 15 NHL seasons were spent on Broadway, while Babe played less than two.

At six-foot-two and weighing 220 pounds, Seibert was big by the standards of *any* era and, if you're inclined to take the word of some of his teammates and clined to take the word of some of his teammates and opponents (as we are), he may have been the toughest player of his era.

Seibert's first defensive partner with the Rangers was the equally rambunctious Ivan (Ching) Johnson. From a toughness standpoint, the twosome was the most imposing in the NHL, a fact that Johnson often credited to Seibert's reputation as a bruiser.

Usually, though, Seibert's size was enough of a deterrent to ward off most aggressors.

"Let's put it this way," Johnson would say, "no one wanted any part of 'Si' in a fight. Even [Boston's] Eddie Shore and [Toronto's] Red Horner steered clear of him, and Shore and Horner were considered the toughest guys in the league at the time."

Receiving league-wide recognition as an elite defenseman, Earl made the All-Star Team ten seasons in a row from 1934–35 to 1943–44, four times as a First Team selection and six times on the Second Team. Chalk up at least some of his success to having strong hockey bloodlines.

His father, Oliver, played regularly with five brothers and was one of the first players out of Berlin (later Kitchener), Ontario, to turn pro. In fact, Earl and his dad were the first father-son duo to make the Hall of Fame.

Like most NHLers, Seibert loved his job and probably would have played for free on a frozen pond in Flin Flon, if he had to. But he was a pro and a proud capitalist who understood his worth to the Rangers and wanted to be paid accordingly. That often led to some tense negotiations with the Rangers' notoriously frugal manager, Lester Patrick.

As much as Lester appreciated what Seibert could do on the ice, he tired of the defenseman's annual holdouts. When Seibert held out again to open the 1935–36 season, Patrick's patience ran out. On January 15, 1936, the Rangers traded Earl to Chicago for another rugged blueliner, Art Coulter.

Both teams benefited from the swap. Coulter and Seibert would each become captain of their new clubs, and each would also win a Stanley Cup: Earl in 1938 with the Blackhawks and Art in 1940 with the Rangers.

Seibert closed out his career in 1946 after two seasons with the Detroit Red Wings. In all, he would play 645 games in the NHL, an extremely high figure for a player of that era.

After his retirement, Seibert accepted an invitation from his old nemesis, Eddie Shore, to coach Shore's AHL team, the Springfield Indians. But working for the cantankerous ex-Bruin was too much for Earl, and he quit after only a few seasons behind the bench.

In 1998, eight years after his death at age 79, *The Hockey News* ranked Seibert No. 72 on its list of the NHL's 100 greatest hockey players—evidence that fading memories and the passage of time haven't completely erased the mark he left on the game.

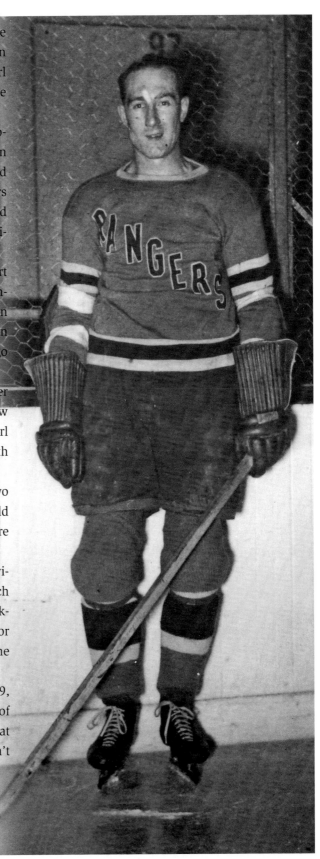

1948–54

DEFENSEMAN

8

60
ALLAN
STANLEY

Games	Goals	Assists	Penalty minutes
307	23	55	272

If ever a player was the victim of too much hype, too much buildup, it was Allan Stanley, the square-jawed defenseman who joined the Rangers midway through the 1948–49 season. Stanley brought with him rugged good looks and an equally handsome résumé, but he was decidedly *not* wearing Superman's cape.

The reason for all the ballyhoo surrounding the six-foot-one 170-pounder from Timmins, Ontario, was two-fold. First, Stanley was indeed a bona fide prospect with definite star power. Second, the Rangers were desperately in need of someone, someone positive, to hitch their wagon to, since the team had made the playoffs only once in the previous seven seasons. That someone was Stanley.

Frank Boucher, the Rangers' general manager, had spent a small fortune in players and cash to pry Stanley's services from the Providence Reds of the

AHL. That led to the team's publicity office, in the person of publicist Stan Saplin, unfairly portraying the 22-year-old rearguard as somewhat of a knight in shining armor who would rescue the Rangers from mediocrity. It was not to be.

Stanley was a prototypical "defensive defenseman" with a deliberate, puck-clearing style and an uncanny ability to read plays before they happened. He was not, as the fans had hoped, a "banger" whose thumping body checks would remind them of popular predecessors such as Ching Johnson, Taffy Abel, Art Coulter and Muzz Patrick. Nor was he a great skater.

Even after he finished runner-up to teammate Pentti Lund for the Calder Trophy as rookie of the year, it wasn't long before the fans turned on Stanley, unmercifully at times. They called him "Snowshoes," mimicking his deliberate style and his lumbering, yet effective, delivery. The Rangers tried everything to turn the tide of continuing fan displeasure, even naming Stanley their captain midway through the

1951–52 season. At age 25, he was the youngest captain the Rangers ever had, up to that point.

"They'd boo every time I touched the puck," Stanley recalled. "Then they began to boo every time I got on the ice. They would even yell at me when I was just sitting on the bench."

The booing got so bad that coaches Boucher, Lynn Patrick, Neil Colville and Bill Cook would sometimes play Stanley only on the road to reduce the pressure on him. That tactic worked to a point, but it also made for a stale player who simply wasn't getting enough overall ice time.

It was inevitable that Stanley would eventually be traded, particularly since the club only made the playoffs once during his five-plus years in New York. That was in 1950, when the Rangers miraculously took the Red Wings to double overtime in the seventh game of the finals before losing. Ironically enough, Stanley played extremely well in that series, since the circus had taken over Madison Square Garden and all seven games were played on the road.

The trade finally happened on November 23, 1954, with the Rangers shipping Stanley and Nick Mickoski to Chicago for All-Star defenseman Bill Gadsby and winger Pete Conacher.

Stanley would then play two seasons for the Boston Bruins before really hitting his stride during ten stellar campaigns—and winning four Stanley Cups—with the Toronto Maple Leafs.

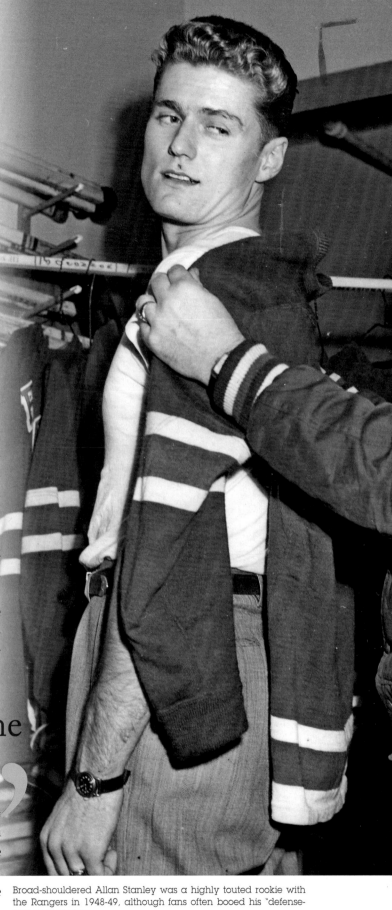

"They'd boo every time I touched the puck."

In 1968–69, Stanley's career played out, oh-so-quietly, with a final season on the expansion Philadelphia Flyers, about 90 miles south of where all the ballyhoo began two decades earlier.

The 21-year NHL veteran was inducted into the Hockey Hall of Fame in 1981.

Broad-shouldered Allan Stanley was a highly touted rookie with the Rangers in 1948-49, although fans often booed his "defense-first" style of play.

59
PHIL GOYETTE

1963–69, 1971-72

20

Games	Goals	Assists	Penalty minutes
397	98	231	51

They called Phil Goyette "The Professor," mostly because off the ice he did indeed look professorial, with a wizened face and wire-rimmed glasses.

But the savvy centerman was also a professor on the ice, a fact that the Rangers knew wholeheartedly over the course of the 397 games he played for the club over six-plus years from 1963 to 1972.

At five-foot-ten, 170 pounds, Goyette was about average for hockey players of his day, yet he played much bigger. Bernie (Boom Boom) Geoffrion, Goyette's longtime teammate with the Montreal Canadiens and even for two seasons in New York, marveled at Goyette's prowess at winning face-offs, calling Phil the best in the league at that skill.

Goyette grew up in the Montreal suburb of Lachine and had a backyard rink at his disposal, where he would emulate the moves of his two favorite players, centers Elmer Lach of the Montreal Canadiens and Ted (Teeder) Kennedy of the Toronto Maple Leafs.

The Canadiens, despite their powerful lineup (especially at center, where Jean Béliveau, Henri Richard and Ralph Backstrom were well-entrenched), nonetheless had Goyette on their radar since he was just a teenager. He came up through the Montreal system, with the Montreal Jr. Canadiens and the Montreal Royals, and even spent a year with the Cincinnati Mohawks of the International Hockey League, leading the IHL with 41 goals in 1954–55.

By 1956–57, Goyette was in the Montreal lineup for good, and he won four straight Stanley Cups from 1956 to 1960. "My role was strictly defensive back then," he recalled. "Playing behind Béliveau, Richard and Backstrom didn't exactly translate into extra ice time, but that was my job."

Traded to the Rangers in the summer of 1963, Goyette quickly blossomed into the all-around player the scouts knew he was. "I remember when I first

heard about the trade," he said. "I really didn't want to go. In the long run, though, it was really the best thing that could have happened to me."

The Rangers promptly installed Goyette at center between left wing Donnie Marshall and right wing Bob Nevin. The trio clicked immediately, and the sportswriters dubbed them "The Smoothies," later the "Old Smoothies." The nickname mostly traced itself to Goyette, whose peripheral vision and uncanny passing skills were a delight to witness.

Said Nevin, the team's captain at the time: "It's like he [Goyette] has eyes in the back of his head. You'd be in a position where you'd never expect to see the puck, but all of a sudden, there it was. He was amazing."

Perhaps the lowest point of Goyette's career with the Rangers occurred on December 26, 1965, barely a year and a half after he arrived in New York. That night, Goyette was viciously speared in the stomach by Boston defenseman Ted Green, and suffered damage to his spleen.

"The Professor" missed about a month's play, but recovered. Rangers fans, however, never forgave Green for the vile act, and team president William Jennings even put a bounty on Green's head for a time. Ranger fans would subsequently vilify Green whenever he came to the Garden, right up to his retirement in 1972.

Goyette was traded to St. Louis for a first-round draft choice on June 10, 1969, and his career wound down with the Blues and the Buffalo Sabres. There was a brief return to New York late in the 1971–72 season. The Rangers thought they could win it all that year, but they lost ace center Jean Ratelle to a broken ankle with a month to go, so they bought Goyette from Buffalo.

Goyette proved to be his old reliable self for eight regular-season games and 13 more in the playoffs. The Rangers made the finals, but bowed to the Bruins in six games on May 11, 1972. Ironically enough, that game would be the last in the NHL for Goyette … and for Ted Green.

1945–51

LEFT WING

18

Games	Goals	Assists	Penalty minutes
368	113	89	420

58 TONY LESWICK

Long before Claude Lemieux and Sean Avery were even twinkles in their parents' eyes, left wing Tony Leswick was inspiring profanity-laced diatribes from opponents with his abrasive style.

"Tony," said Hall of Fame referee Bill Chadwick, "could bring out the worst in a saint."

New York sportswriters called him the Rangers' "Mighty Mite" or "Mighty Mouse" because, at five-foot-six-and-a-half and a generous 160 pounds, Leswick was at once the smallest and spunkiest player on the team. "And don't forget the half [inch]," Leswick would often say. "It's important to me."

A relentless checker and the premier pest of the Original Six era, this spark plug was one of the few bright lights on Broadway during a six-year stretch from 1945 to 1951. At a time when the team's Stanley Cup hopes were bleakest, at least the energetic Leswick helped keep things interesting.

"Tony was a combative little bugger," recalled Frank Boucher, the Rangers' longtime general manager and coach. "He played a lot bigger than his size."

"Leswick never backed down from anyone or anything," said former Boston Bruins left wing Woody Dumart. "Never once. He was feisty. He loved to get into the rough stuff. I don't think anyone liked playing against him."

Leswick, a top boxer back in his native Saskatchewan, wouldn't have had it any other way.

"That was the only way I knew to play," Leswick told *Hockey Digest* about six weeks before his death in 2001. "I couldn't go about things any other way. Oh, it was rough. It wasn't easy. But it was the only way I could do it."

What he lacked in stature, Leswick made up for in skill and cunning, and he knew he could give the Rangers a chance to win if he was able to get Gordie Howe, Ted Lindsay or other stars of the day off their game or—better yet—off the ice.

One of the toughest NHL forwards of his time, Tony Leswick (8) "could bring out the bad side of a Saint," according to Hall of Fame referee Bill Chadwick.

Tony's favorite target of harassment was Montreal's Maurice (Rocket) Richard, and the long-running, fight-filled feud between the men lasted for years. Leswick knew how to get under Richard's skin and could often draw the short-tempered Habitant into taking dumb penalties. A furious Richard then had to watch a Rangers power play from his seat in the penalty box.

On one such occasion, in January 1950, a packed Montreal Forum watched Leswick and Richard battle throughout the match. Four minor penalties, the last assessed with only 20 seconds of play remaining in a game in which his Canadiens trailed 3–1, had Richard fuming. When the final horn sounded, Richard erupted into a vicious rage. He hopped out of the box and made a mad dash for Leswick, his fists swinging. Teammates tried in vain to separate the two, and the Rocket was so incensed that he even took a wild swing at Rangers coach Lynn Patrick.

But agitating and penalty killing weren't Leswick's only contributions to the Blueshirts. He led the team with 27 goals in 1946–47, had 24 the following year, and posted career highs in assists (25) and points (44) in 1949–50, earning a place on the NHL's Second All-Star Team. He also represented New York at four All-Star games.

Leswick came within inches of being the hero of the 1950 Stanley Cup Finals against Detroit when his shot hit the crossbar in overtime of Game Seven. Moments later, Pete Babando fired home the series-clinching goal for the Red Wings.

A year later, the Red Wings acquired Leswick from the Rangers for Gaye Stewart. Stewart never really found his mark in New York, but Leswick went on to have great success in Motown, winning Stanley Cups in 1952, 1954 and 1955.

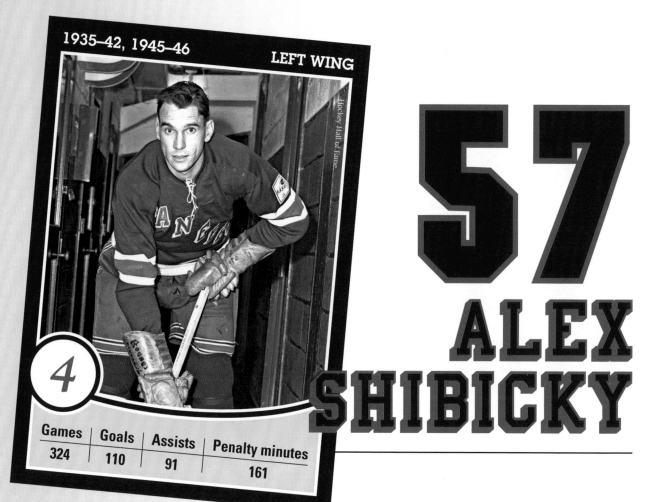

1935–42, 1945–46

LEFT WING

Hockey Hall of Fame

4

Games	Goals	Assists	Penalty minutes
324	110	91	161

57 ALEX SHIBICKY

In eight seasons, covering 324 games, Alex Shibicky distinguished himself as one of the best left-wingers the Rangers have ever had. He did a lot of everything: scoring goals, killing penalties and working the power play. But it was an injury—a seriously broken ankle—that would ultimately define Shibicky's legacy with the Rangers.

Shibicky and his future line mates, the brothers Neil and Mac Colville, were all products of the Rangers' "3-R" system, which placed players with the amateur New York Rovers, then the Philadelphia Ramblers, and ultimately the Rangers.

The Colville brothers (Neil was a center, Mac a right wing) and Shibicky formed one of the most famous lines in Ranger history. They called them the "Bread Line," the moniker coming from New York sportswriters who saw the trio as the Rangers' bread and butter. At the time, they were also the youngest line in the National Hockey League.

The unit was at its peak in 1939–40 when the Rangers streaked to the Stanley Cup Finals and faced the Toronto Maple Leafs. The heart of that team was the "Bread Line."

In Game Three of the finals, Shibicky broke his ankle. He missed Game Four, but aided by painkillers from the Toronto doctors, returned to play with his leg frozen up to the knee for the balance of the series. "Alex was truly amazing, an inspiration," said coach Frank Boucher. "He would play as long as the drugs held out. Then he would come out of the game."

Lester Patrick, the general manager, and Boucher called a special meeting of the players. The issue was whether to tell Shibicky about the fracture or to downplay the injury. "We all voted not to tell him," recalled teammate Muzz Patrick. It was hardly a sound medical practice by today's standards.

"They told me it was a bad sprain," Shibicky recalled. The skillful stickhandler notched five assists in the finals, an amazing effort for a guy who was

Left wing Alex Shibicky (right) starred on the Rangers' "Bread Line" with Neil Colville at center and Mac Colville at right wing.

basically playing on one leg. "I guess it picked up the guys," Shibicky recalled, "because they knew I was injured and they just gave that much more."

Shibicky came out of the junior leagues of Manitoba, catching the eye of Ranger scouts in 1933 and 1934. The Rangers promptly signed him and sent him to the Brooklyn Crescents, predecessors of the Rovers, in the Eastern Hockey League. A year later, he was in the NHL.

With 24 goals in 1938–39, Shibicky led the Rangers in goals and tied Montreal's Hector (Toe) Blake for second in the league that year. Teammates regularly said he should have had more, mostly because of his unselfish nature and his tendency to pass rather than shoot. "SHOOT! SHOOT! Shibicky! Aww, s—t, Shibicky," they would say, even during practices.

A right-handed shooting left wing, Shibicky is well known for being the first person to utilize the slap shot. "I learned it from Bun Cook," he said, "but Bun only used it in practice. I was the first to use it in a game."

Like it did for so many players, particularly on the Rangers, World War II effectively ended Shibicky's NHL career. It cost him three seasons, 1942–43 to 1944–45. During the war years, he played with the Ottawa Engineers and the Ottawa Commandos, winning the Allan Cup (Canada's senior championship) with the Commandos in 1943.

Retiring from the NHL in 1946, Shibicky wound down his career with the Providence Reds and the New Haven Ramblers of the American Hockey League.

He passed away, at the age of 91, on July 9, 2005.

1975–83

GOALTENDER

30

Games	Record	Shutouts	GAA
222	93-90-25	7	3.58

56
JOHN DAVIDSON

Anyone old enough to remember the 1979 play-offs will likely tell you that John Davidson was the difference-maker for a Rangers team that advanced to the Stanley Cup Finals for the second time that decade.

The son of a Canadian Mounted Policeman, "J.D." was the top stopper in the Western Hockey League when the St. Louis Blues made him their first-round draft choice (fifth overall) in 1973, and he became the first goalie ever to make the NHL straight out of juniors.

After two years in St. Louis, Davidson was traded to the Rangers in June 1975 with Bill Collins for Ted Irvine, Jerry Butler and Bert Wilson. He promptly inherited the starter's job when the enormously popular Eddie Giacomin was placed on waivers a few months later.

It didn't take long for fans to warm to the new guy. At six-foot-three and 200 pounds, the big fella filled a lot of net but he also had great agility. His unorthodox style was somewhat similar to that of six-time Vezina winner Dominik Hasek.

"When it came to skills," Dave Maloney said, "John was that type of player. He was chaotic. In John you got a big guy in goal who was very, very acrobatic. He was a tremendous athlete."

"Tremendous" continues to be an adjective used by Davidson's former teammates when discussion shifts to his inspired postseason play in 1979.

Cheered on by chants of "JAY-DEE! JAY-DEE!" the tall, mustached goalie looked downright impenetrable as the New Yorkers dispatched the Kings, Flyers and Islanders en route to the finals and a date with the mighty Canadiens.

A 4–1 Ranger win in Game One had some believing that New York was about to host its first Stanley Cup party in almost 40 years. But a knee injury Davidson suffered during the Islander series worsened over time, neutralizing the best advantage the Rangers had against their heavily favored opponents.

Before Montreal roared back to win the series, Davidson was considered the leading candidate for playoff MVP. While the Flying Frenchmen may have spoiled his Conn Smythe bid, those six weeks in the spring of '79, when the entire city got swept up in the Rangers' cause and it seemed like everyone was a hockey fan, were certainly the most exciting and memorable of Davidson's career.

The following season was his last as a starter. He played in just three games over the next two years due to that nagging knee injury along with chronic back problems that eventually required surgery to remove two badly damaged discs from his spine.

His body beaten down, Davidson retired in 1983 after ten NHL seasons.

But when one door closed, another one opened for J.D., who had dabbled in broadcasting during lengthy stints on the injured list and found he had a gift for gab. Embarking on a new career as a color analyst, he went on to cover almost every major hockey event in the world, including Stanley Cup Finals, numerous All-Star Games and the Olympic Games. More than that, he remained an ambassador for the Rangers franchise and one of its most recognizable personalities.

In 2006, Davidson hung up his microphone to become president of the Blues, ending a 30-year relationship with the Rangers.

"I was lucky enough to work with the best that there ever was in the hockey television business," said longtime on-air partner Sam Rosen. "So many people stopped me to say, 'You helped teach me the game,' and that was because of John. He had the ability to talk to people on the airwaves without talking down to them and without making the experts feel like he was speaking beneath them. He could relate to all people at all levels. Nobody was like him and that's why when any network did hockey, they hired John Davidson."

55 MAC COLVILLE

1935–42, 1945–47 RIGHT WING

5

Games	Goals	Assists	Penalty minutes
353	71	104	130

Throughout their glorious history, indeed from their very inception in 1926, the Rangers have often had a brother combination to lead them. For the most part, the younger brother usually got the lesser billing. Mac Colville fit the pattern perfectly.

Colville, his more famous brother Neil, a center, and left wing Alex Shibicky came to the Rangers as an inseparable trio, all of them signing as free agents on October 18, 1935. They formed the "Bread Line" (also known as the "Stream Line"), the youngest in the NHL at the time. They would become one of the most effective lines in team history, conveniently following in the footsteps of the Rangers' first great line, the "A-Line" of Frank Boucher, Bill Cook and Bun Cook.

Boucher, who would later become coach and general manager of the Rangers, called the Colvilles and Shibicky "Prairie Boys" as they all came from Western Canada, the Colvilles hailing from Edmonton and Shibicky from Winnipeg.

The "Prairie Boys" were Rangers through and through. The three of them played 1,139 games (353 by Mac Colville) for the Blueshirts, and none of them ever played a single game, not a one, for another NHL team. Collectively, they celebrated the Rangers' third Stanley Cup in 1940.

But individually, the trio couldn't have been more different. Where Neil and Shibicky were outgoing and talkative, Mac was the polar opposite. "He wore a frown as his normal expression," Boucher once said. "We called him the Dour Scot."

Mac was a quintessential defensive player, and that role suited him just fine. "I did the back-checking," he recalled. "Lester Patrick told us never to give the puck away, because the other team couldn't score if we had it. That made sense to me, so I did the back-checking."

At five-foot-eight and 175 pounds, Matthew Lamont Colville was about average size for a hockey player of his era. He was surprisingly durable, however, and rarely missed a game during his nine seasons in New York. "I always remembered Murray Murdoch's advice," Colville recalled, "'Don't ever miss a game, somebody might take your job.'"

Less than a year after winning the 1940 Cup, Mac Colville was part of another piece of NHL history. The date was December 1, 1940, in Chicago. For the first time ever, four sets of brothers played in an NHL game: Mac and Neil, plus Lynn and Muzz Patrick for the Rangers against Doug and Max Bentley plus Bill and Bob Carse of the Chicago Blackhawks. The Hawks won, 4–1.

The dawning of World War II simply decimated the Rangers, and no one felt it more than the Colville boys, both of whom played during the war for the elite Ottawa Commandos team in the Quebec Senior Hockey League.

Following the war, Mac tried a comeback with the Rangers, but like brother Neil and Shibicky, he was ineffective, scoring only seven times in 53 games before retiring early in the 1946–47 season.

Mac was a quintessential defensive player, and that role suited him just fine.

Hockey Hall of Fame

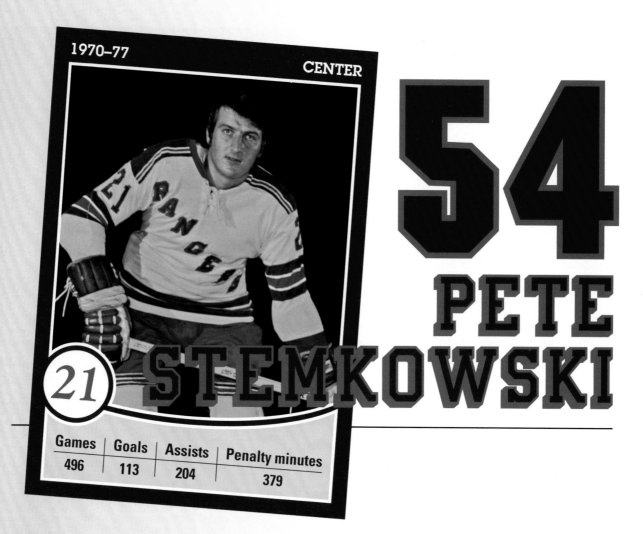

1970–77

CENTER

54 PETE STEMKOWSKI

21

Games	Goals	Assists	Penalty minutes
496	113	204	379

They called him "The Polish Prince" and when it came to scoring clutch goals, Pete Stemkowski was hockey royalty.

A large, lumbering center who also played some left wing, Stemkowski broke into the NHL with Toronto and helped the Maple Leafs win the Stanley Cup in 1967. He was eventually traded to Detroit, settling in as one of the Red Wings' more consistent two-way players. After three seasons in Motown he was dealt once again, this time to the Rangers.

When the six-foot, 200-pound Stemkowski arrived a few days later, he immediately became the Rangers' biggest forward (which tells you how much the average NHL player has grown in recent years). Emile Francis initially had him center a line with Bob Nevin at right wing and Ted Irvine on the left, giving the Blueshirts added versatility.

"Stemmer was kind of my idol," Irvine said of his fellow Manitoban. "He was one of the first guys I knew of to make the NHL out of Winnipeg. We went to the same school and became friends over the years. We roomed together, played together and had a lot of laughs on the bench. He was fun to be with on the ice because when it came to trash talking, Stemmer could do it with the best of them."

No discussion of Stemkowski's career would be complete without mention of April 29, 1971, when the Rangers hosted Chicago in Game Six of the semifinals.

An exciting contest had already seen the Blackhawks rally from a 2–0 deficit to tie the score, putting the Blueshirts on the brink of elimination in the series. The teams played two scoreless overtime frames in a warm and humid Madison Square Garden.

Exhaustion set in on both sides and between periods, an oxygen tank was wheeled into the Rangers' dressing room for anyone who needed a whiff.

Just over a minute into the third extra period, there was a mad scramble in front of the Chicago net. Irvine emerged with the puck, skated to the right side of the crease and fired a shot from a sharp angle. Tony Esposito, the acrobatic Blackhawk goalie, kicked the disk out but it skipped right to Stemkowski. With Esposito flat on the ice in front of him, Stemmer lifted the puck into the net, giving the Rangers a 3–2 win and ending one of the longest NHL games ever at four hours and 23 minutes. It was Stemkowski's second OT winner of the series and for his feat he was promised a summer's supply of Polish sausages or, as he called them, "the breakfast of champions."

Although the Blackhawks rebounded from that devastating loss to win Game Seven in Chicago two nights later—a detail conveniently swept under the rug of history by some Rangers fans—Stemmer's tally was certainly the biggest of his career and one of the most dramatic playoff goals on record.

"I must have had a couple hundred guys say they were at home in bed with a transistor radio in their ear because their parents wouldn't let them stay up late or their son or daughter was born on that night," he says. "It's not winning a Cup or winning a Game Seven—it just prolonged the series. But a lot of people still remind me about it and that's nice."

After seven seasons with the Rangers, Stemkowski became a free agent in 1977 and signed with the Kings. He finished his NHL career in the 1977–78 season and played one final year in the AHL with the Springfield Indians.

Stemmer stayed close to the game after his retirement, most recently working as the color commentator on San Jose Sharks radio broadcasts. Today, he lives on Long Island.

53
ANDY HEBENTON

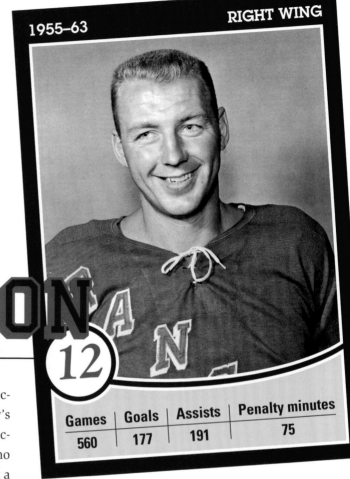

1955–63

RIGHT WING

12

Games	Goals	Assists	Penalty minutes
560	177	191	75

Doug Jarvis holds the record for most consecutive NHL games played, but pro hockey's answer to Lou Gehrig and Cal Ripken is actually Andy Hebenton, a plugging right wing who played more than 1,000 professional games without a single miss. Along the way, the sport's all-time "Iron Man" played 560 games with the Rangers.

Add 22 more playoff games with New York for a total of 582, which stands as the team's all-time record, surpassing by 19 the much-chronicled streak by the team's first Iron Man, Murray Murdoch. "I never thought of it at the time, but I guess it is quite something by today's standards," Hebenton noted, years after his playing career ended. "I just showed up every day and tried to do my job."

In hockey lingo, Hebenton was a "mucker," a complimentary term applied to hardworking players not afraid to get their noses dirty as long as the job gets done. With Hebenton, the job always got done.

Solidly built at five-foot-nine, 180 pounds, Hebenton was originally the property of the Montreal Canadiens, languishing in the minors, mostly in the Western Hockey League. Montreal, given their fire-wagon, nonstop style of play, considered Hebenton too slow for the NHL. Murray (Muzz) Patrick, newly anointed as general manager of the Rangers for the 1955–56 season, had no such reservations.

Plus Patrick, a native of Victoria, B.C., regularly scouted the Western League and was acutely aware of Hebenton's value.

Patrick made Hebenton his very first acquisition, paying $10,000 to Montreal for his services on April 28, 1955. "Let me tell you this," Patrick would often say years later, "that was probably the best spent $10,000 of my time in New York. 'Hebby' repaid us many times over. I never looked back on that deal, no sir."

Turofsky/Hockey Hall of Fame

In 1956–57, Hebenton won the Lady Byng Trophy for "clean, effective play." He also won the Players' Player Award, a club honor, three straight seasons from 1958–59 to 1960–61.

Playing on a line with Red Sullivan at center and Camille (The Eel) Henry at left wing, Hebenton quickly developed into one of the NHL's best back checkers and penalty killers. He also had a knack for scoring, netting 20 or more goals in five of his eight seasons on Broadway, capped by career highs of 33 goals, 29 assists and 62 points in 1958–59.

"Andy was the perfect team player," recalled Sullivan, the team's captain for most of Hebenton's career in New York, and later the Rangers' coach. "He didn't say a whole lot, but he led by example, and never, ever missed a game. That was really something."

In 1956, Hebenton went into the corner with Marcel Bonin, Montreal's feisty left wing. "Marcel tried to lift my stick, but he missed," Hebenton said. "He caught me in the mouth and broke a little bone that holds some of your teeth together. Four of them

> "Andy was the perfect team player. He didn't say a whole lot, but he led by example."

were pushed back, halfway down my throat, in fact." Hebenton finished the game in Montreal, played again the next night in New York and finally saw a dentist on Monday. He lost the four teeth. "They were the only ones I ever lost playing in the NHL," he remembered.

The Rangers lost Hebenton's services on June 4, 1963, when the Boston Bruins grabbed him in what was then called the intra-league draft. He played one season for the Bruins—all 70 games, of course—before returning to the Western League where his pro career began.

All told, Hebenton played 1,062 consecutive games in the WHL and NHL, an achievement that will probably never be duplicated. It was only the death of his father that finally snapped the streak on October 18, 1967.

52 CAROL VADNAIS

1975–82

5

Games	Goals	Assists	Penalty minutes
485	56	190	690

Like Johnny Cash's fictional "Boy Named Sue," Carol Vadnais sometimes endured gallery derision because of his female-sounding first name. But for nearly seven seasons, the All-Star defenseman with the uncommon handle personified professionalism on Broadway.

In his final year of junior hockey, Vadnais was shifted from forward to defense, and the move paid off. He went on to achieve stardom in the NHL as an offensive defenseman with great speed, puck handling skills and toughness to boot. His abilities were somewhat hidden on a deep Montreal Canadiens team but shone brightly after Vadnais moved to the lowly Oakland Seals.

Rangers GM Emile Francis once offered Oakland four players in exchange for the black-haired blueliner. Instead, the Seals dealt Vadnais to Boston, where he helped the Bruins beat the Rangers in the 1972 Stanley Cup Finals.

Three years later, Francis finally got his man as part of one of the biggest blockbuster trades in the history of hockey: Vadnais and Phil Esposito to New York for Brad Park, Jean Ratelle and minor-leaguer Joe Zanussi.

Vadnais' arrival with the Rangers, unlike Esposito's, was delayed for several days. Esposito, accepting the trade however reluctantly, flew immediately from Vancouver, where the Bruins were, to Oakland, where the Rangers were set to play the Seals on November 7, 1975—the same day as the trade.

Unknown to Francis, and inexcusably unknown to Harry Sinden, the Boston general manager, was the fact that Vadnais had a no-trade clause in his contract. He and his Boston-based advisor, Arnold Bloom, just sat tight. They wanted $100,000 to waive the no-trade clause.

Sinden and the notoriously frugal Bruins had no choice. They had to pay, especially since Esposito had already played his first game as a Ranger that very evening. Many hockey people joked that Sinden never would have made the deal in the first place if he knew it would cost him another $100,000. "Harry throws $100,000 bills around like they're manhole covers," cracked Denis Ball, one of Francis's top aides in the Rangers' front office.

Surprisingly enough, both Vadnais and Esposito were welcomed cordially, if not exuberantly, by Rangers fans in the team's 50th anniversary season. Vadnais' play was solid and consistent, and the fans appreciated that, although some were distressed that the team hastily assigned him Park's former No. 2 sweater. Vadnais sensed that discontent and soon switched to No. 5.

One unexpected bonus that Vadnais brought with him to New York was an avuncular quality and the willingness to mentor and bond with the team's younger players.

"In some ways," Esposito said, "Vad was like an assistant captain with those guys. He had their respect, for sure, and he was willing to put in the time. He certainly made my job [as captain] easier."

Vadnais kept an injured Ron Greschner's confidence up. He taught Dave Maloney how to behave like a professional and respect the game. He showed Tom Laidlaw the right way to eliminate the puck carrier. He even helped Lucien DeBlois learn English.

He did much of this tutoring with his keester planted firmly on the bench because, by the early 1980s, Vadnais' effectiveness had slipped, and he was losing ice time to some of the very players he'd taken under his wing.

"His career was winding down," Laidlaw recalled. "It's not like I took his job—I was one of the guys that replaced him on his way out. But he wasn't bitter about his career ending and, in fact, he went out of his way to help me."

Placed on waivers just prior to the 1982–83 season, Vadnais was claimed by the Devils and closed out his playing career in the Garden State.

He later rejoined the Rangers and spent two years as an assistant coach.

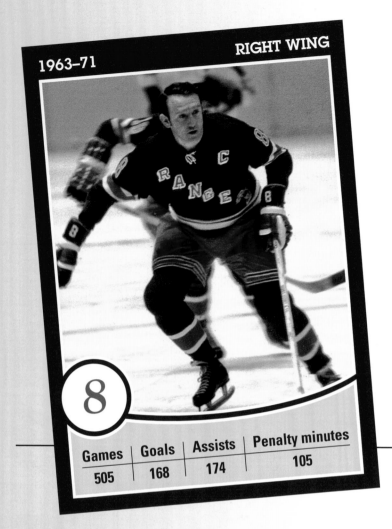

1963–71

RIGHT WING

8

Games	Goals	Assists	Penalty minutes
505	168	174	105

51
BOB NEVIN

On the morning of February 12, 1968, workers flooded the arena floor of the new Madison Square Garden. By nightfall, the liquid had frozen and Bob Nevin, captain of the Rangers, saw to it that his skates were the first to touch the quarter-inch-thick sheet of ice.

Workmen and other onlookers clapped when he fired the puck into an empty net, unofficially christening the team's new home.

Four years earlier, Nevin would probably have given a lot just to hear some applause after he drew the unenviable task of replacing a legend in the hearts of Rangers fans.

A hardworking, hard-checking right wing who helped the Maple Leafs win the Stanley Cup in 1962 and 1963, Nevin came to New York in the big trade for perennial All-Star Andy Bathgate on February 22, 1964.

The colossal, seven-player deal was meant to shake up a fifth-place Rangers club with designs on the fourth and final playoff spot. It began a total reconstruction of the team and ushered in a new era in its history.

But change can be hard, and fans frustrated with the Rangers' inconsistent play were no less grumpy after the trade. Bathgate, a former Hart Trophy winner and team captain, had become a hero to a generation of New York hockey fans, and none of the newcomers could match his star power or game-breaking ability.

Nevin, a native of South Porcupine, Ontario, dealt with the potentially prickly situation graciously, taking great pains to tell sportswriters and others that he was here to be "Bob Nevin," not replace Andy Bathgate. "I mean, who could do that even if they wanted to?" he reasoned.

Nicknamed "Stretch" due to his long reach and angular frame, Nevin was eventually placed on a line with Donnie Marshall at left wing and Phil Goyette at center. The new threesome blended perfectly, and thus was born "The Old Smoothies," one of the team's most famous lines.

Flamboyance was hardly Nevin's forte but he made his mark on Broadway, playing there almost eight seasons and topping the 20-goal mark five times. A natural leader, he ably captained the team from 1965 to 1971, represented the Rangers at two All-Star Games and was regarded as one of the NHL's best defensive forwards.

But no matter how hard Nevin tried, he never quite satisfied the Garden's balcony brigade. His subtle contributions to the team too often went unnoticed, but not by those closer to the action.

"Nevin was the best two-way player I ever coached," Emile Francis said. And that from a guy who also coached Walt Tkaczuk for the better part of a decade.

Dave Anderson of the *New York Times* described how, after Nevin scored a sudden-death goal that gave the Rangers a 4–2 series victory over Toronto in the opening round of the 1971 playoffs, the captain's detractors finally turned lyrical over his play. During the next series, a fan hung a homemade banner of apology from the top deck of the Garden. It read: "We Love You, Bobby / We're Sorry Too / For All The Times / We Gave You The Boo / So Keep On Playing / The Way You Know / And We Will Cheer / From Every Row."

Unfortunately for him, Nevin missed out on the loudest cheers because he was gone before the Rangers of that era really hit their stride.

Following the 1970–71 season, he was dealt to the Minnesota North Stars for right wing Bobby Rousseau. Nevin would eventually play 20 seasons of pro hockey, his career winding down in 1976 with the WHA's Edmonton Oilers.

"I really loved my time in New York," Nevin has often recalled. "It was a great experience. The only thing I regret is that we didn't win a Stanley Cup."

A superb two-way player, right wing Bob Nevin (center) keeps a pair of Maple Leafs at bay.

Dave Sandford/Hockey Hall of Fame

1991–99

DEFENSEMAN

50

JEFF BEUKEBOOM

23

Games	Goals	Assists	Penalty minutes
520	18	72	1,157

A rose by any other name would smell as sweet. And Jeff Beukeboom's thunderous body checks wouldn't have hurt any less had his name been Smiley or Periwinkle.

But that wonderfully descriptive name—Beukeboom—so accurately described the rugged style of this blueline behemoth who used every ounce of his 230-pound frame to the maximum. His bone-jarring hits became a staple at Madison Square Garden, and fans loved them.

"For the most part, it came instinctively when I saw an opportunity," Beukeboom said of his signature hits. "But I definitely tried to deliver that hit to get the crowd into it and get the team going."

A cousin of 20-year NHL veteran Joe Nieuwendyk, a teenaged Beukeboom splattered unsuspecting puck-carriers as a member of the OHL's Sault Ste. Marie Greyhounds. In 1982–83, his first year of juniors, he teamed with future Ranger John Vanbiesbrouck as the Greyhounds won 48 games but lost to Oshawa in the finals.

Drafted 19th overall by Edmonton in 1983, Beukeboom played on three Stanley Cup winners with the Oilers before being dealt to New York for David Shaw in November 1991, completing the Rangers' earlier deal for Mark Messier.

Having grown up on a small dairy farm in rural Ontario, Beukeboom experienced his share of culture shock coming to Manhattan but quickly settled in as the perfect complement to the more offensive-minded Brian Leetch, with whom he was partnered for much of the decade. Beuk's steady, stay-at-home style allowed Leetch to join the rush and kept opposing players out of Mike Richter's goal crease.

"It wasn't a blueprint to go after Edmonton players," Rangers GM Neil Smith said of acquiring yet another ex-Oiler. "But on a battlefront, the best soldiers are the ones who've been in battle before. Winners usually repeat."

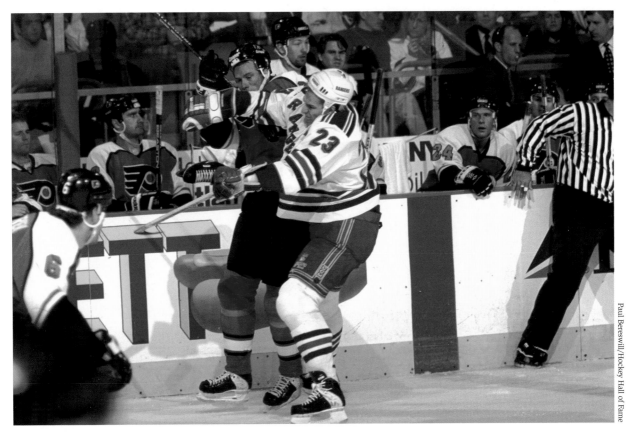

Paul Bereswill/Hockey Hall of Fame

And so it was that Beukeboom, reunited with Oilers alumni Mark Messier, Glenn Anderson, Kevin Lowe, Adam Graves and Esa Tikkanen, won his fourth Cup in 1994 as the Rangers broke their 54-year-old curse by beating the Vancouver Canucks in seven games.

An intimidating presence on Broadway for eight seasons, Beukeboom was willing and able to tangle with the heavyweights when the need arose. His 1,157 penalty minutes as a Ranger rank second on the club's all-time list behind only Ron Greschner (1,226).

"I always tried to play with an edge," Beukeboom said. "Terry Crisp, my coach in junior who went on to coach in the NHL, really brought that out of me. I knew that was my style, my game. That was one of the things that made me more successful than just another six-foot-five defenseman. But I only fought for a couple of reasons, like if I played with Brian Leetch or one of the other top players and felt someone took advantage of them. Sometimes, I fought

when I could deliver a message to the other team or, just like the big hit, when I thought the team needed a boost."

Beukeboom was a fearless shot blocker, too, known to hobble back to the bench and be ready in time for his next shift. The downside of this, of course, was that his physical style made him more susceptible to injury.

"I cracked a bone in my leg once and only missed a week," he recalled. "Then I cracked my ankle and didn't realize it until four weeks afterward and I only missed a couple of games. I think I had a really high pain threshold."

But the human body has its limits and the big defenseman's career was shortened by a series of concussions, with the most devastating coming in November 1998 as a result of a sucker punch by Kings winger Matt Johnson that knocked Beukeboom out cold. He played sporadically after that but was forced to retire in July 1999 due to the lingering effects of post-concussion syndrome.

1977–83, 1986–88

CENTER

Jack/ Peter Mecca - Jack Mecca/Hockey Hall of Fame

10

Games	Goals	Assists	Penalty minutes
499	164	176	370

49
RON DUGUAY

H e played almost 500 games over eight seasons with the Rangers and yet, in terms of exposure, those figures seem woefully low because Ron Duguay's matinee-idol good looks, plus a flamboyance off the ice that was exceeded by no one before or after his time, made him constant fodder for the Big Apple's gossip columns.

"People say I'm a playboy," Duguay once noted. "That doesn't bother me at all. I dress like a playboy, sometimes I act like a playboy, so maybe I am a playboy. I mean, what's so wrong with that?"

His employers didn't seem to mind. Duguay brought talent and great public-relations value to the Rangers, who were trying to rebuild a team that had basically been torn apart just two years before his arrival in 1977. The impresario David (Sonny) Werblin was running Madison Square Garden at the time, and he absolutely loved Duguay's style and sex appeal.

It was Werblin, previously an owner of the New York Jets, who had single-handedly propelled his quarterback, "Broadway" Joe Namath, onto the New York social scene. Sonny envisioned the same for Duguay and encouraged him to join the nightlife of New York. Ever the pragmatist, Duguay was cautious about that role. "Hey, I'm no Namath," he would say. "He only has to play once a week."

Nonetheless, Duguay was off to the races, with gossipmongers and photographers usually in tow. There was Studio 54, the first stop for any A-list New York partygoer, sightings with Cher, an interview session discussing sex, of all things, in *Forum* magazine and a big ad campaign for Sasson jeans. At the height of the decadent disco era, "Doogie" and his thick coif of wavy brown hair were everywhere, a one-man multimedia machine, and the Rangers loved it.

Forgetting about his looks for a moment, it's unlikely that this much attention would have been lavished upon a fourth-line drudge. A versatile center/right wing, Duguay was an exceptional hockey player with world-class skills who never spent a day in the minors. He was great on draws, a reliable penalty killer and surprisingly tough. In his rookie season, he scored 20 goals and followed that up with crisp seasons of 27, 28 and 17 goals before hitting a career-high 40 in 1981–82, earning him his first (and only) All-Star Game appearance.

By then, Herb Brooks, the "Wizard of Lake Placid," was coaching the Rangers, and the off-ice shenanigans tolerated by coaches like Fred Shero—nicknamed "The Fog" for good reason—were no longer considered endearing.

Brooks and Duguay was hardly a marriage made in heaven. The two inevitably clashed, Brooks being the stern disciplinarian and Duguay the freewheeling kid from Sudbury, Ontario, who had become a *bon vivant* and man-about-town on Broadway, hockey's brightest stage.

His penchant for arriving late to practice, a $50 fine for each offense, was particularly galling to

Brooks. Late in the 1982–83 season, Duguay was tardy once more. He paid his fine and promptly asked a trainer how many practices were left for the season. "Four," he was told. Doogie brashly wrote a check for $200. Brooks was not happy.

Duguay did things his way, and Brooks did the same. It was only a matter of time before Duguay was traded, and on June 13, 1983, he was shipped to Detroit along with goalie Eddie Mio and right wing Eddie Johnstone for Willie Huber, Mark Osborne and Mike Blaisdell. Duguay promptly scored 33, 38 and 17 goals for Detroit. Advantage: Red Wings.

By 1986–87, Phil Esposito was running the Rangers and quickly got his old buddy Ronnie back in a trade. There were two more seasons in New York, but Duguay couldn't recapture the old days, and was ineffective with nine and four goals respectively. Two more lackluster seasons followed with the Los Angeles Kings, and he was out of the NHL following the 1988–89 campaign.

1963–64, 1967–69, 1970–75 GOALTENDER

48
GILLES VILLEMURE

Games	Record	Shutouts	GAA
184	98-53-23	13	2.62

I t's fortunate for the Rangers that Gilles Villemure was a stand-up goalie. At five-foot-seven, he wouldn't have stopped much rubber on his knees. But what the red-haired goalie lacked in height he more than made up for with an efficient style and the ability to play the angles with confidence.

As a child growing up in Trois-Rivières, Quebec, Villemure would visit the nearby fairgrounds that featured a rink and a racetrack, side by side. The countless hours spent there gave rise to his dual obsessions: hockey and horses.

In the late 1950s, the young French-Canadian was wrapping up his junior days with the Guelph Biltmores with the anticipation of turning pro. Unfortunately, this was an era when the NHL's Original Six teams each carried only one goaltender. With so few jobs available, one required great patience and the fortitude to endure a potentially lengthy wait in the minors.

The turning point came at training camp in 1970. After beating out fellow minor leaguer Peter McDuffe to earn a full-time spot on the Ranger roster, Villemure went on a tear that forced coach Emile Francis to rethink his opposition to a two-goalie system. The Rangers needed someone to take some pressure off of their overworked starter, Ed Giacomin, and it was clear that Villemure was perfect for the job.

The pair rotated their way through the 1970–71 season with some stupendous play. They possessed different styles—Giacomin was the flopper while Villemure preferred to stay on his feet—but whoever guarded the Blueshirt crease gave his team a great chance to win on any given night.

"I never had two goalkeepers play for me before," Francis recalled. "Giacomin caught with his left hand and they called him a righty because that was normal. Villemure was the opposite. He caught with his right hand so we called him a lefty. And there was no animosity, no jealousy. That's why we could do it. One helped the other."

Said Giacomin: "I think that way down deep, Gilles Villemure's first love was horses. But, what made the rotation so special for him was he happened to have a guy who liked to play a lot, so he could devote more time to studying the racing form. Because of that, we were a good team. The opposition kind of forgot who was in goal. I think it was one of the greatest tandems to play in the National Hockey League."

Overshadowed by a more flamboyant partner, Villemure is among the most underrated Rangers. His personality, low-key and self-deprecating, was responsible for much of this.

He may have been less quotable than Giacomin but when the occasion was right, Gilles would talk with the best of them, providing incisive comments and anecdotes. For the most part, however, he preferred to talk about his teammates rather than himself.

Even Villemure's nickname, "Whitey," owing to the generally pale hue of his skin, lacked color. But when it came to big games, Villemure was a starburst in a paint factory. His record with the Rangers speaks for itself: an eye-popping 98 victories against 53 losses—the best winning percentage ever for a Ranger goaltender who played regularly. From 1970 to 1972, Gilles posted 46 wins against only 15 losses.

Although he and Giacomin shared the Vezina Trophy as the league's best netminders in 1971, honors and awards were hardly a novelty to Villemure. Prior to his NHL career, he won major honors in the Western Hockey League (Rookie of the Year, 1963) and the American Hockey League (Most Valuable Player, 1969 and 1970).

Injuries began to take their toll on his performance and in 1975, Villemure was traded to Chicago. Relegated to a backup role and seeing little action, he decided a year later that it was time to hang up his pads.

His passion for the ponies endured, however, and Villemure continued to own and race trotters long after his playing days.

47

BABE PRATT

11

Games	Goals	Assists	Penalty minutes
305	27	97	289

At six-foot-three, 215 pounds, Walter (Babe) Pratt was a little too big to be called a "teddy bear."

"But that's what he was, believe me," insisted Lynn Patrick, Pratt's teammate on the Rangers' 1940 Stanley Cup winners. "Even [Phil] Watson called him 'un ours blanc' [a white bear]. It was a term of affection, really."

A rollicking defenseman, both on the ice and off, and one of the most unique individuals ever to pull on a Rangers sweater, Pratt was a winner from the first time he laced up skates. His teams won 15 championships, from the junior ranks to the NHL, during his 26 years in the game.

Al Ritchie, the Rangers' legendary scout during the 1930s and 1940s, called Pratt "the finest prospect I have ever seen," when the Rangers signed him to his first NHL contract on October 18, 1935. He spent just 28 games with the Philadelphia Ramblers of the Canadian-American League before the Rangers called him to New York. It would be 12 more years before Pratt would play another minor-league game.

The swift summons to New York would mark the beginning of a love affair between Pratt and the Big Apple, the City That Never Sleeps. After seeing Broadway for the first time, he joked: "Where had this place been all my life? I looked out at all those beautiful lights and said to myself, 'Babe, you are personally going to look behind each and every one of them.'"

No doubt he did.

Babe's running mate on the Rangers was usually defenseman Murray (Muzz) Patrick, son of Lester Patrick, the team's patriarch, general manager and coach. One year, as the Rangers were fast developing into one of the National Hockey League's strongest franchises, Pratt remarked, "This team has balance.

We've got some hungry rookies and two thirsty veterans: me and Muzz."

That remark surely never sat well with boss man Patrick. Neither did Pratt's oft-stated description of Patrick's legendary frugality: "I wouldn't say that Lester was cheap, but he certainly was adjacent to cheap."

On the ice, Pratt's style was boisterous and rough. The fans loved him, and he was the perfect successor to the Rangers' first great defenseman, Ching Johnson, whose style was the same as Pratt's and who left the Rangers following the 1936–37 season.

Pratt's defensive partner was Ott Heller, while Muzz Patrick played with team captain Art Coulter. That foursome is probably the best quartet of Ranger defensemen ever. Pratt was also an offensive force, posting 28 points in 1941–42 as the Rangers won the regular season championship, the club's last hurrah, really, before World War II broke up that formidable group of All-Stars.

Traded to the Toronto Maple Leafs midway through the 1942–43 season, Pratt led all NHL defensemen with 57 points and won the Hart Trophy as the league's most valuable player, an award rarely given to a defenseman. The next season, the Leafs won the Stanley Cup and Pratt scored the Cup-winning goal.

Off the ice, by then, things were not going as well. In 1946, Pratt was caught gambling on hockey games, and he was summarily suspended from the NHL by new league president Clarence Campbell. Pratt admitted the betting charges, but insisted he never

Turofsky/Hockey Hall of Fame

bet against his own team. Campbell reinstated him, and he played his last NHL campaign in 1946–47 with the Boston Bruins.

Pratt was a nonpareil storyteller. He worked for many years as an analyst for *Hockey Night In Canada* and served as a roving goodwill ambassador for the Vancouver Canucks. Many of his stories, of course, revolved around his salad days on Broadway with the Rangers.

"I wouldn't say that Lester was cheap, but he certainly was adjacent to cheap."

Elected to the Hockey Hall of Fame in 1966, Pratt passed away at the age of 72 on December 16, 1988.

1991–97

CENTER

Doug MacLellan/Hockey Hall of Fame

46

SERGEI NEMCHINOV

13

Games	Goals	Assists	Penalty minutes
418	105	120	151

Sharing a nickname with Steve Vickers, a Ranger icon in the 1970s, this "Sarge" was a sometimes underappreciated soldier who did all the little things a good two-way center should do: take draws, back check, forecheck, battle along the boards and chip in timely goals.

Sergei Nemchinov didn't receive much fanfare for those deeds during his six Ranger seasons, but he preferred it that way.

Surprisingly agile for a big man, the blond Muscovite first caught the attention of scouts while touring the NHL with his Red Army team in the late 1980s and early 1990s. Although he ranked among the Soviet Elite League's scoring leaders, Nemchinov was considered a defensive player whose leadership skills and sense of loyalty suggested he was also a person of character.

"He was always a very honest worker," said Rangers scout Christer Rockstrom. "Sergei always worked hard in his play at both ends of the rink. He was never one of those big Russian stars (think Alexander Mogilny, Pavel Bure, etc.) but he turned out to be a very good third-line center. He accepted his role. And he was a nice person who hasn't changed his personality."

Neil Smith, general manager of the Rangers, took Nemchinov in the 12th round of the 1990 draft on the off-chance he would be able to get Sergei released from his commitments back in Mother Russia. Smith initially tried waving some green in front of Red officials, but they showed little interest in negotiating for Nemchinov's services. Pressed on whether he might encourage the player to defect, the Ranger boss coyly replied, "I can't have any influence in that. And if I did, I wouldn't admit it."

Defection, it turned out, would not be necessary to make Nemchinov the first Russian to wear Ranger red, white and blue—just persistence on the part of

the Rangers, who finally bought Sergei's emancipation in 1991.

He arrived in the free world as a 27-year-old rookie with wife and daughter in tow and moved into a condo in Port Chester, New York, just five minutes from the team's old practice rink in Rye. Earning considerably more than the 400 rubles (plus incentives) he was paid per month back in Russia, Nemchinov's first major stateside purchase wasn't a Mercedes or a BMW, but a Toyota.

His taste in cars may have been understated but the soft-spoken Soviet's introduction to the NHL was anything but. He scored his first goal in his second game, beating Patrick Roy in overtime to give the Rangers a 2–1 win over the Canadiens at the Montreal Forum. Spending most of the year on a line between Mike Gartner and Jan Erixon, he finished with 30 goals and helped the Rangers amass the most points in the league during the 1991–92 season.

Nemchinov had proven to be a far better scorer and stickhandler than anyone expected. Teammates were impressed at how smoothly he adapted to the North American game.

Suddenly, everyone wanted to know more about the mysterious (but obviously not superstitious) man wearing uniform No. 13. But Nemchinov's shy nature and rudimentary grasp of English made every press conference an excruciating experience for subject and interviewer alike.

With the help of a private tutor, Nemchinov's English improved dramatically and by 1994, he was able to cope with the glut of interview requests that poured in after he, Alexander Karpovtsev, Alexei Kovalev and Sergei Zubov became the first Russians to win the Stanley Cup.

In time, Nemchinov's role became more defensive, and the team's fortunes declined. In 1997, he was traded to Vancouver with Brian Noonan for Esa Tikkanen and Russ Courtnall.

Nemchinov later played for the Islanders and Devils, with whom he won a second Stanley Cup in 2000, before returning to Russia to close out his career with Yaroslavl Lokomotiv.

He was later named assistant coach of the Russian Olympic team.

45

BUTCH KEELING

Hockey Hall of Fame

1928–38   **LEFT WING**

(10)

Games	Goals	Assists	Penalty minutes
452	136	55	250

The Rangers, still giddy from their victory over the Montreal Maroons in the 1928 Stanley Cup Finals, were enjoying a celebratory dinner at the posh East 69th Street apartment of Madison Square Garden VP Bill Carey when it was announced the club had acquired left wing Melville (Butch) Keeling from the Maple Leafs.

Headed to Toronto with a check for $10,000 was spare forward Alex Gray, whose audition with the Leafs lasted all of seven games before he earned a permanent demotion to the minors.

Keeling, meanwhile, would have an immediate and lasting impact on the Rangers as a durable and consistent goal scorer who excelled under pressure.

"Whenever we needed a goal in a pinch," Rangers manager Lester Patrick recalled, "Butch always seemed to be there."

He was there in the 1929 quarterfinals, a two-game, most-goals-wins series against the New York Americans that saw the first contest end in a 0–0 tie. Game Two was scoreless through regulation and into the closing minutes of the second overtime when an exhausted Keeling beat Amerks goalie Roy (Shrimp) Worters.

"The Cooks [Bill and Bun] and [Frank] Boucher couldn't come close to scoring," Patrick later said of his usually dominant top line. "Who came through with the winning goal for us? Butch Keeling."

Throughout his ten-year Ranger career, which included nine postseason appearances, the underrated Keeling was known primarily as a shooter, as evidenced by his paltry 55 assists (against 136 goals) collected over 452 games. But it was a pass from Butch's stick that led to one of the most exciting plays of the team's golden era.

On April 13, 1933, the Rangers battled Keeling's former team, the Maple Leafs, in Game Four of the Stanley Cup Finals. New York held serve in the best-of-five series but ex-Ranger Lorne Chabot stood tall in net for Toronto that night, turning aside every shot the Blueshirts threw at him in regulation. He continued to frustrate them in overtime, but when Toronto's Alex Levinsky and Bill Thoms were whistled for back-to-back minor penalties, Patrick sent five forwards out on the ensuing power play to end the game—and the series—in short order.

That's when Keeling gathered the puck at mid-ice and raced down the left side into the Toronto zone. Bill Cook followed, skating along the right side. With the imposing Red Horner bearing down on him, Keeling quickly found Cook open with a beautiful rink-wide pass. The streaking Ranger captain never broke stride, rifling the puck past Chabot and causing the visitors' bench to erupt in jubilation.

Keeling had finally won the Stanley Cup, but his best personal season came in 1936–37 when he led the Rangers with a career-high 22 goals (third-most in the league) and matched his previous career best with 26 points. In the playoffs, he scored three goals and five points as the Rangers advanced to the fifth and deciding game of the Stanley Cup Finals against the Detroit Red Wings.

That turned out to be the last hurrah for many of the "original" Rangers, the boys who had been with the club since the very beginning. It was time to rebuild, and the emergence of young wingers like Bryan Hextall, Alex Shibicky and Dutch Hiller signaled the end for Keeling. In April 1938, the club reluctantly cut him loose.

"Butch is one of the great players of all time," Patrick remarked. "You never knew what he would do as an individual, but in team play he was tops."

Keeling played a little while longer in the minor leagues, first with the Philadelphia Ramblers and then the Kansas City Greyhounds, whom he also coached. He resurfaced in the NHL a short time later as a referee and worked in that capacity for three years.

Eventually settling in Toronto, Keeling passed away in November 1984 at the age of 79.

Hockey Hall of Fame

44 JAMES PATRICK

1983–93

DEFENSEMAN

3

Games	Goals	Assists	Penalty minutes
671	104	363	541

Over the course of almost three decades playing the sport, James Alan Patrick was blessed to have lived three hockey lives.

In the first, "Jeep" was a highly decorated collegian at the University of North Dakota, where he captured a national championship with the Fighting Sioux in 1982. In the last, he was a sage veteran providing leadership and stability to a rebuilding Buffalo Sabres team. In between, Patrick spent a decade on Broadway as a defense-first blueliner with great speed and offensive skill who helped the Rangers re-establish themselves as a league power.

Canada, it turns out, has produced not one but two great sporting families with the surname Patrick. James was no relation to Lester Patrick, his sons Lynn and Muzz or grandson Craig, all of whom had links to the Rangers. He was, however, the son of Steve Patrick, once a star lineman with the Canadian Football League's Winnipeg Blue Bombers, and kid brother to Steve Jr., who played five years in the NHL with the Rangers, Sabres and Nordiques.

Selected ninth overall by the Rangers in the 1981 draft, James joined the club immediately after competing in the 1984 Olympic Winter Games in Sarajevo. His arrival was met with much anticipation.

"He's good enough," declared coach Herb Brooks, "that I can't screw him up."

In just his second NHL game, played in his hometown of Winnipeg, Patrick recorded three assists in a 6–5 win over the Jets. His final helper came on Mark Osborne's game winner 43 seconds into overtime.

Averaging over 50 points per season for the Blueshirts during a seven-year stretch from 1985 to 1992, Patrick may be one of the most underrated defensemen of the last two decades. That's due, in part, to the emergence of a more prolific point producer in Brian Leetch but also Patrick's preference to stay in the background and play a support role.

A devoted Ranger in every sense of the word, Patrick was also fiercely loyal to Canadian hockey,

representing his country not only at the Olympic Games but also at two World Junior Championships, five World Championships and the Canada Cup. Despite being chosen to play at so many international events, he was never picked for an NHL All-Star Game.

"James was a great guy and a very good model for young players," said former Rangers captain Kelly Kisio, Patrick's roommate on road trips for over four seasons. "He looked after himself and was in phenomenal condition. He had some health problems too, and fought through a lot of things just to play every day."

Indeed, he lived with a chronic autoimmune disease called colitis, which can cause severe fatigue—a pretty big challenge for a professional athlete. Health issues notwithstanding, Patrick felt comfortable in New York into the early 1990s, but he began to feel his career needed a jump start. So when the Rangers hired Mike Keenan as coach, James welcomed it as an opportunity to take his game to the next level.

Instead, he frequently found himself benched for the first part of the 1993–94 season as Keenan relied more heavily on the likes of Leetch, Jeff Beukeboom, Kevin Lowe and Sergei Zubov. It was a frustrating time for Patrick, who wasn't a "Keenan-type" player and probably never would be. The man who had nobly worn uniform No. 3 for a decade began to suspect that he was not in the Rangers' future plans.

In November 1993, James was shipped off to the Hartford Whalers with Darren Turcotte in the deal that brought Steve Larmer to New York. Patrick played in Hartford only briefly before being traded again to Calgary. After several years with the Flames, he signed with the Sabres as a free agent.

Patrick's professionalism, intelligence and strong positional play allowed him to prolong his career even after his speed and offensive skills had waned. He retired in 2005 after 21 years in the NHL, the last six with Buffalo.

He is now an assistant coach with the Sabres.

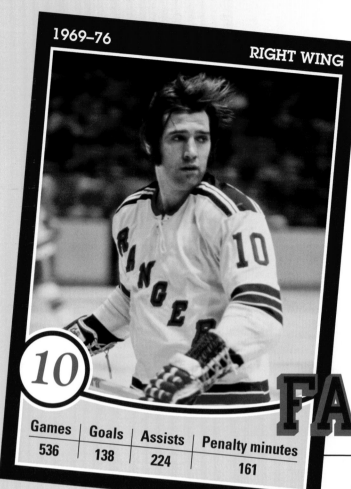

1969–76

RIGHT WING

43 BILL FAIRBAIRN

10

Games	Goals	Assists	Penalty minutes
536	138	224	161

A rock-solid competitor who could take a hit as well as anyone in the league, Bill Fairbairn performed the thankless duties that freed up marquee players like Rod Gilbert and Jean Ratelle to grab headlines.

Turning pro in 1967 with the Central Hockey League's Omaha Knights, the right wing from Brandon, Manitoba, showed steady progress over the next two seasons. He made the league's Second All-Star Team in 1969 and also earned a one-game look with the parent Rangers that same year.

Originally pegged as a checker, Fairbairn earned a full-time job in New York the following year and so impressed the Rangers with his outstanding two-way play that when Bob Nevin went down with an injury, Fairbairn replaced the team captain on a line with Dave Balon and Walt Tkaczuk.

That unit was probably the most silent in team history. Off the ice, they rarely said a word. Dana Mozley, who covered the team sporadically for *The Daily News*, said: "If these guys get paid like I do [by the word], there ain't gonna be a lot of food on the table."

But the newly formed "Bulldog Line" was so proficient that Nevin was bumped to another slot when his health returned. The Rangers nominated Fairbairn for the Calder Trophy but he finished runner-up to Chicago's Tony Esposito.

Tkaczuk remembers Fairbairn as terrific at digging in the corners and willing—maybe too willing—to absorb the physical punishment that usually entailed.

"He wouldn't leave the boards," Tkaczuk said, "and he would wait for a guy to hit him. Then, at the last second, he'd give me the pass so I could get a two-on-one. I would ask him, 'Would you please, every once in a while, get off the boards and go center ice?'"

"When the game was on the line," said Fairbairn's former coach, Emile Francis, "guess who was out there—Fairbairn. When we came down to the last minute of a period or a one-goal game, trying to protect the lead, guess who was out there—Fairbairn. I put him against the other team's best lines. He and Tkaczuk could kill penalties but were so offensive that the other team couldn't get out of their own end when we were shorthanded. They used to call Fairbairn 'Dog' because he would bite you in the ass. He would come after you. He wouldn't let you alone!"

Fairbairn was such an expert penalty killer that he and Tkaczuk once controlled the puck just by themselves for one minute and 44 seconds of a Los Angeles Kings power play, prompting cheers from King fans when Don Kozak finally managed to get the puck off Fairbairn's stick.

He remained a Ranger regular for over seven years and helped the Blueshirts reach the Stanley Cup Finals in 1972. His best offensive season came in 1972–73 when he scored 30 goals and formed a superb line with Tkaczuk and rookie Steve Vickers.

With the 1976–77 season set to begin, Fairbairn was the Rangers' reigning iron man with a consecutive games-played streak of 394. But he seemed older than his 29 years and no longer played with the same tenacity of his youth.

Had the dog lost its bite? Coach John Ferguson thought so and on opening night, he informed Fairbairn that he would be watching the game from the stands. Supplanted by a young hotshot named Don Murdoch, Fairbairn knew his days in New York were numbered.

Weeks later, Fairbairn was traded along with defenseman Nick Beverley to the Minnesota North Stars for Bill Goldsworthy. He closed out his career in 1978 after a brief stint with the St. Louis Blues.

42

JIM NEILSON

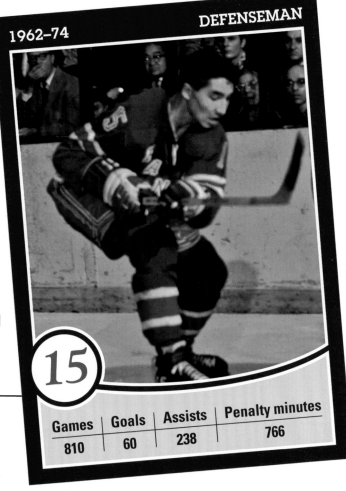

1962–74   DEFENSEMAN

15

Games	Goals	Assists	Penalty minutes
810	60	238	766

In less politically correct times, James Anthony Neilson was known as "The Chief" because of his mixed Danish-Cree ancestry. But that nickname was a sign of respect for a sturdy defenseman who spent 12 seasons in New York and was an underrated member of the great Rangers teams of the early 1970s.

Only three blueliners—Harry Howell, Ron Greschner and Brian Leetch—have played more games in Ranger blue than this native of Big River, Saskatchewan, who scored a total of 60 goals for the club over 810 regular-season games. But it was the two-time All-Star's defensive ability, steady but not flashy, that would ultimately define his Ranger legacy.

At six-foot-two and 205 pounds, Neilson was a big and muscular specimen who could hit but preferred to use his broad frame to maneuver attackers out of the play. Responding to criticism that he didn't use his substantial size and strength to full advantage, Neilson once offered this retort: "I get tired of hearing I don't hit enough. My temperament is such that I don't fly off the handle and try to take people apart. You make mistakes doing that."

As workmanlike and passive as he was on the ice, Neilson was just the opposite, a blithe spirit, in his leisure time. He remains that today.

There have been more difficult paths to the NHL, but not many tougher than Neilson's.

When Jim was just a boy, his mother left a husband and three children behind to return to her tribe's reservation. Olaf Neilson, a fur trapper who spent weeks at a time out in the wilderness of Northern Canada, decided to place Jim and his two sisters in St. Patrick's Catholic Orphanage in Prince Albert. There, Neilson enjoyed few luxuries but received a good education and never went to bed hungry. And, of course, he fell in love with hockey.

Leaving the orphanage in his late teens to play for the Prince Albert Mintos of the Saskatchewan Junior Hockey League, Neilson registered consecutive 20-goal seasons in 1960 and 1961.

Having a hot stick in juniors helped get Neilson to the NHL but it wasn't going to keep him there. He arrived in New York in 1962 eager to show his skills—he was talented enough offensively to earn an occasional shift at left wing—but was raw and may have been guilty of trying to do too much, too soon. As a sophomore, he was taken out of the lineup and risked being sent to the minors for a spell.

But taking his cues from Howell and Doug Harvey, a pair of legendary defensemen in the twilight of their careers, Neilson learned a lot about how to be successful in the world's fastest, most competitive league. In time, he developed into a solid defensive defenseman who could still help out on offense by moving the puck up ice to his forwards.

By 1968–69, it was Chief's turn to act as mentor. Paired with a rookie named Brad Park, Neilson was credited with making a huge difference in the youngster's game. Park had a positive impact on Neilson's game, too, as the veteran set career highs in goals (10), assists (34) and points (44). He was eventually partnered with Rod Seiling, and the twosome became one of the most dependable defensive duets in Ranger history.

Slowed by chronic back problems, Neilson was left unprotected in the 1974 intra-league draft and claimed by the California Golden Seals. He later played for the Cleveland Barons and WHA's Edmonton Oilers before retiring in 1979.

In 2001, Neilson was profiled in *They Call Me Chief*, a Canadian documentary about the origins of hockey in Native culture and the many obstacles Native players have overcome to become stars in the NHL.

A popular defenseman for 12 seasons with the Rangers, Jim Neilson (right) gets the jump on Boston's Ron Stewart.

41 ROD SEILING

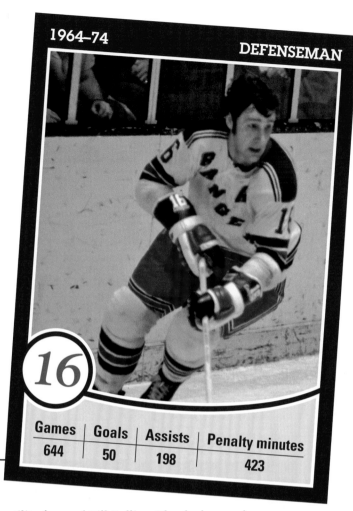

1964–74   DEFENSEMAN

16

Games	Goals	Assists	Penalty minutes
644	50	198	423

When he was traded to the Rangers on February 22, 1964, defenseman Rod Seiling was still a member of the Toronto Marlboros, who were about to capture the Memorial Cup championship, junior hockey's version of the Stanley Cup. His mostly teenaged teammates started calling him "The Lone Ranger."

A can't-miss prospect in what at the time was the biggest trade in Rangers' history, Seiling was the cornerstone of a seven-player blockbuster that cost the Rangers their captain and best player, Andy Bathgate, plus center Don (Slip) McKenney.

Emile Francis, the Rangers' assistant general manager at the time, had been bird-dogging Seiling and Arnie Brown for over a year in anticipation of the big trade. "I must have seen them 30 times apiece," Francis recalled. "Believe me, I knew what kind of underwear they both wore."

Coming to Manhattan with the Lone Ranger were established wingers Bob Nevin and Dick Duff, defenseman Arnie Brown, like Seiling a youngster, and utility forward Bill Collins. The deal was a long-range steal for the Blueshirts, who not only got 11 quality seasons out of Seiling, but seven out of Brown and eight out of Nevin, who soon became the Rangers' 13th captain, replacing Camille Henry.

But it was Seiling whom the Rangers most coveted, and wanting to showcase their phenom right away, they called him up immediately. The teenager did not disappoint.

A finesse defenseman, not a bruiser, Seiling proceeded to win the hearts of the New York faithful on his very first shift, about a minute and a half into his debut on March 4, 1964, by cleanly slamming Pierre Pilote, the Chicago Blackhawks' perennial All-Star defenseman, into Madison Square Garden's 50th Street sideboards to rousing cheers.

That check not only trumpeted Seiling's arrival, but it also allowed him to avoid the perennial boos that hounded two of his "finesse defensemen" predecessors, Allan Stanley and Harry Howell. Even an

All-Star left wing, Lynn Patrick, heard it from the Garden boo birds because of his lack of boisterous play in the late 1940s. Said Pilote: "This guy is gonna be a star. I didn't even see him coming."

The Rangers won in Seiling's debut, 4–3, and they won their next game too, a 3–2 decision over the Canadiens in Montreal. So Seiling had two wins in his first two pro games, and didn't even know that he was about to win the Memorial Cup.

Even if the boos did come (which they didn't), the phlegmatic Seiling was prepared.

"Hey, they [the fans] paid more to get in than I did," he quipped, displaying a trademark sense of humor that he carried throughout his career.

By the mid-1970s, the Rangers were starting to retool, and the Washington Capitals claimed Seiling on waivers on October 29, 1974. Seiling was barely out of the dressing room that day, and certainly not out of the building, before quirky Derek Sanderson classlessly wrested Rod's No. 16 jersey from Seiling's locker and claimed it as his own.

Eventually Seiling's career wound down with the Toronto Maple Leafs, the St. Louis Blues and

Seiling proceeded to win the hearts of the New York faithful on his very first shift.

the Atlanta Flames. He would go on to pursue prosperous careers in harness racing and the hotel and tourism industry in Toronto, not far from his native Elmira, Ontario.

1992–99, 2003–04   **RIGHT WING**

27

Games	Goals	Assists	Penalty minutes
492	142	188	533

40
ALEXEI KOVALEV

Unlike the disciplined and grim-faced Soviets who dominated international hockey throughout the Cold War, Alexei Kovalev was a free-spirited, spotlight-adoring kid who had, as GM Neil Smith once termed it, "the curse of great talent."

The first Russian drafted in the first round (15th overall in 1991) might have gone a few picks earlier had he not still been bound to his club team, Moscow Dynamo. But when the Soviet Union crumbled, Kovalev made his way to America to play for the NHL team he had followed since childhood: the New York Rangers.

A human highlight reel from the sports-crazy town of Tolyatti, Kovalev was a six-foot 200-pounder so strong on his skates that it was almost impossible to knock him over (unless, of course, he felt like taking a tumble to draw a penalty). He had a deft passing touch, a hard, accurate shot and no shortage of confidence.

The "curse," in Alexei's case, was having all the physical tools to be a megastar but sometimes forgetting that games are won on goals, not style points.

That was a lesson Smith and the Ranger coaches tried to convey during Kovalev's rookie season in 1992–93, when his poor defensive play and habit of overhandling the puck—like a game of keep-away with *everyone* on the ice—finally earned the likable but stubborn youngster a demotion to the minors.

"He's got to learn the fundamentals of picking up your check—the one on the ice, not the one in the office," Smith cracked. "He knows the other one."

For one season at least, Kovalev found an unlikely fan in coach Mike Keenan, a man not generally known for his patience. Iron Mike loved Alexei's enthusiasm for the game and compared him to a wild bronco. "He's got a flash to him," Keenan said. "He's got personality. He's got charisma. I think you can let him run."

And that's what Kovalev did during the 1994 playoffs, when he trailed only Brian Leetch and Mark Messier in postseason scoring with nine goals and 21 points in 23 games. Among his more important tallies was the first goal against New Jersey's Martin Brodeur in Game Six of the Eastern Conference Finals, the famed "Messier Guarantee Game."

It's hard to imagine Russian hockey icon Vladislav Tretiak being as animated after any of his world championships as Kovalev was after winning the Stanley Cup. With lucky troll doll in hand and drenched in champagne, Alexei bounced through the victors' locker room wearing a grin so big it seemed to envelop his entire face.

Kovalev notched at least 20 goals four times in his first six seasons with the team but every time he scored 20, the Rangers wanted 40—not an entirely unrealistic expectation when a player with his ability

was getting feeds from Messier and Wayne Gretzky.

As a result, every year became *THE* year that Kovalev had to break out to legitimize his high draft position, and the waiting spawned an almost endless stream of trade rumors. By 1998, the Rangers could wait no longer and dealt their underachieving winger to Pittsburgh for Petr Nedved.

Given a fresh start in the Steel City, Kovalev *finally* blossomed into a star, lighting the lamp 102 times over the next three seasons. He was on pace for 40 goals in 2002–03 when the cash-strapped Penguins traded him back to New York for a gaggle of minor-leaguers.

Unfortunately, Kovalev's second Gotham go-round did not get the Rangers any closer to ending a six-year playoff drought. He played 90 games over the next two seasons, managing only 23 goals before being sent to Montreal in New York's payroll purge in March 2004.

39

MURRAY MURDOCH

1926–37

LEFT WING

Games	Goals	Assists	Penalty minutes
508	84	108	197

Inexplicably, John Murray Murdoch is not in the Hockey Hall of Fame. As much as any of the 900 or so men who have played for the Rangers over the years, he belongs.

There were more than a few constants on the "original" Rangers, the Cook brothers, Frank Boucher, Taffy Abel and Ching Johnson among them. But the biggest constant among that group of two-time Stanley Cup winners was Murdoch, a five-foot-ten 180-pound left-winger, who at the time of his death on May 17, 2001, was 96 years old and the lone survivor of that first Ranger team.

Murdoch was only 22 when Conn Smythe, the Rangers' first general manager, offered him his first contract for $5,000 plus a $1,500 signing bonus. "I was about to say no," Murdoch recalled, "when Conn leaned over a coffee table at the Fort Garry Hotel in Winnipeg and slowly counted out the $1,500 in $100 bills. That clinched it. For a young guy, just married and with a summer job selling insurance, that looked like an awful lot of money."

Murdoch played 11 seasons with the Rangers and never missed a single game—508 in the regular season and 55 more in the playoffs for a total of 563 consecutive games. He was the NHL's first "Iron Man." In 1934–35, when Murdoch reached 400 straight games, the Rangers honored him on the ice at Madison Square Garden and brought in Lou Gehrig, the famous "Iron Man" of the New York Yankees, to present Murray with a watch.

Two years later, when he reached 500 straight games, there was another ceremony. This time, the team gifted Murdoch with a set of luggage. "That was certainly a message to me," he often joked. "The next season I was playing for the Philadelphia Ramblers."

In Murdoch's day, hockey was a far more defensive game than it is today. Low scores, sometimes even scoreless ties, were commonplace. Murdoch was one of the top defensive players of his day. Recalled Alex Shibicky, a teammate of Murray's for

The Canadian Press

one season, 1936–37: "When Murray went on the ice, the other team just didn't score. It was that simple."

Murdoch, who was the first Ranger to wear number 9, had center Paul Thompson and right wing Billy Boyd as his first linemates. "Back in those days, all teams were built around the first line," Murdoch recalled. "The first line did exactly as they pleased. The second line did exactly as they were told. The third line was just so happy to be there that they never said a word. I was on the second line."

> "When Murray went on the ice, the other team just didn't score. It was that simple."

In 1974, Murdoch was presented with the Lester Patrick Trophy for "outstanding service to hockey in the United States." The award was named after Lester Patrick, who once called Murdoch "an ideal major leaguer in every department of the game." Said Murdoch: "Lester definitely had a way with words. What he said was nice, but he wasn't nearly as generous when it came time to talk contract."

Twenty years after getting the Patrick Award, Murdoch beamed with pride as his old team, the Rangers, skated to the 1994 Stanley Cup and ended a drought that had reached 54 years. Murray watched the entire playoffs on television at his home in Hamden, Connecticut. "I didn't miss a minute, no sir. Oh, the memories that brought."

Following his playing career, Murdoch proved he was still an "Iron Man." He coached at Yale for 28 straight years. Author S. Kip Farrington, in his book *Skates, Sticks and Men*, wrote: "He [Murdoch] literally ate, slept and breathed hockey. At Yale, Murray brought a quiet dignity and professionalism. He popularized the sport there."

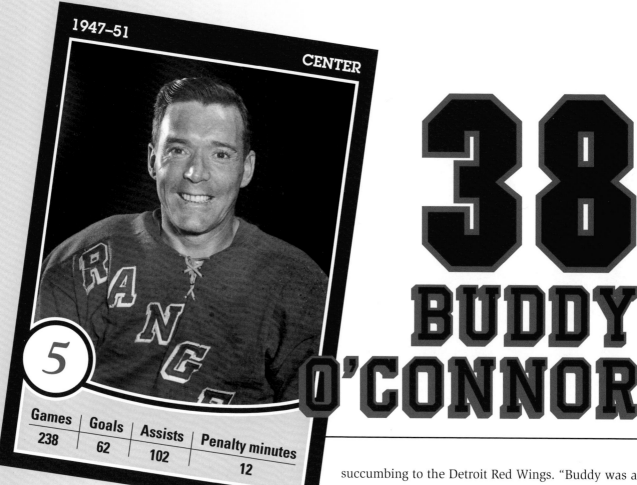

1947–51

CENTER

5

Games	Goals	Assists	Penalty minutes
238	62	102	12

38 BUDDY O'CONNOR

Imagine the discipline it took for Herbert William (Buddy) O'Connor to be whistled for only six minor penalties in 238 games spread out over four seasons as a New York Ranger. To put that remarkable statistic into perspective, consider that Christian Backman took three minor penalties *in his first game* as a Ranger!

O'Connor, a diminutive center who stood five-foot-seven and weighed just over 140 pounds, was one of the cleanest players the league has ever seen. Including the six years he also spent with the Montreal Canadiens, he amassed a paltry 34 penalty minutes in 509 career regular-season games. That's clean.

"I don't know how he did it, I really don't," recalled Chuck Rayner, O'Connor's teammate on the 1949–50 Rangers, who made it to double overtime in the seventh game of the Stanley Cup Finals before succumbing to the Detroit Red Wings. "Buddy was a little guy, but he was like a gnat, all over the place. He didn't get penalties, he drew penalties. And what a stickhandler, let me tell you."

Such was O'Connor's art that he played two seasons with the Rangers without drawing a single penalty, not a one!

A native of Montreal, O'Connor played seven seasons of junior hockey in his hometown before turning pro with les Habitants in 1941–42. The Canadiens signed Buddy and his linemates, left wing Pierre (Pete) Morin and right wing Jerry Heffernan, as a unit. The trio, all expert stickhandlers, was known as the "Razzle Dazzle Line."

For six straight seasons, O'Connor quietly starred for Montreal, albeit well within the lengthy shadows of Maurice (Rocket) Richard, Elmer (The Old Lamplighter) Lach and Hector (Toe) Blake. The Canadiens won two Stanley Cups in O'Connor's six years, never missing the playoffs. By then, Buddy was quite used to cashing playoff checks.

Turofsky/Hockey Hall of Fame

So, it was probably with a bit of disappointment and certainly a touch of angst that O'Connor accepted his fate when he was traded to the Rangers with defenseman Frankie Eddolls in exchange for bespectacled defenseman Hal Laycoe, left wing Joe Bell and left wing George Robertson on August 19, 1947.

The change of venue from Montreal to New York had to be a shocking one. But if the trade was a disappointment to O'Connor (the post-World War II Rangers were a ragtag bunch who had missed the playoffs the previous five seasons), it hardly showed. Buddy simply had his best season ever, a career-high 24 goals and 60 points in 1947–48, leading the Rangers to the playoffs.

That effort was also good enough for Buddy to haul home the Hart Trophy as NHL MVP, beating Boston's Frankie Brimsek, and the Lady Byng Trophy for "clean, effective play," beating Toronto's Syl Apps. It was the first time any NHL player had won those two awards in the same season. O'Connor barely missed a third trophy, the Art Ross as scoring champion, edged by a single point, 61–60, by his former Montreal teammate, Elmer Lach. At the start of the 1948–49 season, Clarence Campbell, the NHL's new president, presented the Hart and Byng trophies to O'Connor at center ice in Madison Square Garden.

Unlike most other finesse players, both preceding him and succeeding him, O'Connor quickly became a favorite in New York. His skills were readily apparent to all, not unlike Clint Smith of an earlier day and Camille Henry, who would follow. Recalled Emile Francis, another former teammate of O'Connor's: "Buddy was the nicest guy you'd ever want to meet, on the ice and off. He was one of the most intelligent players I'd ever seen."

After his NHL career wound down, O'Connor played for and coached the Cincinnati Mohawks of the American League. He died on August 24, 1977.

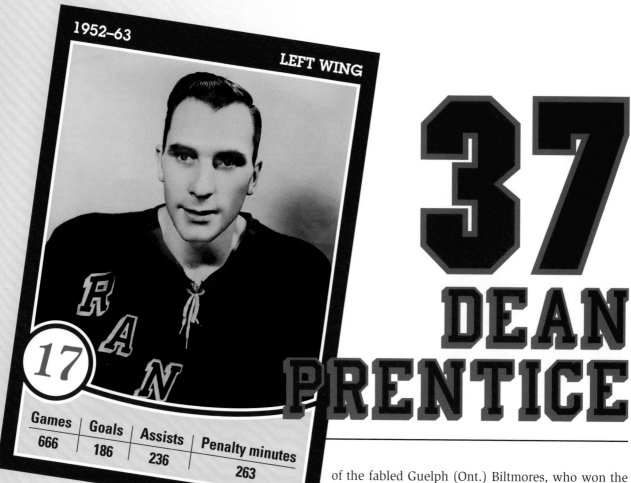

1952–63

LEFT WING

17

Games	Goals	Assists	Penalty minutes
666	186	236	263

37 DEAN PRENTICE

In his typically modest and soft-spoken way, Dean Prentice almost blushes at the mere suggestion, which he hears on a somewhat regular basis. "Dean Prentice," his boosters claim, "is simply the best player not in the Hockey Hall of Fame." It is hard to argue with them.

Statistically speaking at least, Dean Sutherland Prentice should be a shoo-in for hockey's highest honor: 22 seasons (only eight players have played more) with 391 goals, 469 assists and 860 points. Hall-of-Fame numbers don't come more emphatic than that. Among his contemporaries, only Gordie Howe, Alex Delvecchio and Tim Horton, Hall-of-Famers all, played more seasons than Prentice.

Eleven of Dean's 22 NHL campaigns were spent in New York with the Rangers. He never spent a minute in the minors, joining the club at age 22 early in the 1952–53 season. He arrived straight off the roster

of the fabled Guelph (Ont.) Biltmores, who won the Memorial Cup, Canada's junior championship, in May of 1952.

Prentice was part of the so-called Guelph Gang that also included Andy Bathgate, Harry Howell, Ron Murphy and Lou Fontinato. They would soon form the core of some solid Ranger teams in the mid-1950s, teams that reached the playoffs three times under fiery coach Phil Watson, but falling short in the first round every year.

"We were a very close bunch coming out of Guelph," Prentice recalled, "and that certainly made our transition to the big club a lot smoother. I think only Looie [Fontinato] spent any real time in the minors before heading to the Rangers."

A sturdy left wing at five-feet-eleven, 170 pounds, Prentice was known for his robust body checks and his hard shot. He was immediately tabbed to play with right wing Bathgate, the Rangers' superstar-in-the-making. With Larry Popein (and later Earl Ingarfield) at center, the trio was one of the best the

Rangers have ever had. Prentice and Popein were basically charged with keeping Bathgate's cannon loaded, providing the ammunition for Andy to become one of the game's best right wings.

Four times a 20-goal scorer with the Rangers, Prentice had a career-high 32 goals and 66 points in 1959–60, making the second All-Star Team that season (Bobby Hull, Chicago's Golden Jet, was the first-team selection).

Durability was a Prentice trademark, particularly during his Ranger years. Still, he suffered some significant injuries. "Our skates were made of kangaroo leather," he said, "and once I got 22 stitches in my foot after Looie Fontinato's skate went through it. Another time, I fell over Fleming Mackell and the ulnar bone popped out of my wrist and came down into my hand. The doctor gave me a Band-Aid and an aspirin."

He suffered a broken back one season after being tripped while on a breakaway by Chicago's Stan Mikita. Despite the injury, Prentice took the awarded penalty shot, and scored. "I sat back on the bench and cooled off, but suddenly I couldn't move," he remembered. "They got a stretcher and took me out. I spent half a year in a body cast."

With the Rangers heading into a serious and badly needed rebuilding mode, Prentice was traded to the Boston Bruins for Don McKenney and Dick Meissner on February 4, 1963. Still a solid performer, he would play 11 more seasons with the Bruins, Detroit Red Wings, Pittsburgh Penguins and Minnesota North Stars.

More than three decades after his retirement, he is still without a phone call from the Hockey Hall of Fame.

Surrounded by four Detroit Red Wings, left wing Dean Prentice takes a tumble.

36

ANDERS HEDBERG

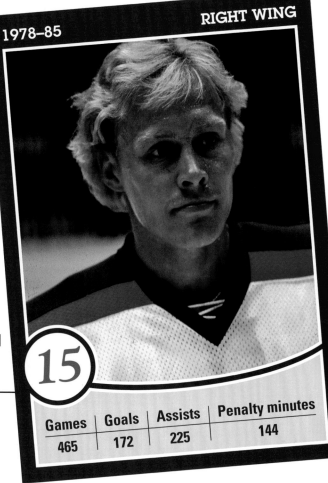

15

Games	Goals	Assists	Penalty minutes
465	172	225	144

The NHL of the late 1970s was not especially welcoming for players with funny accents and peculiar surnames. But with style, guts and grace, Anders Hedberg overcame an anti-European bias to become one of the game's most exciting stars.

Hedberg is reluctant to think of himself as a trailblazer but he and players like countrymen Thommie Bergman, Börje Salming and Inge Hammarström were precisely that: the forerunners of an international explosion that has completely reshaped the face of the league.

An intelligent and offensively creative player, Hedberg first achieved fame as a member of the Swedish national team in 1970 when his inspired play earned him the nickname "the New Tumba" after 1950s Swedish hockey star Sven (Tumba) Johansson. Not an honor to be taken lightly, in Sweden it was roughly akin to dubbing someone "the new Gretzky."

Because there was no professional hockey in Sweden at the time, Anders and friend Ulf Nilsson came to North America in 1974 to star for the WHA's Winnipeg Jets. Every team in the NHL lined up to lure them away from the rival league when they became free agents four years later, but only the Rangers were willing to make Hedberg and Nilsson the highest-paid players in all of hockey. In June 1978, the duo signed for a combined $2.4 million over two years.

That alone could have bruised some egos in the dressing room but Hedberg and Nilsson fit in because they were completely team-oriented and, as former captain Dave Maloney noted, "they weren't coming in here trying to get a candy bar named after them."

If they had, it might have been sold under the unpalatable label "True Grit." That was the term Ron Greschner used to describe the Swedes, who didn't let off-color remarks, cheap shots and other intimidation tactics throw them off their game.

"Guys were going to run the Europeans right back over the Atlantic so they wouldn't take any more jobs," Hedberg said. "But we had already seen it all, done it all and had experienced the most discrimination and prejudice playing in Winnipeg by the time we arrived in New York. It wasn't that bad there. And I felt that if you're going to survive, you can't play it by the rules of your opponent who wants you to fight, because you're going to lose. So I had to beat them in other ways."

Like on the scoreboard, where Hedberg's impact was felt immediately as he paced the Blueshirts with 79 points in 80 games in his first season. After the team suffered a pair of bitter overtime losses to the Islanders in the 1979 semifinals, he scored the game-winning goal in the closing minutes of Game Five to shift momentum in the Rangers' favor, and they went on to win the series.

Over the next several years, Anders continued to rank among New York's top scorers. And with the influx of younger European players, he emerged as a leader who could be the bridge between different groups on the team. The Swedes and the Finns stuck so close to Hedberg that on one Father's Day, they actually sent him flowers.

The 1984–85 season was Hedberg's last as a player. Although he declined a hero's sendoff that would have included a ceremony on Garden ice, preferring to go out with less fanfare than what accompanied his headline-grabbing debut, he did accept the 1985 Masterton Trophy for "perseverance, sportsmanship, and dedication to ice hockey."

His playing days over, Hedberg continued his pioneering ways by becoming the first European to serve in a top front-office position in the NHL when Rangers GM Craig Patrick tabbed him to be his assistant. He went on to hold similar managerial posts with the Toronto Maple Leafs and Ottawa Senators.

In 2007, Hedberg rejoined the Rangers as a scout.

35 CLINT SMITH

1937–43

CENTER

10

Games	Goals	Assists	Penalty minutes
281	80	115	12

Well into his mid-90s, Clint (Snuffy) Smith was still as crisp as a Jeff Beukeboom body check, and as sharp as a Sean Avery wake-up punch. He was forever thus.

Prior to his passing in May 2009 at age 95, Smith was the oldest living winner of the Stanley Cup, which he did with the Rangers in 1939–40, the oldest living ex-Ranger, and the oldest living member of the Hockey Hall of Fame.

In addition to his longevity, Smith is also known as probably the cleanest player to ever wear a Ranger jersey, totaling a mere 12 penalty minutes during his time in New York. Overall, in ten National Hockey League seasons and 483 games, he drew only 24 minutes in penalties.

He won the Lady Byng Trophy for "clean, effective play" twice, with the Rangers in 1938–39 and with the Chicago Blackhawks in 1943–44. For four seasons, Smith drew *zero* penalty minutes. He once went an amazing 85 straight games without a penalty.

How did he avoid drawing penalties? "It was easy," he said, "I knew the referees."

At five-foot-eight, 165 pounds, Clinton James Smith, a speedy center, was hardly a big guy, even by the standards of his day. He was, however, one of the fastest skaters in the league. But his line mate, Wilbert (Dutch) Hiller, was even faster. Smith recalled: "Nobody could keep up with Dutch, not in the entire league."

Smith's fondest memories of his days in New York revolved around the 1940 Cup champions. "We were a family, all of us," he remembered. "Anytime we went anywhere, we went as a body. We stuck up for each other and knew where everyone was all the time."

Snuffy, whose nickname came from the popular cartoon character Snuffy Smith, also recalled, with more than a chuckle, the amount of playoff money each of the 1940 Rangers received. "It was $377 American funds and $636 Canadian," he said. "Plus, the Madison Square Garden Corporation coughed up a $500 bonus for all of us. That was a very big deal."

The Rangers signed Smith to a contract when he was just 18 years old, but he matured out west, mostly in Saskatoon and Vancouver, until cracking the Rangers' lineup at the age of 24 in 1937–38. In his second season with the club, he led the team in goals with 21 goals and 41 points.

With the Rangers, Smith usually played on a line with Hiller and Alf Pike. Defensively, the trio was one of the best in the NHL. "Remember, it was a defensive game back then," Smith said, "not at all like it is today. The games were very low scoring, and the team with the best defensive players usually won. In 1940, we had the best defensive players." Pike passed away in March 2009, less than three months before Smith.

Signed by Chicago in 1943–44, Smith continued to excel. He had three straight 20-goal seasons, a league-leading 49 assists and a career-high 72 points in his first year with the Blackhawks. His linemates in Chicago were Bill Mosienko and Doug Bentley. They set what was then an NHL record with 219 total points in 1943–44.

Smith retired as a player in 1947 with 161 goals and 397 points. Eighty of the goals and 195 of the points came with the Rangers. In 1975, Snuffy returned to the Rangers as a west coast scout under general manager John Ferguson.

In July of 2007, the NHL sent the Stanley Cup all over Canada to visit with players who had previously won it. Clint got his visit in Vancouver, his longtime home, on July 26. He proudly sported a Rangers jersey for the occasion, a jersey he had worn with great distinction from 1937 to 1943.

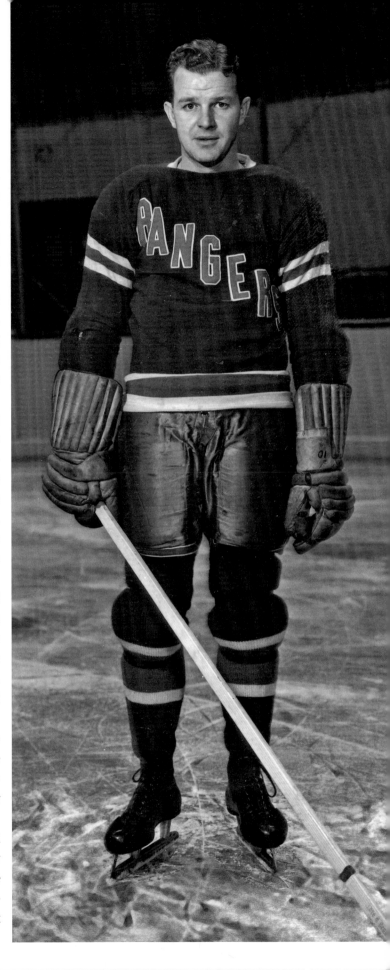

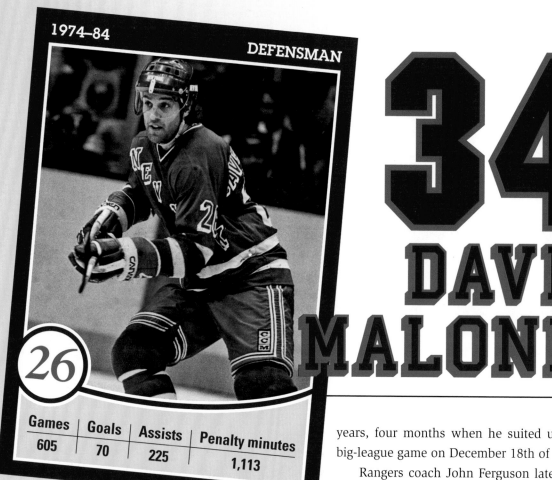

1974–84

DEFENSMAN

26

Games	Goals	Assists	Penalty minutes
605	70	225	1,113

34 DAVE MALONEY

With a personality befitting the wild and unpredictable era in which he played, Dave Maloney was a mainstay on the Ranger blue line throughout the late 1970s and early 1980s.

A good playmaking defenseman whose skating and hockey sense made him an important member of both the power play and penalty-killing units, Maloney was also a scrappy leader in the defensive zone—scrappy enough to lead the club in penalty minutes on three occasions.

"Dave was in the middle of everything whether he won a fight or lost a fight," former teammate Ron Greschner said. "You could always count on Dave."

Drafted 14th overall in 1974, he was the second-youngest player in Rangers history at the age of 18

years, four months when he suited up for his first big-league game on December 18th of that year.

Rangers coach John Ferguson later marveled at the almost infectious killer instinct of the teenaged defender.

"One wonders where that kid has been hiding," Fergy noted. "Maloney's running guys into the boards and giving out some fierce checks. And once one guy starts it, everybody does. He's only 19, but he's already a leader on the ice and in the dressing room."

Maloney played his position so well during his first two years of full-time duty that in 1978–79 he succeeded Phil Esposito as the Blueshirts' captain, a title he says has taken on deeper meaning in recent years.

"I don't know if that's just a result of extended media coverage or over-observation," Maloney said. "The role of captain was typically one in which I was kind of in the middle. I never, ever felt that I was in a position to tell the coaching staff, 'You should be

doing this or that.' Obviously, with Mark Messier and all the things that happened with him here, that role of captain became more impactful than perhaps it was for the rest of us."

In his first year with a "C" stitched to his uniform, Maloney helped the team reach the Stanley Cup Finals for the first time since 1972 and he registered his first of four consecutive seasons with at least ten goals. He also got to play with his younger brother, Don.

"While Don and I were only two years apart in age," Dave explained, "I'd always played up, so we were four or five years apart on a competitive level. He and my brother Bob and I played together on a little squirt team as kids but that was the only time prior to playing with the Rangers. It was really very special. We probably could have been closer in those days but we were young and independent. I

think there was a healthy respect for one another's abilities."

Maloney kept busy in the off-seasons working as an instructor at various hockey camps, including one he ran with his brother. He also spent two summers working for brokerage firm Bear, Stearns & Co. in preparation for life *after* hockey.

But when the Rangers declined in the mid-1980s, Maloney was traded to the Buffalo Sabres. He played out the 1984–85 season and the first round of the playoffs with Buffalo before retiring at the relatively young age of 29 so he could pursue a full-time job on Wall Street.

Maloney eventually came back to hockey, and his sense of humor and enthusiasm for the game have served him well in his new career as a color analyst on radio and television.

33
CECIL DILLON

1930–39   **RIGHT WING**

Hockey Hall of Fame

8

Games	Goals	Assists	Penalty minutes
409	160	121	93

Perhaps because he had the good fortune to play with a slew of future Hall-of-Famers including Frank Boucher, Bill Cook and Art Coulter, Cecil Dillon is simply one of the most overlooked and under-rated players in the annals of the New York Rangers.

Yet Dillon, a left-handed-shooting right wing, never missed a single game during his nine years with the Rangers—409 consecutive contests from 1930–31 through 1938–39, an "Iron Man" mark exceeded only by Murray Murdoch, another teammate, and later by Andy Hebenton.

At five-foot-eleven, 175 pounds, Dillon was solidly built and quite difficult to knock off the puck. He was a crafty playmaker with the eye of a sharpshooter and a very heavy shot. He led the Rangers in scoring three years in a row (1935–36 to 1937–38) and that alone puts him in very exclusive Ranger company. Only Boucher, Bill Cook, Andy Bathgate, Phil Esposito and Wayne Gretzky can make the same claim.

Dillon played initially on a line with Murdoch and Melville (Butch) Keeling, the trio serving as a bridge between the team's first great line, the "A-Line," and their second great line, the "Bread Line."

First impressions were encouraging.

"The boys on skates say that Cecil Dillon of the Rangers is the flashiest first-year man since Howie Morenz, the flying Frenchman, came darting over the frozen horizon," exclaimed the venerable *New York Times* columnist John Kieran.

Dillon and company helped the Rangers win their second Stanley Cup in 1932–33, the "Forgotten Cup" as it's been called, coming as it did between the much greater ballyhooed triumphs of 1928 and 1940. With eight goals in eight games (plus two assists), Dillon led all playoff scorers in goals and points in 1933. With three goals and an assist, he was also the leading scorer in the finals, which the Rangers took in four games over the Toronto Maple Leafs despite getting only one home game in Madison Square Garden.

Cecil Dillon (center) chats it up with former teammates Frank Boucher (7) and Murray Murdoch (9) before the closing ceremonies at the third Madison Square Garden in 1968.

Murdoch remembered the low-key response to the 1933 title. He said: "There was no parade, or anything like that. We took cabs down to City Hall. They shook our hands, and that was that."

Off the ice, Dillon was an affable sort who absolutely loved stories of the Old West, sometimes even bringing his guitar to practice to sing western songs. In time, Dillon became fast friends with Frank Boucher, once he discovered (from Keeling) that Boucher had been a member of the Royal Canadian Mounted Police (true) and even once had to shoot a man (not true).

Recalled Boucher: "Cec became very excited at this news, and he began asking me incessant questions about the Mounties. I told him many exciting tales about tracking down mad-dog killers and such. Some of them were even true.

"Cec followed me everywhere. There was no way I could tell him enough to satisfy him. I even had to start reading western stories to find enough plots to quench his insatiable thirst."

After 409 games with the Rangers, Dillon was sold for cash to the Detroit Red Wings on May 17, 1939, missing by one season the Rangers' third Stanley Cup in 1940. He retired from pro hockey in 1942 after two seasons in the American Hockey League.

Although he grew up in Thornbury, Ontario, Cecil Graham Dillon was born in Toledo, Ohio, on April 26, 1908. That wouldn't make news today but it was noteworthy in the early 1930s when the game was almost completely dominated by Canadians. A handful of other U.S.-born players in the NHL at the time included "Yonkers" Billy Burch of the New York Americans and Michigan product Clarence (Taffy) Abel, a Ranger rearguard from 1926 to 1929.

Dillon passed away at 61 years of age on November 14, 1969.

1947-56

CENTER

7

Games	Goals	Assists	Penalty minutes
535	101	219	96

32 DON RALEIGH

"Well-rounded" is hardly a term you would normally apply to a guy nicknamed "Bones" or "The Thin Man," but in the case of Don Raleigh, it fit perfectly.

Raleigh, who played 10 seasons and 535 games for the Rangers, was not only a superb hockey player, but also an aficionado of nontraditional hockey pursuits such as classical music, poetry, gourmet foods, and of all things, Civil War battlefields. Small by hockey standards of any era, Raleigh was a wispy five-foot-eleven, and weighed only 150 pounds, hence his nicknames.

In 1943–44, Raleigh, at the tender age of 17, became the youngest man ever to play regularly for the Rangers. A crafty center, Raleigh played 15 games, but a broken jaw made him reconsider his options, and he decided on school at the University of Manitoba.

Rangers general manager Frank Boucher was determined to lure Raleigh back to Manhattan. It took

him three seasons to do it. By 1947–48, Bones was a ripe old man of 20, yet he launched a Blueshirt career that nearly resulted in a Stanley Cup in 1950.

Just how much did the Rangers prize James Donald Raleigh? Well, they bestowed uniform No. 7 on him for the 1948–49 season, a high honor indeed. Only Boucher and Phil Watson had worn it previously for 22 consecutive seasons, and the Rangers thought hard before giving it to Raleigh. They wanted a guy headed for stardom, and they wanted a center. Bones was both, and much more, as the Rangers soon discovered.

Most of the Rangers of that era lived in Manhattan hotels. Raleigh did that for a while, but soon settled in Staten Island, the first—and only—Ranger to live there while playing. He commuted on the Staten Island ferry, and even composed poems while doing so. "Manhattan was too crowded for me," he said. "I couldn't sleep there, I had to get out to the country."

Raleigh's penchant for Civil War history and battlefields saw him spend two summers traveling in search of historic sites, sometimes even sleeping on those hallowed grounds. "I'll never forget Gettysburg," he said. "You could smell the history there. I traveled over 7,000 miles studying the Civil War, and it was an experience I'll never forget."

On the ice, Raleigh, still technically a rookie, became the first Ranger to score four goals in a game, on February 25, 1948, a 7–4 loss to the Chicago Blackhawks at Madison Square Garden. That same season, he set what was then a National Hockey League record, assisting on three goals in just 81 seconds in a 4–2 win over the Montreal Canadiens at the Garden on November 16, 1947.

But it would be the 1949–50 season that would ultimately determine Raleigh's legacy with the Blueshirts. The Rangers had finished fourth, but upset the Canadiens in the first round, setting a final-round matchup with the Detroit Red Wings, who finished first, 21 points ahead of the Rangers.

The Rangers played only two "home" games at Maple Leaf Gardens in Toronto (the remaining games were played at the Olympia in Detroit) and trailed the Wings two games to one entering Game Four. Incredibly, Raleigh would score two overtime goals to win Game Four and Game Five, giving the Blueshirts the lead in the series.

Raleigh recalled: "The silence in the Olympia was deafening. No one cheered except our guys. I don't think there were ten people in the building rooting for us, but right then we had them on the ropes."

Despite heroic efforts by Raleigh, linemate Pentti Lund and goaltender Chuck Rayner, the Rangers dropped the next two games and the series. Game Seven went to double overtime, but reserve forward Pete Babando scored against Rayner, and Raleigh's finest moment in New York came to an end.

Now in his 80s, Raleigh is retired in Winnipeg.

Small of stature, but a crafty stickhandler, center Don Raleigh clears the puck from behind the Rangers' net.

34

Games	Record	Shutouts	GAA
449	200-177-47	16	3.45

31
JOHN VANBIESBROUCK

He was a cocky kid from Detroit who starred in the Canadian juniors, and by the time John Vanbiesbrouck quit the game two decades later, he was the winningest American-born goaltender ever to play in the NHL.

Vanbiesbrouck had quick reflexes and an aggressive style, and his performance with the OHL's Sault Ste. Marie ("Soo") Greyhounds left little doubt that he would be selected in the NHL draft. He was considered a solid prospect when the Rangers chose him 72nd overall in 1981, a high pick for a goalie at the time.

The Blueshirts had no intention of rushing the 18-year-old into action. But with the team's expected starter, John Davidson, out with a chronic back injury that would eventually force him into retirement, and backup Steve Baker nursing a pulled groin muscle,

necessity trumped discretion and "The Beezer" was summoned to New York as an emergency call-up.

"They wouldn't put me in if they didn't think I had the ability," a confident Vanbiesbrouck said shortly before his professional debut in Denver against the Colorado Rockies on December 5, 1981. "I'll shake for a while, but I'll calm down after the first few shots. It's definitely gonna be a win."

And win he did, backing up his words with 30 saves to beat the Rockies, 2–1. After the game, the Rangers returned Vanbiesbrouck to the Soo for seasoning, but he was back on Broadway two years later splitting duty with Glen Hanlon.

Barely out of his teens, the chatty netminder carried himself with an air of authority more befitting a much older player and he emerged as a team leader.

The legendary Herb Brooks was Vanbiesbrouck's

first coach with the Rangers. "John was a real professional in every way," Brooks recalled. "There was no baloney about him, no superstitions, no quirks. I liked that. His positive attitude rubbed off on a lot of his teammates."

What didn't rub off tended to chafe because Vanbiesbrouck, ferociously competitive and opinionated, was inclined to criticize teammates' play as much as his own. Some elder Rangers began calling him "The Mouth," a not-so-subtle reminder that rookies should know their place.

It wasn't until 1984–85 that Vanbiesbrouck became the club's regular goalie, pushing Hanlon into a backup role. The following season he won 31 games, backstopped the Rangers to the Conference Finals and became just the fourth Ranger to capture the Vezina Trophy. Night in, night out, chants of "BEE-ZER! BEE-ZER!" followed his most stupendous saves, and his popularity soared.

Vanbiesbrouck reigned supreme until another Yank, ex-collegian Mike Richter, hit the scene and established himself as a future star. They became the best duo in the game and in 1990–91 set an odd record for the longest one-two goalie rotation by religiously alternating starts for 76 straight games. The

next year, they combined for 50 wins and helped the Blueshirts earn their first Presidents' Trophy.

The tandem, playfully dubbed "VanRichter-Brouck," gave the Rangers the luxury of two franchise goalies, neither of whom wanted to spend the rest of his career starting every other game. Even if the veteran Vanbiesbrouck resented having to share the limelight with an equal but younger (and more affordable) talent, he kept his griping to a minimum and made the best of an arrangement all parties knew couldn't last much longer.

Two new teams were joining the league in 1993 and the Rangers had to decide which goalie to keep. New coach Mike Keenan wanted Richter, so Vanbiesbrouck became the odd man out. Traded to Vancouver, he was then claimed in the expansion draft by the Florida Panthers, a team he almost single-handedly legitimized by leading them to the 1996 Stanley Cup Finals.

Vanbiesbrouck's 20-year NHL career also included stints with some of the Rangers' most hated divisional rivals: the Philadelphia Flyers, New York Islanders and New Jersey Devils. Along the way he amassed 374 victories, placing him 11th on the all-time list and first among American-born goaltenders.

1935–42 DEFENSEMAN

2

Games	Goals	Assists	Penalty minutes
287	18	67	342

30
ART COULTER

Defenseman Art Coulter, the second captain of the New York Rangers, succeeding Bill Cook in 1937–38, was among the toughest rearguards the team has ever known. His seven-year run in New York included the Stanley Cup of 1939–40, the team's third, and three Second Team All-Star selections.

On the ice, Arthur Edmund Coulter was a "punisher," as one of his teammates, left wing Lynn Patrick, called him. "When he hit you in practice, you just knew that it was him," Patrick used to say. "Art's checks felt different, and it wasn't a good type of different, I can tell you that."

From a purely pugilistic standpoint, the 1939–40 Rangers indisputably had the greatest four-man unit in NHL history. Coulter was paired with Muzz Patrick, who was only the former amateur heavyweight boxing champion of Canada. The other pairing featured Ott Heller, an accomplished and renowned boxing enthusiast himself, and Walter (Babe) Pratt, one of the most feared body checkers in the league at the time.

How tough was the unit that featured Coulter with Patrick and Heller with Pratt? Well, not another defenseman, not a one, played a single game in 1939–40. "And we won the Stanley Cup," Coulter would sometimes brag. "Not too bad, eh?" He led the championship Rangers with 21 penalty minutes in 12 playoff games that season.

But for Coulter, as outspoken off the ice as he was punishing on it, that single Cup wasn't nearly enough. "We should have won three Cups, maybe four," he often griped. "Lester [Patrick] worked us too damn hard before the playoffs every year. He made a great team into a good team. He overdid it for sure." Patrick would take the playoff-bound Rangers to Atlantic City, 100 or so miles south of New York, for grueling training-camp-style torture sessions. "They were killers," Coulter moaned.

Coulter's arrival in New York, in a mid-season trade with the Chicago Blackhawks for Earl

Seibert on January 15, 1936, was a timely one for the Rangers, given that Ivan (Ching) Johnson, the Rangers' first great blueliner, was winding up his illustrious career on Broadway. Patrick knew what he was getting in Coulter, a winner who had won the Stanley Cup with the Blackhawks in 1934, Chicago's first championship.

Said teammate Frank Boucher on Coulter's leadership with the Rangers: "Art lent strength to our smaller players, always on the spot if opposing players tried to intimidate them. He was a great team man, a great captain. The team always came first with him."

Coulter's nickname was "The Trapper," not only because of his skill at blocking shots, but also because of his great prowess as an outdoorsman. "Besides hockey," Muzz Patrick recalled, "hunting and fishing was all Art talked about."

Retiring from the NHL in 1942, Coulter played two more seasons with the fabled United States Coast Guard Cutters of the Eastern Hockey League. Even deep into his retirement, which he spent in the south in Georgia and Alabama, Coulter remained as outspoken and starchy as he was years earlier about Lester Patrick.

Coulter was certainly a man of conviction. In February of 1968, the Rangers were planning a gala final for the closing of the third Madison Square Garden. They invited every living member of a First All-Star Team to attend. Coulter, never having been a first teamer, was not invited, and this miffed him. He never set foot in the Garden again.

Reached at his home in the mid-1990s by hockey writer Chuck O'Donnell, Coulter snapped, "I never watch today's game. That's not real hockey. They're not as tough as we were." Asked what he thought of a fellow named Wayne Gretzky, Coulter snarled: "Who? Never heard of him. I don't know who you're talking about."

Elected to the Hockey Hall of Fame in 1974, Coulter lived until he was 92, passing away on October 14, 2000.

1926-36 **LEFT WING**

6

Games	Goals	Assists	Penalty minutes
433	154	139	436

29
BUN COOK

From the inaugural Rangers team of 1926–27, Frederick Joseph (Bun) Cook was perhaps the most underrated, a position that probably suited him just fine. The five-foot-eleven, 180-pound left wing was stoic and silent, sometimes to a fault, but his contributions to the club itself extended beyond mere words.

Bun—the nickname came from Fred's habit of hopping "like a bunny" to gain momentum on his skates—was the left wing on the Rangers' very first power line, with the smooth playmaker Frank Boucher at center and Bun's older (by seven years) brother Bill at right wing. The trio was known as the "A-Line."

Bun was an original in more ways than one. He registered the Rangers' very first assist, passing to brother Bill for the Rangers' first-ever goal on November 16, 1926, a 1–0 shutout of the Montreal Maroons at Madison Square Garden. "Nobody ever remembers the assist," he would say years later. "The goal, yes, but not the assist."

On an even broader plane, Bun Cook is credited as the first NHL player to utilize the slap shot, years and years ahead of Montreal's Bernie (Boom Boom) Geoffrion and Chicago's Bobby Hull, who popularized the shot in the 1950s and 1960s. Cook utilized the maneuver mostly in practice. "It had a great element of surprise," he remembered. "Everybody used to use the wrist shot or a backhander."

Cook's claim as the originator of the slap shot is without challenge. Alex Shibicky, Cook's successor at left wing on the Rangers' top line in 1936, admitted he got the idea from Cook in practice. The two played together for only one season, 1935–36, Cook's last Ranger campaign and Shibicky's first. "Bun never used the slapper in a game," Shibicky said. "I did, but it was definitely his idea."

The Cooks, along with Boucher, were basically the foundation of those early Rangers teams. All of the men were well established when they came to New York in 1926, the Cooks having been purchased for $30,000 from the Saskatoon Crescents of the Western Hockey League. Bun became a rock-solid Ranger performer for 10 seasons, scoring 154 goals and 139 assists for 293 points.

Despite his low-key nature, Bun still held a lot of sway with Lester Patrick, the Rangers' first general manager and coach. It was Bun, along with Boucher, who convinced Patrick (at age 44) to tend goal for the Rangers when Lorne Chabot got injured and was

Cook's claim as the originator of the slap shot is without challenge.

unable to finish a famous 1928 playoff match with the Montreal Maroons. It was also Bun who convinced Patrick to sign Lester's youngest son Lynn, a left wing, to a professional contract in 1934, even though Lester had severe misgivings about Lynn's ability to perform at the NHL level.

In retrospect, Cook was right. Lynn developed into an All-Star left wing, much to the delight of Lester, who didn't often relish being wrong … especially about his own son.

By 1936–37, Bun's talents were ebbing quickly. He had scored only four goals the previous season, and was plagued by an persistent throat problem that was eventually diagnosed as rheumatic fever. Left with little choice, Patrick sold Cook to the rival Boston Bruins for $15,000. "It was a very sad day," Lester often reminisced, "the beginning of the break-up of the 'original' Rangers."

Following his NHL career, Cook went on to manage, coach and occasionally play for the Providence Reds of the International/American League. Then, from 1943 to 1956, he coached the AHL's Cleveland Barons to nine Calder Cup Finals, winning five championships.

Bun was elected to the Hockey Hall of Fame in 1995, long after brother Bill and Boucher were enshrined. To this day, they are the only entire line in Rangers' history to make the Hall of Fame. Bun never knew of the honor. That was probably fine with him, just as he never sought credit for developing the slap shot.

DEFENSEMAN

1926–37

3

Games	Goals	Assists	Penalty minutes
405	38	48	798

28 IVAN (CHING) JOHNSON

Before Beukeboom, before Beck, when speak-easies doled out illegal hooch and silvery Zeppelins cruised above the Manhattan skyline, Ivan (Ching) Johnson joyfully upended opposing forwards with body checks so stiff, it's lucky he was never arrested for assault.

A mainstay on the Blueshirt blue line for the first 11 years of the team's existence, Johnson was one of the top defensemen in the game and, partnered with Clarence (Taffy) Abel on the Rangers' first defense pairing, a key member of New York's Stanley Cup winners in 1928 and 1933.

Johnson's nickname—fans would shout "Ching, Ching, Chinaman!"—had nothing to do with his ethnicity (actually, he was of Irish ancestry). It derived instead from summer camping trips Johnson and his pals would take along the Red River in Alberta. In those days, it was common practice on

extended excursions of this sort to hire a man, usually of Chinese descent, to serve as the group's cook. But Johnson usually volunteered for that duty, probably to save a few bucks, and the unseemly nickname was born.

He also went by "Ivan the Terrible," but that tag had nothing to do with his temperament. Johnson was the kind of jovial, fun-loving guy you'd enjoy meeting anywhere … except in his end of the ice.

"A big, raw-boned fellow with a bald head, he always wore a grin, even when heaving some poor soul six feet in the air," former teammate Frank Boucher recalled of Johnson's signature hits. "He was one of those rare warm people who'd break into a smile just saying hello or telling you the time."

He had a mischievous streak, too, and one of his favorite tricks was to hide a puck in his gloves. Then, during a multi-player scrum along the boards, Ching would drop the concealed puck, causing an immediate whistle and more than a little confusion, not to mention a breather for the smirking defenseman.

"I only did it four, maybe five times," Johnson said. "But it was great fun. I even used to do it in practice, but that was tough because Lester [Patrick] used to count the pucks, no foolin'."

A World War I veteran who saw action in France with the Third Canadian Ammunition Train as well as a trench mortar outfit, Johnson was fond of saying that he'd had enough of real combat since the wars fought on ice were tough enough on him. A physical player, he incurred any and all varieties of scrapes, bumps, bruises and broken bones.

It was during the early weeks of 1930 when Johnson suffered a fractured jaw after a head-on collision with Bruins defenseman Dit Clapper. Doctors wired Ching's jaw back together but it wasn't long before he was smiling and joking—through clenched teeth, of course—and asking when he'd be back in the lineup.

"My ankles and shoulders are all right," he reasoned, "and they're the most important things in hockey. Your jaw doesn't count. What if I can't open my teeth? You're not allowed to bite in this game."

Sure enough, Johnson was in uniform wearing a jaw protector when the Rangers opened the playoffs against Ottawa that spring.

By the mid-1930s, many of the "original" Rangers were showing signs of age and moving on to other teams or even other professions. At 38, Johnson had slowed considerably but he could still break up an offensive rush with a well-timed poke check or hit, which still carried enough force to knock much younger men on their rears.

But he began to see less and less regular action and a one-year stint as player-coach left him feeling unsatisfied. After turning down an offer to coach the Rangers' amateur squad, the Rovers, in 1937, he decided to extend his playing career with the New York Americans. Johnson played only 32 games for the Rangers' star-spangled rivals before closing out his career in the minor leagues.

Elected to the Hockey Hall of Fame in 1958, Johnson passed away in 1979 at age 81.

27
LYNN PATRICK

1934–43, 1945–46   LEFT WING

9

Games	Goals	Assists	Penalty minutes
455	145	190	240

Virtually all professional athletes, including some of the Rangers' biggest stars, get booed at one time or another. But it's safe to say that left wing Lynn Patrick probably had the thickest skin of them all.

At six feet and 200 pounds, Patrick had a better-than-average hockey body, plus a sterling athletic reputation tracing to his roots in Victoria, British Columbia. It was Lynn's style that brought him criticism. He was a finesse player, preferring to dazzle on his skates and with his stick, eschewing the more robust exploits of some of his teammates, particularly his rollicking, hard-checking brother Muzz.

Madison Square Garden crowds often teased him with nicknames such as "Twinkletoes" or "Sonja," the latter a reference to the world-famous figure skating star of the era, Sonja Henie. Patrick merely shrugged it off, much as he had the criticism and doubt that came earlier from, of all places, within his own family.

As great as Lynn's athleticism was, his father, Lester, boss of the Rangers at the time, simply didn't think Lynn could make it in the NHL. Veterans Bill and Bun Cook, plus Frank Boucher, thought otherwise, and pestered Lester mightily enough that he finally signed his eldest son to a contract in 1934.

It was one of the best decisions Lester ever made. Lynn was a key contributor to the Rangers' Stanley Cup championship in 1940, scored a career-high 32 goals in 1942 and won First Team All-Star honors that year.

Lynn's linemates at the height of his career were Phil Watson at center and Bryan Hextall at right wing. The trio was known as the "Powerhouse Line" and all three were on the ice when Hextall scored the goal that won the Stanley Cup on April 13, 1940, at Maple Leaf Gardens in Toronto.

Such was Lynn's stature in New York at the time that the team bestowed sweater No. 9 on him when Murray Murdoch retired following the 1936–37 season. Over ten seasons, Lynn would eventually play

455 games for the Blueshirts, scoring 145 goals and 190 assists for 335 points. He was elected to the Hockey Hall of Fame in 1980.

In retrospect, Lester, no doubt with a tinge of familial pride, admitted in his biography *The Patricks* that the signing of Lynn "was one of the best things I ever did. Nothing has given me the flush of satisfaction that came with the realization that my bumbling but persistent redheaded son had made the grade to hockey stardom."

World War II, as it did for so many Rangers, effectively ended Lynn Patrick's playing career. Following two years of service in the United States military, he came back briefly in 1945–46 but was ineffective. Retiring as a player, he embarked on a long and successful coaching and managerial career with the Rangers (1948 to 1950), the Boston Bruins and the St. Louis Blues.

In his first full season coaching the Rangers, Lynn took the club to the Stanley Cup Finals, only to lose in double overtime of Game Seven to the Detroit Red Wings. Sadly, a dispute over money ended Lynn's days in New York the following season.

The Bruins offered Patrick about $12,000 to come to Boston, about $3,000 more than Lynn was making behind the Blueshirts' bench. General manager Frank Boucher, proving every bit as frugal as his predecessor Lester Patrick, refused to budge, and much to the very public dismay of New York sportswriters, Lynn was off to Beantown, where he made great contributions in promoting amateur hockey in New England. He did the same later in St. Louis, starting in 1967–68.

In 1989, he was posthumously awarded the Lester Patrick Trophy, named for his father, for "outstanding service to hockey in the United States."

1978–88

LEFT WING

26 DON MALONEY

Games	Goals	Assists	Penalty minutes
653	195	307	739

12

His size, skating and stickhandling were merely average—maybe even below average, if one were to believe his self-evaluation—but Don Maloney's versatility and work ethic served him very well in a 13-year career spent almost exclusively with the Rangers.

Anders Hedberg shared a dressing room with this self-made star for seven seasons and called Maloney "a fabulous addition of energy to the team and someone you could absolutely trust every day because you knew he would give whatever he had and he would give it every night. He was a man of integrity."

"The best cornerman I've ever seen or ever played with," was Eddie Johnstone's appraisal.

After scoring 104 points for the OHA's Kitchener Rangers in 1977–78, Maloney was drafted 26th overall by New York. He adjusted quickly to the pros by recording 44 points in 38 games for the AHL's New Haven Nighthawks the following season.

At the time, the Rangers were jockeying for position in the old Patrick Division and had begun to slip behind rival Philadelphia. With a third of the season remaining, the club summoned Maloney to Manhattan, and he had an immediate impact, establishing himself as an aggressive checker and penalty killer whose baby face and polite nature off the ice belied a pit-bull style.

Asked if he approved of the new recruit, coach Fred Shero said, "Yes, I always have. He's hardnosed. He doesn't play like an All-Star, does he?"

Coming from Shero, that was meant as a compliment.

To Phil Esposito, Maloney was like an early Christmas present: a digging left wing who could scoop the puck out of the corners and shovel it to him in the slot. Espo hadn't had a winger like that since his glory days with Wayne Cashman in Boston.

Maloney continued to dig in the 1979 playoffs but showed he could do much more than that for the surging Blueshirts. With seven goals and 13 assists,

Sure-handed and sure-footed, left wing Don Maloney gains control in a game against the Vancouver Canucks.

he set the record (since broken) for most points by a rookie in the playoffs with 20 while joining his older brother, Dave, in helping the Rangers reach the Stanley Cup Finals.

Beginning in 1979–80, Maloney registered five straight 20-goal seasons in New York. The crafty forward also took part in the 1983 and 1984 All-Star Games, winning the MVP award at the latter at the Meadowlands Arena—not bad for a fellow once overheard to say, "I'm one of the slowest, if not *the* slowest, skaters in the league. I never was too fancy, never had that good a shot."

After an injury-plagued season in 1984–85, the classy veteran rebounded the following year with an outstanding defensive performance in helping the Rangers reach the Conference Finals.

Maloney was by no means a brawler. But his willingness to play through pain—a chronic bad back shortened his career substantially—proved that toughness cannot be measured simply by penalty-minute totals. And he was, by all accounts, a pro's pro.

But his ice time dropped markedly under new coach Michel Bergeron, who felt the team needed a big, strong center. So in December 1988, the Rangers traded Maloney and two others to Hartford for Carey Wilson. Ironically, it was Esposito, then Rangers GM, who reluctantly sent his old line-mate packing.

Maloney played only 21 games for the Whalers before closing out his career with the Islanders.

Articulate and charismatic, Maloney was destined for a post-playing career in hockey. Sliding into the Islanders' front office, he was eventually named general manager—the youngest in the league at the time—and held the post for three years before rejoining the Rangers as an assistant GM in 1997.

In 2007, he left the Rangers again to become general manager of the Phoenix Coyotes.

1931–46

DEFENSEMAN

③

Games	Goals	Assists	Penalty minutes
647	55	176	465

25 OTT HELLER

O ver the course of his 15 seasons in the National Hockey League, steady defenseman Gerhardt (Ott) Heller wore the uniform of only one team, and it was the Rangers. He played 647 games for the club, the most in team history at the time, more than Bill Cook, Frank Boucher and Murray Murdoch. And he won two Stanley Cups.

His style was a simple one, that of a stand-up defenseman who excelled at steering opponents away from the middle of the ice and toward the boards. His upper body and arm strength was incredible, allowing him to avoid many of the penalties that sometimes plagued his rearguard teammates.

Heller, red-haired and as personable a guy as you'd ever want to meet, was front and center in the Rangers' famous 1940 celebratory photo that captured the Rangers whooping it up with the Cup itself in the Tudor Room of the Royal York Hotel in Toronto the night of April 13. Heller, more than any of his teammates, had reason to celebrate a little bit extra. Ott was the only man to play on both the 1932–33 and the 1939–40 clubs.

"It's true," he reminisced years later. "I never made a big deal of that, but it's a fact."

Born of solid German stock in Berlin (later Kitchener), Ontario, Heller received his earliest instruction on handling a stick and guiding the puck from his older brother, Wilfie. A natural who could play any position (except goal), Ott had no trouble making his public school team. Nor was it much of a challenge, when he grew older, to secure a spot in the Kitchener City League. That started him on the road to the NHL.

A rash of injuries to the Blueshirt defense corps led to Heller's call-up from the minors. He made his Ranger debut on January 28, 1932. It was unreasonable to expect much from the 21-year-old rookie but he played well enough to stick with the club for the rest of the regular season and playoffs. If his amazing dash the length of the rink at Madison Square Garden

to score the lone goal over the Montreal Canadiens in the third game of the semifinals didn't prove that Heller belonged in the big league, perhaps his two-goal performance the next game did the trick.

The Rangers lost to Toronto in the finals that year but stormed back to win the Stanley Cup the following season, Heller's first full NHL campaign.

Besides hockey, Heller's athleticism traced to boxing. He often trained at Stillman's Gym, just up Eighth Avenue from the third Madison Square Garden, and occasionally even in the offices of *The Ring* magazine, the redoubtable boxing publication that had its offices on the third floor of the Garden. There was a punching bag there, and Heller would train on it, as did some members of the New York Americans, whose own offices were right down the hall.

Besides hockey, Heller's athleticism traced to boxing

Most of those visits (to Stillman's and *The Ring*) were arranged by Harry Westerby, the Rangers' Runyonesque trainer at the time, who himself had been a celebrated featherweight boxer in his native Toronto before becoming the Rangers' first trainer.

Heller was also one of the most durable players in Rangers' history. The former team captain rarely missed a game, and eventually played an amazing 26 professional seasons: 15 in New York and 11 more all over the hockey map, from Springfield to New Haven to Indianapolis to Cleveland.

"Ott was a hockey player, simple as that," recalled Emile Francis, who played with him only briefly, but was acutely aware of his talents. "He was as tough as nails, and not an ounce of fat on him. What an athlete. It seemed like the guy played forever, and at such a high level. He was amazing."

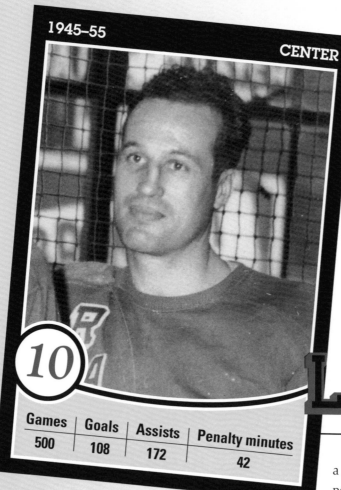

1945–55

CENTER

10

Games	Goals	Assists	Penalty minutes
500	108	172	42

24
EDGAR LAPRADE

Edgar Laprade played hard-to-get with the Rangers for half a dozen years in the early 1940s. But once they finally got their man and signed him to a contract in 1945, the Rangers knew they had themselves a gem, a vastly underrated center, a treasure they kept for 10 seasons and exactly 500 games. The Blueshirts were the only NHL team Edgar ever knew.

The Rangers had wanted Laprade as far back as 1939–40, when they were winning the Stanley Cup for a third time. Laprade, however, preferred playing senior hockey in his native Port Arthur, Ontario, even winning the Allan Cup, emblematic of senior hockey supremacy in Canada, with the Port Arthur Bearcats in 1943.

After a two-year stint in the Canadian Army during World War II, Laprade finally relented and decided to turn pro. His first season (1945–46) was a solid one, 15 goals, 19 assists, 34 points, plus *zero* penalty minutes, something no other regular in the NHL could claim that season. His crouching, weaving style confounded opponents. He was the epitome of keep-away hockey, not unlike two distinguished predecessors of his with the Rangers, Murray Murdoch and Clint Smith.

Despite his considerable offensive skills, Edgar Louis Laprade became known as a defensive ace, a top penalty killer and one of the NHL's best at poke checking and stealing the puck from the opposition. At five-foot-ten, 160 pounds, Laprade was another of the many smallish forwards the Rangers seemed to attract in those years. Yet the accomplishments of "Eager" Edgar, as his teammates used to call him, were hardly small.

He promptly won the Calder Trophy as NHL rookie of the year in 1946, and followed that with the Lady Byng Trophy for "clean, effective play" in 1950. He was, in the words of many, "a hockey player's hockey player." Four consecutive All-Star Game appearances, from 1947 to 1950, attested to that.

In 1949–50, Laprade scored two shorthanded goals in 45 seconds against the Chicago Blackhawks, an NHL record at the time.

Said Frank Boucher, the Rangers' longtime general manager and coach: "I've always felt that Edgar missed the general acclaim he really deserved because it was his misfortune never to be cast with a winning team." The closest he came was in 1950, when he had three goals and five assists in 12 playoff games, the Rangers eventually losing in double overtime of Game Seven of the finals to the Detroit Red Wings.

Laprade retired in 1955, and returned to his native Ontario where he ran a sporting goods store and also served his community for many years in politics. He was elected to the Hockey Hall of Fame in 1993.

The Rangers knew they had themselves a gem, a vastly underrated center, a treasure they kept for 10 seasons and exactly 500 games.

Long after his hockey career ended, Laprade was still remembered by a college history professor in New Jersey with a fondness for difficult research. Every year, mostly in the 1970s, the professor would challenge his students to identify the Rangers' line known as "The Three Little Schaefers." The nickname was created by broadcaster Bert Lee with an eye toward boosting sales for the Rangers' main sponsor at the time, Schaefer beer, "the one beer to have when you're having more than one."

The answer to the quiz was Laprade at center and fellow little guys Tony Leswick (five-foot-seven, 160 pounds) at left wing and Grant (Knobby) Warwick (five-foot-five, 155 pounds) at right wing. The threesome was the smallest in Rangers' history.

Every season, years before powerful Internet search engines were in vogue, New Jersey college students would call the Rangers' publicity office to find out who "The Three Little Schaefers" were. "Leswick-Laprade-Warwick," they were told, and the college kids would hang up happy.

23

PHIL ESPOSITO

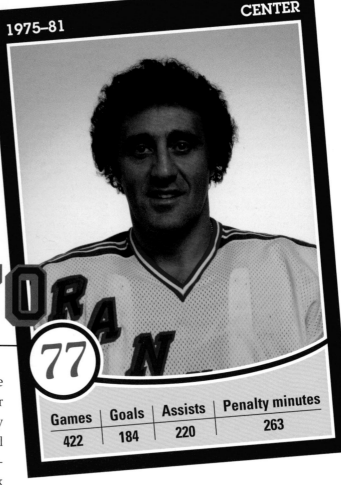

Games	Goals	Assists	Penalty minutes
422	184	220	263

He cemented his legacy in Boston with five scoring titles, two MVP awards and a pair of Stanley Cups. But given his propensity for bombast and embellishment, one wonders if Phil Esposito was exaggerating a smidge when he described the 1975 trade that brought him to New York as "the biggest hurt of my life ... including the death of both my parents."

It was a blockbuster of the highest magnitude, with Esposito and Carol Vadnais heading south in exchange for Brad Park, Jean Ratelle and minor leaguer Joe Zanussi. Not only did the deal involve three future Hall-of-Famers, but the Bruins and Rangers were blood rivals. Esposito loathed New York and frankly, New York wasn't too fond of him, either.

But he was a professional, and professionals understand that trades are part of the business of sports.

When he caught up with his new team on the road, Esposito walked into the visitor's dressing room at the Oakland Coliseum and was stunned to find a captain's "C" stitched to his jersey. He felt awkward accepting such an honor without ever having played a game for the Rangers, believing Rod Gilbert or Walt Tkaczuk—both career Blueshirts—to be more deserving.

Esposito begrudgingly embraced his new leadership role and set out to change the culture of a club that was tall on talent but lacked a killer instinct. Coming from a close-knit group in Boston that exerted tremendous internal pressure to win, he was vocal about wanting to create a similar atmosphere on the Rangers. Self-expression was never a problem for the big centerman.

"I hate to qualify it ethnically," said Dave Maloney, the man who eventually succeeded Esposito

as captain, "but Phil is a fiery Italian who has that emotional thing. In a team sport, that's a dynamic that can be somewhat hard to manage and to understand. But holy cow, did this guy care. He was a tremendous character but also a tremendous player. I don't know if it's acknowledged how smart Phil was offensively."

Brains weren't going to endear Esposito to the fans and media of New York, who were slow to embrace the ex-Bruin. Then in his mid-30s, he had slowed down a step and the critics were descending upon him like hungry vultures, perhaps because he had been such a brash character in his prime. Where, they wondered, was the 60-goal scorer who used to terrorize the Rangers with regularity?

While not as sparkling an offensive force as in his glory days, Esposito still managed to lead the Rangers in points three times in six years with the team and remained an effective scorer until his final season.

In 1978–79, he was rejuvenated skating between young guns Don Murdoch and Don Maloney, scoring 42 goals at age 37. That trio, dubbed the "Godfather Line," helped power the Rangers to the Stanley Cup Finals. Esposito, who by then was living on Manhattan's East Side and finally comfortable in his Ranger silks, was elated to have one last shot at a championship. The Montreal Canadiens, however, conspired to keep his dream out of reach.

When he retired in 1981, Esposito was second only to Gordie Howe in career goals and total points.

Esposito briefly worked as an assistant coach and then as a TV analyst for Madison Square Garden Network before moving up to the front office. His stormy, three-year run as vice president and general manager earned him the nickname "Trader Phil" and was marked by frequent roster reshuffling and a very public feud with coach Michel Bergeron.

Inducted into the Hockey Hall of Fame in 1984, Esposito later helped found the expansion Tampa Bay Lightning.

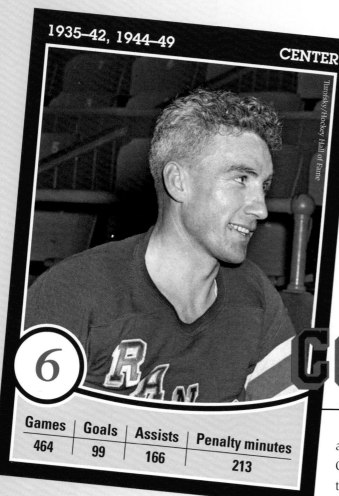

1935–42, 1944–49   CENTER

Turofsky/Hockey Hall of Fame

6

Games	Goals	Assists	Penalty minutes
464	99	166	213

22 NEIL COLVILLE

The career of Neil Colville, which covered 11 seasons in New York, was an outstanding one by any standard, and it included an NHL first, a record he will hold for all time: Colville was the first NHL player to make an All-Star Team both at forward *and* defense.

A skilled pivot who helped propel the Rangers to their third Stanley Cup in 1940, plus the NHL's regular-season title in 1941–42, Colville was twice a Second Team All-Star as a forward. Then, after missing two full seasons in the Canadian military during World War II, he returned to the Rangers as a defenseman in 1945–46, teaming effectively with Frankie Eddolls.

Upon his return, Colville was quickly named the club's fourth captain, succeeding Ott Heller. He was named to the Second All-Star Team in 1947–48. Of all the Rangers called to military duty, Neil McNeil Colville was the only one to make a successful return to the NHL wars.

Colville, his brother Mac, a right wing, and left wing Alex Shibicky came to the Rangers as an inseparable trio, all of them signing as free agents on October 18, 1935. They formed the "Bread Line" (also known as the "Stream Line"), the youngest in the NHL at the time. They would become one of the most effective lines in team history, conveniently following in the footsteps of the Rangers' first great line, the "A-Line" of Frank Boucher between the Cook brothers, Bill and Bun.

Boucher, who later became coach and general manager, called the Colvilles and Shibicky "Prairie Boys," as they all came from western Canada, the Colvilles hailing from Edmonton and Shibicky from Winnipeg. They were also the first star products of Lester Patrick's highly trumpeted "3-R" system, which brought players up through the ranks, starting with the Philadelphia Ramblers, continuing with the

New York Rovers and, finally, blossoming with the Rangers.

Like his predecessor Patrick, Boucher thrived on hockey innovations, one of which was "offensive penalty killing," which was specifically promoted by Neil Colville. When the Rangers were shorthanded, they would inevitably throw defenseman Art Coulter on the ice with the "Bread Line." Instead of ragging the puck and wasting time, the foursome would attack vigorously, as though a penalty hadn't even been called.

"One season," Boucher recalled, "we outscored our opponents almost two to one when we were shorthanded. Credit for that had to go to Neil Colville." It was "offensive penalty killing" that also led the Rangers to become the first team to popularize a "box defense" when they were shorthanded, forming a tightly knit box in front of their goalies, "Sugar" Jim Henry and Chuck Rayner. It was a solid strategy and one that survives to the present.

Despite spending four seasons as a defenseman, Colville would score 99 goals and 166 assists for 265 points in 464 games. A superb stickhandler and a deft playmaker, Colville had a style that was smooth, and very popular with Ranger fans.

Following his NHL career, Neil played for and coached the New Haven Ramblers of the American Hockey League, before being named the Rangers' fourth coach prior to the 1950–51 season. At just 36 years old, he was the youngest bench boss in team history and the youngest in the NHL at the time.

As a coach, Colville's task was nearly an impossible one. His predecessor, Lynn Patrick, had led the 1949–50 Rangers to the Stanley Cup Finals before unexpectedly bolting to the Boston Bruins for more money. Colville, hampered by a painful ulcer condition, lasted less than a season and a half behind the Blueshirts' bench.

Colville was elected to the Hockey Hall of Fame in 1967. Twenty years later, on December 26, 1987, he passed away at the age of 73.

21 CAMILLE HENRY

1953–55, 1956–65, 1967–68   LEFT WING

Frank Prazik/ Hockey Hall of Fame

21

Games	Goals	Assists	Penalty minutes
637	256	222	78

Pound for pound, Camille (The Eel) Henry was certainly the smallest man ever to play for the New York Rangers ... including Theo Fleury. Unlike Fleury, however, Henry was also one of the team's most popular players. Teammates, fans and even the press just loved the little guy.

Generously listed throughout his career as five-foot-eight, 150 pounds, Henry was probably much smaller. Teammate Vic Hadfield once cracked, "Cammy was wearing platform heels and diving boots the day those figures were taken. One good wind would blow him away."

The diminutive left wing played 12 seasons in New York, winning the Calder Trophy as NHL rookie of the year in 1954 (beating out Montreal's Jean Béliveau) and the Lady Byng Trophy for gentlemanly play in 1958. Rangers fans simply identified with Camille, who was kind of an Everyman on skates.

Henry's style was simple: he parked himself in front of the net and deflected pucks left and right, pucks that were blasted by the Rangers' bigger guns

at the time, particularly Andy Bathgate. "The little guy was uncanny, the best in the league at that," Bathgate recalled. "He made bad shots, wide ones, into good shots, and lots of goals. He was the key to our power play in those years."

Given his style, Henry endured more than his share of punishment from opposing checkers. Despite his size, he even threw the odd body check himself. Asked whom he hurt the most with his checks, Camille deadpanned: "Camille Henry, that's who."

Emile Francis, the Rangers' longtime general manager and coach, had great respect for Henry's talents. Henry was the only player who didn't have to weigh in and weigh out following training camp sessions. Trainer Frank Paice just left blank spaces next to Henry's name on the weight chart, fearing the press might discover his real weight was closer to 130–135 pounds than the 150 pounds the club claimed.

About midway through the 1964–65 season, broadcaster Bob Wolff brought former vice president (and president-to-be) Richard Nixon to a game at the third Garden. Wolff and Nixon had been friends when Wolff was broadcasting baseball in Washington, D.C.

Henry scored a hat trick that day and was the game's first star. Wolff dragged Nixon into the Rangers' cramped locker room after the game. Thinking Camille's first name was Henry, Nixon extended his hand over a tangle of sweaty bodies and said, "That was a great game, Henry, I really enjoyed it." Puffing his ever-present post-game cigarette, Henry responded with trademark wit: "You realize I can't vote in the United States, Mr. Nixon, only in Canada."

By the mid-1960s, the game had taken its toll on Henry. Francis dealt him to the Chicago Blackhawks for defenseman Wayne Hillman and promising forwards Doug Robinson and John Brenneman. "The Eel" played less than half a season in Chicago before retiring.

Francis had one last hurrah in mind for Henry, coaxing him back for the 1967–68 season. The "new" Madison Square Garden opened that season, on February 18, 1968, and there was Henry at left wing for the first face-off with linemates Jean Ratelle and Rod Gilbert. Ratelle won the inaugural face-off cleanly, pulling the puck back to Henry, who skated with it and thus became the first Ranger to handle the puck in the new Garden.

He played his last two seasons in the St. Louis Blues organization before retiring for good in 1970.

Life after hockey was not overly kind to Henry. He had a variety of ailments, and held a couple of menial jobs. He died on September 11, 1997, at the age of 64.

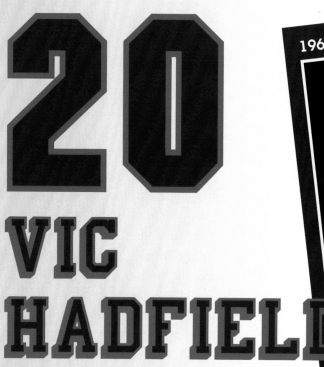

20
VIC
HADFIELD

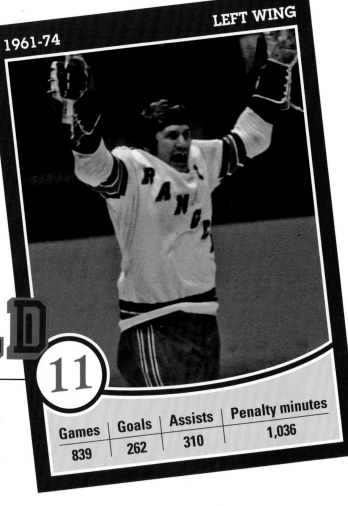

LEFT WING

1961-74

11

Games	Goals	Assists	Penalty minutes
839	262	310	1,036

It's hard to take Vic Hadfield seriously when he insists that players in his day were too worried about keeping their jobs to waste time on practical jokes. He was, after all, one of the biggest pranksters around.

Another key figure on the powerful Rangers teams of the 1960s and early 70s, Hadfield was fond of sending teammates off on wild goose chases, but his repertoire also included a wide array of clubhouse pranks like switching teammates' neckties, fake phone messages (usually from girls) and smearing the inside of shoes with Vaseline or just nailing them to the floor.

On the road, he might march up to the hotel's unsuspecting front desk clerk and announce, "I'm Vic Hadfield, captain of the Rangers, and I need a suite for an important team meeting. While you're at it, send up 20 beers." Of course, these "team meetings" rarely had anything to do with business. Or he would tell the clerk that all the players' room assignments had changed (when in fact they had not), so an incoming phone call for Walt Tkaczuk might be routed to Bill Fairbairn's room.

Gleefully causing so many minor inconveniences for his teammates had the effect of giving the mischievous No. 11 locker room credibility, which in turn made him a more effective leader.

But Hadfield's metamorphosis from minor-league tough guy to major-league All-Star took much of the hockey world by surprise.

Toiling for St. Catharines of the OHA and later the AHL's Buffalo Bisons, the blond and brawny left wing regularly posted far more penalty minutes than points, and he continued in an enforcer role for the Rangers after they claimed him from Chicago in the 1961 intra-league draft.

Old-guard Blueshirts like Andy Bathgate, Harry Howell, Earl Ingarfield and Johnny Wilson welcomed young Vic into the fold and made the roughhousing rookie feel like he'd been born to play on Broadway.

But how did Hadfield, who led the league with

151 penalty minutes in 1963–64, discover a flare for goal scoring and become the first Ranger to score 50 goals in a season?

"I could go back to the only reason I ever made it to the Rangers," he theorized, "and that was because I was aggressive. And being aggressive for so long, I had more space on the ice because people stayed away from me. You have to stick with what got you there."

Clearly, Hadfield's game also received a huge boost from coach Emile Francis who, in 1968, assigned Vic to a line with a pair of silky-smooth French Canadians: center Jean Ratelle and right wing Rod Gilbert. The new combination was so effective that it was nicknamed the "G-A-G (Goal-A-Game) Line," and it remained largely intact for the next five seasons.

In 1971–72, Ratelle, Hadfield and Gilbert finished one-two-three in team scoring with Vic notching 50 goals—the last two scored in the season's final game against the Montreal Canadians at Madison Square Garden.

"Denis Dejordy, who I played with back in St. Catharines, was in net for Montreal," Hadfield recalled. "I wasn't even supposed to play that night because I had a broken thumb. Nobody knew about it."

Hadfield had 13 seasons of Ranger hockey under his belt when a rebuilding program led to him being traded to Pittsburgh in 1974. He was disheartened at having to leave New York but managed two more 30-goal seasons for the Penguins until knee injuries ended his career.

A golf pro during his off seasons, Hadfield today runs a sprawling golf academy in his native Oakville, Ontario, and is a PR representative for BusinessEdge Solutions in Manhattan. He is also very active in Rangers alumni events. When Adam Graves broke his 22-year-old club record for most goals in a season in 1994, Hadfield hopped on a plane and was among the first to offer his congratulations.

Hadfield's metamorphosis from minor-league tough guy to major-league All-Star took much of the hockey world by surprise.

19

DAVEY KERR

1934–41   GOALTENDER

Hockey Hall of Fame

Games	Record	Shutouts	GAA
324	157-110-57	40	2.07

For the first eight seasons of their existence, the New York Rangers were largely unsettled at the most important position on the ice: goaltender. Then Davey Kerr arrived, and the position was unsettled no more.

What David Alexander Kerr did was set the stage for a long line of popular netminders to follow— Charlie Rayner, Gump Worsley, Eddie Giacomin, Mike Richter and Henrik Lundqvist among them.

The Rangers purchased Kerr for $10,000 from the Montreal Maroons on December 14, 1934. It was money well spent. Kerr became the bellwether of Ranger squads for the next seven seasons. An amazingly durable player, Kerr would miss only one game during the entire course of his Ranger career, an incredible stretch for anyone, especially a goaltender. Davey emphatically favored "goaltender" to describe his chosen craft. "Goal*keepers* are soccer players, not hockey players," he was fond of saying. "Goal*tenders* are hockey players."

The pinnacle of Kerr's career was 1939–40. He had a league-leading eight shutouts in the regular season, a miserly 1.54 goals-against average and eight wins in the playoffs en route to a Stanley Cup championship. He also won the Vezina Trophy, the first Ranger to do so. "He was our leader," recalled stalwart defenseman Ott Heller, "simple as that."

Recalled Frank Boucher, Kerr's coach that year: "Davey was tremendously important to the 1940 team. He was always in fantastic shape and was really an inspiration for the other fellows to stay in shape. Plus, the fans really liked him." Off the ice, Kerr was a very diverse guy. He attended McGill University, was a stockbroker in Toronto during the summer and, to keep in shape, he played lots of tennis and handball, which not a lot of hockey players did at the time.

Kerr, following his playing career of course, revealed a secret that no one knew: to relax, he would occasionally sip some wine with his pregame meal

Goalie Davey Kerr is front and center as the Rangers celebrate their record 19-game unbeaten streak in January of 1940.

in the afternoon. This was done in the privacy of his own home, of course, as the use of alcoholic beverages would hardly be tolerated on game days by even the most liberal of coaches, of which Boucher was certainly one.

On March 14, 1938, Kerr became the first active Ranger to appear on the cover of *TIME* magazine, an amazing accomplishment when you consider that two of hockey's greatest superstars of that era, Montreal center Howie Morenz and Boston defenseman Eddie Shore, never did it.

The accompanying *TIME* article sought to explain the game of hockey to the magazine's readership through the eyes of the New York Rangers. And, there on the cover, looking more than a little out of place, was hawk-eyed (and hawk-nosed) Davey Kerr in a painting specially commissioned for *TIME* by the artist S.J. Wolff. It would be decades before another hockey player would have that honor. Maurice

(Rocket) Richard of Montreal and Chicago's Bobby Hull managed to do it in the 1950s and 1960s.

"The guys ribbed me a lot about that magazine," Kerr said years later. "Cec Dillon in particular. Cec was pictured inside and said he should have been on the cover since he was better looking than me. He admitted that I was better looking than [race-horses] Seabiscuit, War Admiral and Man O'War, whose photos happened to be on the same page the hockey article began." Kerr just grinned and grinned, knowing full well that he, and only he, had been the Rangers' very first "cover boy."

Unfortunately, Kerr was the first member of the Rangers' 1940 Stanley Cup team to pass away, at the age of 68, on May 11, 1978.

Through the years, many Kerr supporters have lobbied for his election to the Hockey Hall of Fame, but to no avail. Not even the cover of *TIME* magazine, it seems, can make that happen.

18

STEVE VICKERS

1972–82

LEFT WING

Games	Goals	Assists	Penalty minutes
698	246	340	330

Thanks to Steve Vickers, the night of February 18, 1976, was the worst that Ron Low ever experienced at Madison Square Garden, if one excludes the two gloomy seasons he later spent as Rangers coach.

Low was in net that evening for the second-year Washington Capitals when Vickers, New York's gritty left wing, scored three goals and assisted on four others to set a franchise record of seven points en route to an 11–4 Rangers win. Although Vickers jokingly attributed his good fortune to having just shaved off his trademark mustache, it probably also had something to do with the Capitals being the worst team in the league at the time.

Selected 10th overall by the Rangers in the 1971 draft, Vickers caught on full-time with the club the following year and made a great first impression. Skating on a line with Walt Tkaczuk and Bill Fairbairn, he established himself as a confident and effective rookie who could fight well and park himself like an immovable object in the opposition's goal crease, an area that came to be known as "Vickers' Office." Many of his 246 career goals were scored from that spot using a powerful and accurate backhand shot.

"Sarge," so nicknamed because of the old army jacket he used to wear, racked up 53 points in 63 games and won the Calder Trophy as the league's top rookie in 1972, a season that also saw him become the first NHL player to score back-to-back hat tricks when he achieved the feat against the Los Angeles Kings and Philadelphia Flyers.

Any first-year jitters the kid had were not outwardly noticeable. But Vickers had them, and used them to his advantage.

"If you're not a little nervous," he said, "and don't feel a little pressure, you shouldn't be there. My first year in New York, I think I was sixth or seventh on the depth chart so there was pressure to perform.

But I had excellent linemates. Fairbairn and Tkaczuk were really hard-working players and they helped me a lot."

The Rangers brought Vickers along slowly but his clout—and ice time—grew steadily.

"The first couple of years," he said, "we were more or less told where to live out on Long Island and I lived in New Hyde Park then Long Beach. Nowadays, they encourage you to move into Manhattan but back then they didn't want you to because they were afraid you would have too much fun. But in 1975, I scored 40 goals and said, 'I'm going to live where I want to live.' So I moved into the city and lived with Pat Hickey."

Although he was a member of the 1978–79 team that reached the Stanley Cup Finals, Vickers reserves a special fondness for the 1973–74 squad that received career-best performances from Brad Park, Ted Irvine and Pete Stemkowski and won 40 games but lost a tough, seven-game semifinal series to the Flyers.

"I didn't mind taking a bit of a beating in the crease," he said, "especially if I got to play against guys like Eddie Van Impe and Moose Dupont. That 1974 team was the best that I ever played on. And to lose that way was disheartening. I think we had the team to go all the way but we couldn't win in Philly. That hurt us."

Vickers sailed along through the seasons with consistency until 1981–82 when his numbers and effectiveness began to slip. He was demoted to the AHL's Springfield Indians for the balance of the campaign before packing it in for good. He still stands as the Rangers' highest-scoring left wing.

His post-hockey career saw Vickers become an insurance broker, and he later worked as a consultant for an international mineral company.

With 586 points, Steve Vickers (8) is the Rangers' all-time leading scorer among left wings.

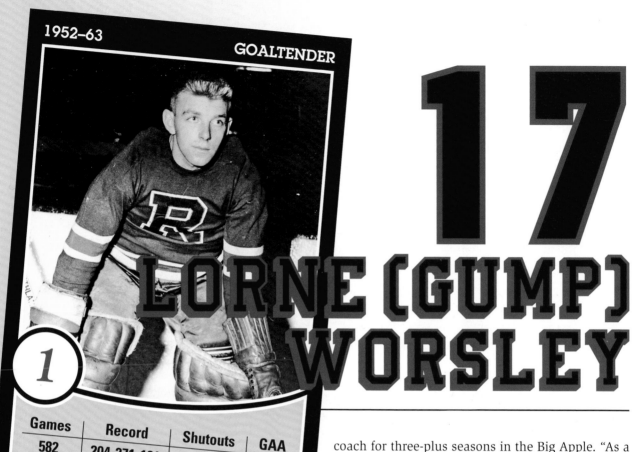

1952–63

GOALTENDER

1

Games	Record	Shutouts	GAA
582	204-271-101	24	3.05

17
LORNE (GUMP) WORSLEY

Roughly 80 men, give or take a few, have roamed the crease of the New York Rangers, but it's hardly a stretch to say that none was more beloved than Lorne John (Gump) Worsley, the team's last line of defense for 10 memorable seasons.

Gump's appeal was universal and infectious, owing to several factors. He was lovable, quotable to a fault, pudgy like a doll and, above all, possessed a marvelous talent that eventually landed him in the Hockey Hall of Fame. In addition to the fans, the press also loved Worsley, grateful as they were to be covering a guy as colorful as the team has ever had.

Always quick with a quip, Gump—the nickname came from the popular comic strip character Andy Gump—usually saved his best (and most pointed) barbs for Phil Watson, his bombastic

coach for three-plus seasons in the Big Apple. "As a coach," Gump famously said of Watson, "he was a good waiter." It was just one of many salvos the two exchanged throughout the length of their fractious relationship.

At five-foot-seven, 180 pounds, Gump hardly had an athlete's physique. That made him a target of Watson's verbal barrages. Typically, these played out in the press. Despite his size and a career-long battle with his weight, Worsley was surprisingly nimble "in the barrel," as he described his home office, the net.

"Believe me, Gump would do anything, *anything*, to stop the puck," recalled his longtime teammate and friend, defenseman Harry Howell. "And he faced more shots than any goalie in the league. Remember, we weren't exactly a first-place team at the time."

Worsley's debut with the Rangers was a strange one. He won the Calder Trophy as NHL rookie of the year in 1952–53, but spent the entire following season with the Vancouver Canucks of the Western Hockey League. His replacement was Johnny Bower, who played all 70 games and 4,200 minutes of the 1953–54 campaign. Worsley was back on the job full-time the next season.

Among his fellow Blueshirt goaltenders, only Mike Richter played more games than Worsley (666 to 582).

Over the years, Gump developed a great fondness for New York City and regretted that he didn't visit enough after his playing days. He and his wife, Doreen, spent part of their honeymoon in New York in the summer of 1951. He lived in Manhattan, the Bronx and Queens, using the subway to get to practices and games at Madison Square Garden.

Traded to the Montreal Canadiens in a deal that brought Jacques Plante to New York on June 4, 1963, Worsley embarked on an amazing run with Les Canadiens, winning four Stanley Cups and sharing two Vezina Trophies with Charlie Hodge in 1966 and Rogatien Vachon in 1968.

The closest Gump came to a Cup in New York was 1962, when the Rangers extended the Toronto Maple Leafs to six games in the semifinals.

In overtime of Game Five, after stopping a hard shot by Leafs' ace Frank Mahovlich, Worsley was on his back, covering the puck. He lifted his head off the ice for a moment and Red Kelly promptly stuffed the puck into the net. "What was I gonna do?" Worsley moaned. "My head was cold. Plus, Eddie Powers [the referee] should have blown the damn whistle way earlier."

Gump's most memorable quip, "My face is my mask," has become one of the most repeated quotations in hockey history. Not until the final days of his career with the Minnesota North Stars did he don facial protection. Even then, it was mostly at the urging of Doreen that he did so at all.

Elected to the Hall of Fame in 1980, Worsley passed away on January 27, 2007. He was 77.

16 CHUCK RAYNER

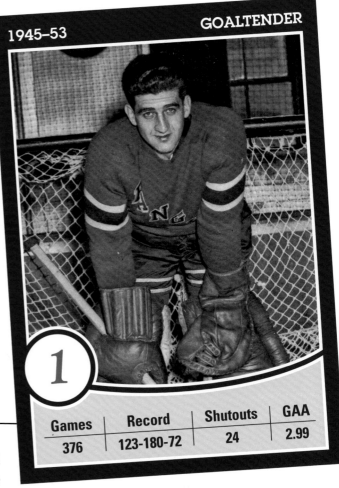

1945–53   GOALTENDER

Games	Record	Shutouts	GAA
376	123-180-72	24	2.99

Fans of the New York Rangers have always had a thing for goaltenders. Perhaps that's because there have been so many good ones over the years. Despite his relatively short NHL career, Claude Earl (Chuck) Rayner was more than one of the good ones. He was one of the great ones.

"Bonnie Prince Charlie" was voted the team's most valuable player three times and won the Hart Trophy as league MVP in 1950, only the second goalie in NHL history to do it.

The 1949–50 season was Rayner's most memorable. Despite finishing fourth in the regular season, the Rangers surprised the Montreal Canadiens in the first round of the Stanley Cup playoffs and played the Detroit Red Wings in the finals. Madison Square Garden was booked with the Ringling Brothers Barnum and Bailey Circus, so the Rangers had to play their two "home" games at Maple Leaf Gardens in Toronto. The balance of the series was played at the Olympia in Detroit.

The series went seven games, and the Red Wings prevailed on a goal by utility forward Pete Babando that eluded Rayner in double overtime. "Not a day goes by that I don't think about that goal," Rayner said years later. "What a shame that was. Just one goal, and there never would have been a 54-year drought."

It was Rayner and "Sugar" Jim Henry who started the practice of platoon goaltending in the NHL. The two goalies, best of friends off the ice, were of equal talent so Frank Boucher, the Rangers' coach, kept them both to start the 1945–46 season.

Boucher would play them in alternate games, alternate periods, and on a few occasions, change them from shift to shift as he switched defensemen.

Big for a goalie at five-foot-eleven, 190 pounds, Rayner was remarkably agile and a powerful skater who often left his net to carry the puck, an unheard-of practice at the time. He became the first goalie in history to score a goal. Playing for a Royal Canadian

Big for a goaltender, Chuck Rayner was nonetheless a superb stickhandler. Here he clears the puck in a game against the Boston bruins.

Armed Forces team in Halifax, Nova Scotia, in 1944, Rayner skated the length of the ice and scored. And, like all of the goalies of his time, he played his entire career without a mask. "What else could you do?" he said. "There were no masks, simple as that."

Even deep into retirement, Rayner would extol the merits of playing hockey in Manhattan. "New York was a great part of my life, it really was," he recalled. "I will never forget my days as a New York Ranger.

"Madison Square Garden was a great place to play," said Charlie of the old (third) Garden. "People were like family. We'd wave or nod at them, usually in the same seats. The icemen, the concession guys, we all knew each other. They say 'Old soldiers never die,' well, old ushers never die either. I mean, once an usher said hello to me in the current Garden, and I hadn't played a game in 35 years."

Born in Sutherland, Saskatchewan, on August 11, 1920, Rayner began his NHL career with the now-defunct New York Americans in 1939. After three years in the Canadian military, he signed with the Blueshirts as a free agent in 1945. He spent the next eight seasons with the Rangers, representing New York at three All-Star Games (1949–51) despite playing for a club that often finished sixth in a six-team league.

Knee problems forced Rayner into premature retirement following the 1952–53 season, and he was elected to the Hockey Hall of Fame in 1973. He passed away on October 6, 2002, in Langley, British Columbia.

1937–44, 1945–48

RIGHT WING

Turofsky/Hockey Hall of Fame

12

Games	Goals	Assists	Penalty minutes
449	187	175	227

15
BRYAN HEXTALL, SR.

It was a record that was his and his alone for 54 long seasons—54 years and 62 days to be exact. That's how long Bryan Aldwyn Hextall, square-jawed and tough as a flint stone, held the mantle as the last Ranger to score a Stanley Cup-winning goal. It wasn't until June 14, 1994, that Mark Messier relieved him of that distinction.

How tough was Hextall, who would eventually become one of the greatest Rangers? Ace hockey writer Herb Goren, who covered Hextall's Rangers for the *New York Sun*, put it quite succinctly: "Hextall was the hardest bodychecking forward I ever saw in 40 years of covering hockey."

Yet it wasn't toughness that made the five-foot-ten, 180-pound forward a star. It was scoring—lots of it—and durability. Arriving in New York at the end of the 1936–37 season, Hextall would stay for 10

glorious seasons and 449 games, plus 37 more in the playoffs. He would never play for another team.

A left-handed-shooting right wing, Hextall led the NHL in goals with 24 in 1939–40 and again with 26 in 1940–41. In 1941–42, with 56 points, he led the NHL in scoring and toted home the Art Ross Trophy. He was also named to the First All-Star Team three times, from 1940 to 1942.

"I scored 20 goals for seven straight years," Hextall recalled. "That was a league record. Twenty goals was a big thing back then."

Hextall's numbers would have been even stronger had he not missed all of 1944–45 and all but three games of 1945–46 due to wartime border restrictions that prevented many players from entering the United States. "That was really a shame," said Muzz Patrick, a teammate on the Cup-winning team. "Bryan was at his peak when the war broke out."

Hextall never missed a game until his final season, 1947–48. "He always played through injuries," remembered Lynn Patrick, Hextall's left wing on the

"Powerhouse Line" that also included Phil Watson at center. "He was an inspiration to play with."

But it would be April 13, 1940, a Saturday night in Toronto, that would ultimately define Hextall's career. The Rangers were leading the Maple Leafs, three games to two, when Game Six, tied at 2–2, went to sudden-death overtime. Hextall won it—and the Rangers' third Stanley Cup—at 2:07 of the first overtime.

Everybody who was there that night remembered it as a fast play. "It was 'bang, bang,' just like that," Watson recalled time and again through the years. "Bryan came burning in like an elephant. There was no way he was going to miss." He didn't. Hextall's high backhander beat Toronto goalie Turk Broda and stunned the capacity crowd at Maple Leaf Gardens.

"Was it the biggest goal of my career? Of course it was," Hextall said. "I never forgot it."

Hextall retired following the 1948–49 season after a year in the American Hockey League with the Cleveland Barons and the Washington Lions. An avid outdoorsman his entire life, he operated a shooting lodge and a lumber business in retirement near his longtime home in Poplar Point, Manitoba. He passed away on July 25, 1984, just six days shy of his 71st birthday.

Was there a strong hockey gene in Hextall's bloodline? You'd have to think so since his sons, Bryan Jr. and Dennis, both played in the NHL while grandson Ron was an outstanding goaltender (and frequent target of Ranger fan abuse) for 13 seasons with the Philadelphia Flyers, Quebec Nordiques and New York Islanders.

Hextall attained hockey's highest honor, induction into the Hockey Hall of Fame, in 1969.

14
WALT
TKACZUK

1968–81   CENTER

18

Games	Goals	Assists	Penalty minutes
945	227	451	556

Like a deposit of precious metal concealed beneath dense layers of soil and stone, Walt Tkaczuk's latent hockey-playing ability was a treasure waiting to be discovered.

Possibly the greatest checker to ever play for the Rangers, Tkaczuk began his junior hockey career as a scrawny and defensively challenged kid who showed little or no obvious potential as an NHL prospect. In fact, he showed more promise as a teenaged laborer in a Northern Ontario gold mine, delivering dynamite to more senior miners who would actually detonate the explosives.

By the time his career with the OHA's Kitchener Rangers wound down, however, a much-improved Tkaczuk had developed into a can't-miss prospect. This caught the attention of William Jennings, the Rangers' longtime president and governor, who hoped to find the lad a safer aboveground profession.

General manager Emile Francis promptly did just that, and Tkaczuk quickly entrenched himself at center ice as a strong two-way player who could take pressure off of the Rangers' high-scoring Ratelle-Gilbert-Hadfield line.

A stalwart on the 1971–72 team that battled Boston in the Stanley Cup Finals, Tkaczuk may have been a more essential piece of the 1978–79 squad. That year, the Cup was supposed to belong to the Islanders, who finished atop the regular-season standings and were heavy favorites in their semifinal meeting with the Rangers.

But the Rangers checkers, led by Tkaczuk and his "Bulldog Line" partners, clamped down on the "Trio Grande" of Bryan Trottier, Mike Bossy and Clark Gillies, holding one of the most dominating lines ever to just two goals in six games. With that unit all but neutralized, the Islanders never had a chance.

"That shouldn't reflect on just what I did or what the line did as a group," Tkaczuk said. "It's how the whole group played. I was told I was strong on my

skates but players were smaller and I was probably over the league average. It had more to do with the way I skated and positioned my legs and stick on the ice. It was hard moving me around—like a tripod. I didn't let people get by me and I made sure they didn't get back into the play."

In addition to having great hockey sense, Tkaczuk was consistently among the team's best-conditioned athletes.

"When John Ferguson came in as the new coach-GM in 1976," Tkaczuk recalled, "he had a doctor from Quebec do our physicals. This guy, Dr. Enos, would comment about what kind of shape we were in like, 'You're in the same shape as the average housewife,' or 'the average hockey fan.' He was really saying the

guys weren't in good shape. I worked all summer long with a few other people building a barn. I was working ten- to 14-hour days to get it finished in nine weeks. I was too busy to exercise. But I went to camp and took the physical and the doctor said, 'Whatever you did, do it again next year.'"

Tkaczuk's durability allowed him to play 945 games in the NHL, all with New York. Only an eye injury in 1980–81 prevented him from joining Harry Howell and Rod Gilbert (at the time) as the only Rangers to play 1,000 games with the team.

Despite being a defensive gem, Tkaczuk put up his fair share of points as well, cracking the 20-goal mark six times in 14 seasons on Broadway.

13
ADAM GRAVES

Dave Sandford/Hockey Hall of Fame

1991–2001

LEFT WING

9

Games	Goals	Assists	Penalty minutes
772	280	227	810

There have been more skilled athletes in the history of New York sports, but few as beloved as "Gravy."

The son of a Toronto police officer, Adam Graves earned respect throughout the NHL and the entire New York area for his goal-scoring ability, tough work in the corners and the slot and unprecedented dedication to numerous charitable causes.

What father wouldn't want his daughter to bring home a nice young man like Graves, whose boyish grin and courteous manner made him seem like an adult-sized Boy Scout. But woe to the opposing player who mistook his soft side for weakness. If Mark Messier was the man to lead your team into battle, then Graves was surely the one you wanted watching your back. He didn't have the fleetest feet in the world but nobody, *nobody*, moved to the aid of a teammate in trouble faster than No. 9.

Signed as a free agent from the Oilers in 1991, Graves was asked to play the role of two-way power forward for the first time in his career. He responded to the challenge with 26- and 36-goal performances in his first two seasons in New York.

Although he blossomed into one of the game's more versatile forwards, earning the trust of coaches to play in almost every situation, there was nothing especially fancy about Graves' style. He was an awkward skater and his slap shot was almost nonexistent.

"I like to think my game doesn't revolve around putting the puck in the net," he cracked. "If it does, I'm in trouble."

Still, one doesn't become the third-highest goal scorer in team history without *some* ability. Graves managed 280 goals over his ten Ranger seasons, with the majority of those scored on rebounds and tip-ins off shots from the point (thank you, Brian Leetch).

Together with Messier, Leetch and Mike Richter, Graves helped complete the tight-knit nucleus of a surging Ranger team with championship aspirations,

and in 1993–94, he broke out with a franchise-record 52 goals—a mark since eclipsed by Jaromir Jagr—then added ten more in the playoffs to help the Blueshirts win their first Stanley Cup since 1940.

Through the remainder of the decade the Rangers failed to make a significant impact in the playoffs, but Graves continued to be a reliable scorer while supplying leadership and grit for New York. Even when his name didn't show up on the score sheet, he found other ways to contribute.

What really set this absurdly modest player apart from other stars was his selflessness off the ice. Growing up in a house full of foster children taught Graves the importance of helping those less fortunate, and as an adult, he never shied away from the humanitarian responsibilities that often accompany such a high-profile occupation.

Ron Low, who coached Graves in Edmonton and New York, marveled at the breadth of Adam's extracurricular activities.

"He was a huge part of the community [in Edmonton], and he's become a lot more gifted in that part of the community services here," Low said. "The things he does, he goes three nights, four nights a week. He does it because he's a good person, not because he thinks it's going to come back with good things to him in any way."

As the 1990s came to a close, so too did Graves' time with the Rangers. After receiving the Bill Masterton Trophy in 2001, he was traded to the San Jose Sharks and played two more seasons before calling it quits.

Graves returned to the Rangers in 2005 to work with the team's prospects and help out in community outreach programs. In 2009, he became the sixth Ranger to have his number retired—a fitting honor for one of the most adored sports figures that New York City has ever seen.

1974–90

DEFENSEMAN

12 RON GRESCHNER

Games	Goals	Assists	Penalty minutes
982	179	431	1,226

Y ou might not expect someone from a town whose most recognizable landmark is a 20-foot-tall wooden lumberjack named Goodsoil Gus to adapt easily to Big City life. But Ron Greschner did that and so much more, combining skill and toughness to enthrall a generation of Rangers fans.

"Opponents feared Gresch because every time he got the puck they knew something was going to happen," said Pat Hickey, who shared a dressing room with the popular rearguard for six seasons. "He was probably one of the most naturally talented guys we had and also the most likeable guy you would ever want to meet."

The pride of Goodsoil, a tiny village in western Saskatchewan, was a big, mobile defenseman who

was only 12 years old when he first competed in a local senior league against players in their 20s and 30s. He arrived in New York in 1974 after being selected 32nd overall in that year's draft, sparking a mutual love affair with the city that spanned his entire 16-year career and bridged the eras of Brad Park and Brian Leetch.

"[New York] was the only place I ever wanted to go," Greschner said. "I always liked Vancouver and Toronto but if you're going to be somewhere you might as well be in the best city in the world. Apart from New York, there is no other city. The rest of the world is a suburb."

Greschner's ability was as obvious as his affinity for his adopted home. At six-foot-two and weighing over 200 pounds, he used his long reach to great advantage and was a strong skater who excelled on the power play and handled the puck with ease—so easily that it earned him an occasional shift at center or left wing. During the 1980–81 season, he played on a line with Ulf Nilsson and Anders Hedberg.

Greschner reached the 20-goal plateau on four occasions, and his best offensive season came in 1977–78 when he tallied 24 goals and 48 assists in 78 games. The Rangers were building a powerhouse at the time.

Led by Greschner, goalie John Davidson, the Maloney brothers and Phil Esposito, the Rangers of 1978–79 stormed into the Stanley Cup Finals against Montreal.

It was the closest Greschner would get to hockey heaven. Although intensely competitive, he was one of many Ranger legends who never experienced the thrill of winning a championship in New York. That, ex-teammates insist, should not detract from No. 4's legacy.

"I mean no disrespect to guys like Brian Leetch and Mike Richter," said Tom Laidlaw, one of Greschner's former defense partners, "but playing his whole career there, doing the things he did and the points he put up, Greschner belongs in the same category as them. He was a quiet leader but definitely proud to be a Ranger."

Like Rod Gilbert before him and Mark Messier afterward, Greschner showed that pride by establishing close ties with the community. He co-owned restaurants, ran a local hockey school and became involved in numerous Big Apple charities. His marriage to model Carol Alt in 1983 was a hot gossip-page item, as was his cameo on the soap opera *Ryan's Hope*.

Back injuries caused Greschner to miss most of the 1981–82 and 1982–83 seasons, a period when he had been playing some of his best hockey. He still managed to appear in 982 contests, trailing only Harry Howell, Gilbert and Leetch for most games played as a Ranger.

Greschner retired in 1990 as the team's all-time leader in points, goals and assists by a defenseman, records all broken by Leetch. But his franchise-record 1,226 penalty minutes is a mark that will stand for many years to come.

11
BRAD PARK

1968–75

DEFENSEMAN

2

Games	Goals	Assists	Penalty minutes
465	95	283	738

Having finished runner-up to Bobby Orr four times for the Norris Trophy (and six times overall), Brad Park has theorized—probably in jest—that he must be the second-best defenseman who ever lived.

Comparisons to Orr were drawn with regularity throughout Park's Hall of Fame career, as each man could skate and handle the puck better than most forwards and dominated at both ends of the ice.

A Ranger for seven-plus seasons, Park welcomed being placed in a class with the Bruins legend but always preferred to be known as "the first Brad Park," as opposed to "the next Bobby Orr." To that end, Park carved out his own niche by playing a slightly more physical style than his Boston-based counterpart. He loved to hit and when it came to fighting, Brad took on all comers.

Douglas Bradford Park played junior hockey in his native Toronto but failed to make an impression with the Maple Leafs, who owned his rights. When he became available in the 1966 amateur draft,

New York wisely scooped him up with the second overall pick.

His meteoric rise to NHL stardom coincided with the Rangers' ascent to league power.

"It's a little hard to believe," Park told an interviewer in 1969. "Here I am, 21 years old, two years out of the amateurs, playing with and against the best players in hockey—guys I was only reading about the other day, it seems like—and holding my own. I read how good I am, that I'm one of the best players in hockey, and try to keep my head from swelling up like a balloon."

Park's foes heard the hype, too, and went to great lengths to knock him off his game.

"Brad was in a class above everybody as an offensive defenseman," said Ted Irvine, a teammate in New York for six seasons. "Superstar that he was, he took a lot of punishment in other teams' buildings.

He had a bull's-eye on his back if we went to Boston or Montreal. In both places, they wanted him badly. But Brad handled himself very well and didn't back down, didn't ask for anything. He just stood up and held his own and that's why he got so much respect."

As a Ranger, Park was a First or Second Team All-Star five times and played in six All-Star Games. Although many of his franchise scoring records have since been eclipsed by Ron Greschner and Brian Leetch, he still holds the club record for most goals in a season by a defenseman with 25. Above all, Park was a fierce competitor, and losing to the hated Bruins in the 1972 Stanley Cup Finals affected him deeply.

Brad was named captain in 1974 after Vic Hadfield was traded to Pittsburgh, but he couldn't get the Rangers any closer to winning the Stanley Cup in subsequent years. When the team got off to its worst start in a decade to open the 1975–76 season, change was inevitable.

Under pressure to make a deal—*any* deal—GM Emile Francis pulled the trigger on a trade that sent shockwaves through the hockey industry: Park, Jean Ratelle and Joe Zanussi to Boston for Phil Esposito and Carol Vadnais.

"I knew that our era was over," Francis said. "I knew that to protect Brad and Jean that they should no longer be in New York. The media was down on them, and all of us, because we hadn't won. That was the toughest deal I ever had to make."

Although that day remains his most painful hockey memory, Park went on to have much success with the Bruins, helping Boston reach the finals twice. He closed out his 18-year career in 1985 as a member of the Red Wings but kept his hand in the game as a coach and pro scout.

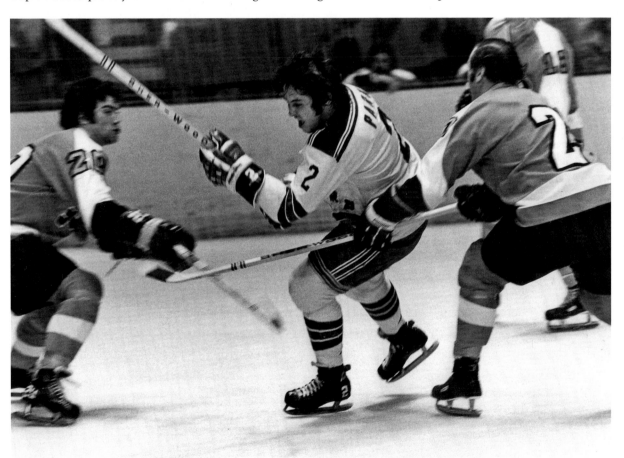

A superb rushing defenseman, Brad Park breaks through despite the efforts of two Philadelphia opponents.

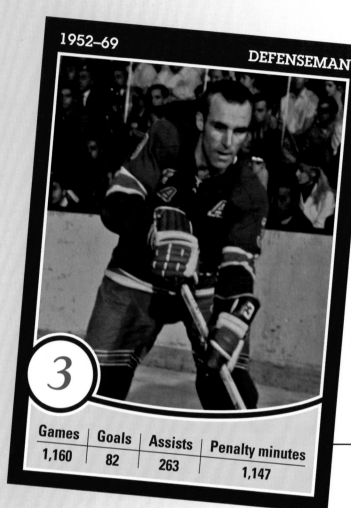

1952–69

DEFENSEMAN

3

Games	Goals	Assists	Penalty minutes
1,160	82	263	1,147

10
HARRY HOWELL

L eadership, loyalty and longevity. That's what Harry Howell brought to the New York Rangers. And he did it for 17 seasons and 1,160 games, more than any other player in the team's 80-plus-year history. It's a record that has stood for more than 40 years, and will probably stand for 40 more.

Howell is certainly one of the most well respected players to ever wear the Rangers uniform, joining Rod Gilbert, Brian Leetch, Mark Messier, Adam Graves, Mike Richter and one or two others in that category. Ranger fans, long among the most discerning sports fans around, loved the big defenseman. Recalled ace sportswriter Mel Woody of *The Newark News* many years ago: "Harry is really unique. It seems like he is friends with everyone, and everyone wants to be friends with him."

Back in the mid-1960s, one season-ticket holder, whose name has long been lost to time, was being transferred by his firm to a new job in Washington. "You know, most of all I am going to miss watching Harry Howell," the fan said. "I've never met him, but he became my favorite player because he looks like such a nice person."

Starting early in the 1952–53 season, when he arrived in New York from the championship Guelph Biltmores of the Ontario Hockey Association, Howell went about his business with a quiet efficiency. The six-foot-one, 195-pounder's style was precise, smooth and almost matter-of-fact. Mostly, he left the jarring body checks to others, a method that sometimes led to catcalls, but which suited him just fine. "If they're booin', they must be hurtin'," his longtime defense partner Lou Fontinato would often say, and Howell would nod appreciatively.

Never known for his goal-scoring prowess, it is somewhat ironic that Howell scored his first NHL goal on his very first shift. It was Saturday, October 18, 1952, during a 4–3 loss to the Toronto Maple Leafs.

The Rangers' all-time leader in games played, defenseman Harry Howell maneuvers the puck away from Norm Ullman of Detroit.

"I'll never forget it," he said. "I just lofted a long one that somehow went over Harry Lumley's shoulder … and in! I probably didn't get another goal that whole season." Actually he got two more, but more important, a Ranger career like no other was launched for Henry Vernon Howell, a career that would eventually land him in the Hockey Hall of Fame.

Howell's play with the Blueshirts, especially early in his career, was so impressive that team management, perhaps somewhat hastily, made him the club's ninth captain for the start of the 1952–53 season. At just 22 years of age, the youngest captain in team history at the time, Howell was not overly comfortable in his new role.

Two years later, in 1957, he chose to resign the captaincy. "It was the right thing to do," he recalled. "I had played two bad seasons in a row, and I knew it. I wanted to be free to concentrate on improving my play." And improve he did, leading the Rangers defensively on the ice and by example in the dressing room.

The NHL was awash in great defensemen at the time, Doug Harvey, Pierre Pilote, Carl Brewer and Tim Horton among them, so Harry was sometimes overlooked when it came to postseason honors. He did win the Norris Trophy as the outstanding defenseman and made the First All-Star Team in 1967, just as Boston's budding superstar Bobby Orr was coming onto the scene.

Howell considers that his best play over a long period of time in New York came in partnership with the rollicking Fontinato, whose bone-jarring style was a perfect complement to Harry's elegant play, which featured superb poke checks, adroit stick-handling and skillful playmaking.

"It takes a while for a partnership like that to develop," Howell said. "You really have to *know* each other, which we certainly did coming up together from the Biltmores."

Of his time in New York, Howell said: "We had some pretty good teams in the mid-1950s. Andy [Bathgate] was in his prime, so was Gump [Worsley].

Harry Howell (3) battles behind the Rangers' net with Montreal center Ralph Backstrom.

Camille [Henry] was a great sniper. We made the playoffs a couple of times, but never got out of the first round."

Off the ice, Howell was a public relations god-send for the Rangers, rarely saying no when public appearances were needed. "Harry was always very interested in kids," said his wife, Marilyn. "He finds it very rewarding every time he visits a kids' hospital. And he did that a lot."

One of the biggest nights in Howell's career occurred on January 25, 1967. Harry Howell Night, the first-ever special night for an active Ranger player, was at Madison Square Garden. The team, his fans and the press showered the classy rearguard with

gifts and applause. Howell called it the most memorable night of his career.

Howell's days in New York were winding down with the onset of expansion, six new teams, in the late 1960s. Out of respect for his loyalty and his length of service, Howell was offered a front-office position with the Rangers in the spring of 1969 by the club's general manager, Emile Francis. Harry chose instead to continue playing, so Francis sold him for cash to the Oakland Seals on June 10, 1969. The longest playing career in team history was over.

True to his longtime nickname "Harry the Horse," and despite a serious back injury that required spinal-fusion surgery, Howell would play four more NHL campaigns with Oakland and the Los Angeles Kings. He followed that by playing for three teams in the old World Hockey Association. All told, his playing career spanned 1,581 big-league games.

Howell would go on to become general manager of the AHL's Cleveland Barons and, briefly, coach of the Minnesota North Stars. He also scouted for the Edmonton Oilers for many years, picking up a Stanley Cup ring in 1990. "I wish it could have been with the Rangers," he said, "but a ring is still a ring."

Under Glen Sather, he returned to his ancestral home to scout for the Rangers for four seasons, from 2000 to 2004. Then, quietly as was his way, he retired at the age of 72, following the 2003–04 season.

> "I had played two bad seasons in a row, and I knew it."

In 2009, the Rangers at long last honored Howell by retiring his No. 3 jersey. Long overdue, it had to happen someday.

Two future Hall of Famers, Harry Howell of the Rangers and Stan Mikita of Chicago pursue a loose puck. Cesare Maniago is the Ranger goalie.

9
FRANK BOUCHER

Hockey Hall of Fame

CENTER

1926–38, 1943–44

7

Games	Goals	Assists	Penalty minutes
533	152	261	115

The date was November 16, 1926, a Tuesday. The New York Rangers played their very first National Hockey League game against the defending Stanley Cup champion Montreal Maroons at Madison Square Garden.

The question is: who took the Rangers' first face-off? The answer: Frank Boucher, Frank Boucher, and Frank Boucher.

The very first face-off was a ceremonial one with Lois Moran, a movie star of the day, dropping the puck for Boucher. Moments later, it was Boucher again facing off, this time for real, with Montreal's ace center, Nels Stewart.

Then, after 20 minutes of scoreless play, Boucher did yet another ceremonial face-off with New York City mayor Jimmy Walker to start the second period. Walker, who eventually became a big hockey fan, would have performed the first ceremonial face-off, but he arrived fashionably late as always and the game had already started, so Ms. Moran did the honors. For the record, Boucher recalled Moran as "slim, blonde, and very attractive."

Of all the "original" Rangers, Francis Xavier Boucher was the first to completely embrace New York City and its myriad pleasures. He developed a love for the city that stayed with him until his death at the age of 77 on December 12, 1977.

As a hockey player, Boucher became one of the very best of all time. A wily center, he stood five-foot-nine and weighed 185 pounds. Comparisons, physical and stylistical, between Frank and Wayne Gretzky are not uncommon. Both were left-handed shooting pivots, marvelous playmakers and extremely adept at avoiding opposition body checks.

Boucher was also one of the cleanest players in NHL history. He had, in fact, only one fight, one major penalty, during his 13-plus NHL years. The fight, with Montreal's "Bad" Bill Phillips, occurred in that first Ranger game. Boucher would win the Lady Byng Trophy seven times, and the NHL eventually gave it to him permanently before commissioning a

Turofsky/Hockey Hall of Fame

new trophy (years later, Bobby Orr would win eight consecutive Norris Trophies, and even he didn't get to keep it!).

That Boucher made it to New York at all was in no small part because of the Cook brothers, right wing Bill and left wing Bun, who signed with the Rangers before Frank did, in the fall of 1926. The stature of the Cook brothers was so great that Connie Smythe, the Rangers' first general manager, told them they could choose any available center they wanted, including established stars such as Stewart and Frank Nighbor.

The brothers insisted on Boucher, and a magical line, the "A-Line," was formed. It would become one of the most famous lines ever. Legendary Toronto broadcaster Foster Hewitt, in 1972, compared that unit to the great Russian lines that were then beginning to make an impact on North American hockey. The Cooks and Boucher, Hewitt said, "played like they had the puck on a string."

The "A-Line" would propel the Rangers to a Stanley Cup championship in 1928, a remarkable achievement in only the team's second season. A second Cup quickly followed in 1933. Boucher would lead

the team in scoring five times, make the NHL's First All-Star Team three years in succession (1933–35) and eventually earn a place in the Hockey Hall of Fame.

Following his illustrious playing career, Boucher turned to coaching with the New York Rovers of the Eastern Amateur League in 1938–39. That was just a local stop, as it was widely assumed that Boucher would eventually inherit the Rangers' coaching reins from Lester Patrick.

That happened for the 1939–40 season, and the Rangers promptly annexed a third Stanley Cup. Save for Boucher behind the bench, no one remained from the Rangers' first two championship teams. "What Lester Patrick gave me [in 1939–40]," Boucher often recalled, "was the best team I had ever seen."

Statistically, Frank Boucher was not a great coach. He had only 166 victories in 486 games. But as an innovator, Boucher was a coaching giant. He was the first coach to use a "box defense" in front of the goalie and the first coach to pull the goaltender when a penalty was called on the opposition.

Boucher also introduced what he called "offensive penalty killing" when the Rangers got a penalty. "We'd send out three forwards and one defenseman

that had seen so many of its best players go off to fight in World War II. The experiment was short-lived, however, with Boucher scoring 14 points in 15 games before returning to his rightful spot behind the bench.

In 1946–47, Boucher took over the general manager's chair in a not-so-pleasant ouster of Lester Patrick. Frank remained general manager for nine seasons before turning the post over to Murray (Muzz) Patrick for the 1955–56 season. That gave Frank Boucher 31 active years on the New York hockey scene. He was the club's longest-running employee until Rod Gilbert, who like Boucher wore sweater No. 7, came on the scene in 1962.

Besides his playing heroics and his coaching achievements, Boucher's legacy will also be defined by his loyalty and his popularity. "Once a Ranger, always a Ranger" was a favorite saying of his, and the phrase remains a team motto to the present.

In 1950, it was Boucher, along with team publicist Herb Goren, who founded the Rangers Fan Club. The group is still very active today, and once swelled in numbers to 1,500 rabid Ranger rooters.

and forecheck like crazy in the other team's end," he explained. "This worked so well that first season that we scored more goals shorthanded than were scored against us."

Like Patrick before him, Boucher loved innovation on the part of his players. "I'd encourage suggestions," he said. "The boys would come up with them, and then we would practice the new ideas." It was that philosophy that made the Rangers the first team to develop the slap shot and later the drop pass, both of which were perfected by left wing Alex Shibicky.

At age 42 and nearly five years removed from his retirement as a player, Boucher mounted a brief comeback with the Rangers during the dreadful 1943–44 season. Starting out on the third line between left wing Billy Gooden and rookie right wing Kilby MacDonald, Boucher hoped his presence in the lineup would help stabilize a club

Boucher was also one of the cleanest players in NHL history. He had, in fact, only one fight, one major penalty, during his 13-plus NHL years.

The club still honors Boucher with the annual Frank Boucher Trophy, awarded to "the most popular Ranger on and off the ice," a fitting memorial to a guy who was certainly one of the nicest Rangers ever. "I'm proud of that, I really am," he said years later. "Ranger fans are the best."

Hockey Hall of Fame

Frank Boucher was one of the most popular and enduring Rangers ever, serving the team as player, coach, and general manager.

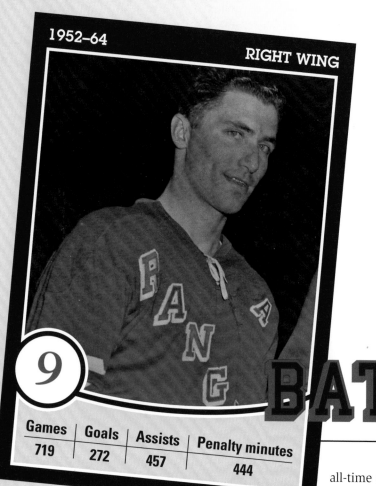

1952–64

RIGHT WING

9

Games	Goals	Assists	Penalty minutes
719	272	457	444

8
ANDY BATHGATE

A fan looking skyward at Madison Square Garden will notice that uniform No. 9 has been retired twice by the Rangers. The first time was on February 3, 2009, when the club celebrated the career of Adam Graves. Three weeks later, it was Andy Bathgate's turn.

Unusual? A little awkward? Perhaps, but then the Rangers are lucky to have had two men wear that numeral with so much distinction.

Since they opened play in 1926, the Rangers have had four great homegrown right wings, and all of them ended up in the Hall of Fame. Bathgate was the third of these, succeeding Bill Cook and Bryan Hextall and preceding Rod Gilbert, giving Ranger fans a line of succession of right-side excellence for fifty years.

Bathgate was captain of the Rangers from 1961 to 1964, winner of the Hart Trophy as the NHL's most valuable player in 1958–59, ranks fourth on the club's all-time scoring list with 729 points, represented the Rangers at eight All-Star Games and set a team record that still stands by scoring at least one goal (11 total) in 10 consecutive games from December 15, 1962, to January 5, 1963. He was also the first Ranger to appear on the cover of *Sports Illustrated*. The date was January 12, 1959, and the cover headline read simply: "Andy Bathgate, Hockey Hero."

But it was his elegance—a quiet elegance—that defined Bathgate's career in New York. Al Laney, the graceful hockey writer with the *New York Herald-Tribune*, might have put it best when he wrote, "All of the superstars are at once great individuals *and* great team players. What they have in common is an uncommon skill and flair. They alone try the new, the unexpected. Andy Bathgate has this ability to an unusual degree."

That New Yorkers could only enjoy Bathgate's uncommon skill and flair for just over 11 seasons was a shame, but the strapping right wing with the ferocious slap shot left his mark in so many ways,

Always a hit with the fans, right wing Andy Bathgate was a four-time winner of the Frank Boucher Trophy, presented annually by the members of the Rangers Fan Club.

endearing himself to the Ranger faithful for 719 games, plus 22 more in the playoffs.

Of Scottish origin, Bathgate's surname came from the hamlet of Bathgate, about 16 miles outside of Edinburgh, where his father had lived. Andy was born in Winnipeg, long a rich pipeline of talent for the Rangers, and at age five stood up in a pair of his sister's skates. At age six, an older brother put a hockey stick in his hands. About a year after that, while standing on an improvised rink outside his house, Andy broke his first window with a slap shot.

Turning down scholarships to play for the University of Denver and the University of Colorado, Bathgate came east in 1949–50 to play his junior hockey with the Guelph Biltmores of the Ontario Hockey Association. He led the talent-rich Biltmores to the Memorial Cup, Canada's junior championship, in 1952 and was stamped a "can't-miss" prospect.

Phil Watson was first drawn to Bathgate during those Memorial Cup playoffs and it was a fight—not a fancy goal—that left the greatest impression on the bird-dogging Rangers coach.

"Andy didn't strike me as much as two or three other guys on his team," Watson confessed years later. "But then he had this fight with a big defenseman. One of the best I ever saw in the juniors. Bathgate beat his brains out. Didn't break anything but he hit him so hard he fell over the boards."

Only a balky left knee seemed to stand in Bathgate's path to stardom in the NHL.

Doctors in Guelph diagnosed torn cartilage in the knee and recommended surgery. Frank Boucher, the

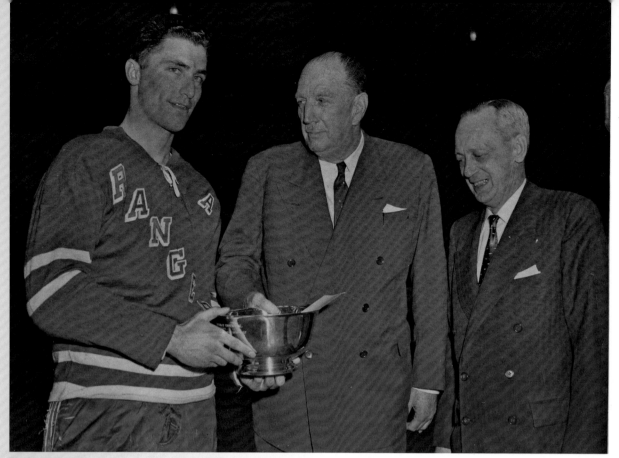

Trophies seemed to come naturally for Andy Bathgate. Here, he receives the West Side Association of Commerce Award as the Rangers' most valuable player.

Rangers' general manager, wasn't so sure, and Bathgate was brought to New York and put in the care of Dr. Kazuo Yanagisawa, the Rangers' legendary orthopedic surgeon. Yanagisawa detected a "loose kneecap," requiring a different kind of surgery and the insertion of a permanent steel plate in Bathgate's knee.

"I spent two weeks in St. Clare's Hospital," Bathgate recalled, "and I'd venture to say they were the loneliest two weeks of my life. I had no visitors other than Dr. Yanagisawa and the nurses. The only New Yorkers I knew were hockey players, and they were all back in Canada for the summer."

The operation was a success. Bathgate recovered well and Yanagisawa cleared him to return to Guelph for his final season of junior hockey. It was a short stint with the Biltmores, only two games. The 1952–53 Rangers were struggling on the ice and at the gate, so they quickly imported Bathgate, their budding superstar, to help right their listing ship. Thus was launched a Hall of Fame career.

Eventually, the Rangers decided they had brought Bathgate along a little too quickly, and that he needed more seasoning. He got it with the WHL's

Vancouver Canucks and the AHL's Cleveland Barons before arriving for keeps in New York for the 1954–55 season.

What followed, despite playing on what now were *two* gimpy knees, was a stretch of ten seasons in which Bathgate missed only five games, all of them in 1957–58. He quickly became the Rangers' leader, the superstar the club had predicted, and eventually the holder of all the team's offensive records until his successor, Gilbert, came along. Along with Gordie Howe, Maurice (Rocket) Richard and Bernie (Boom Boom) Geoffrion, Bathgate was for a time among the top right wings in all of hockey.

His battle with Bobby Hull for the scoring title in 1961–62 was an epic one that came down to the final game of the season, Chicago at the Rangers, on March 25, 1962.

Bathgate was tied with Hull at 84 points entering the third period, and the Rangers did everything in their power to get another point or two and sole possession of the Art Ross Trophy for their captain. It didn't work. The Blackhawks had Eric Nesterenko and Reg Fleming shadowing Bathgate's every move,

leaning on him, holding and hooking. Chicago was taking advantage of a loophole in the NHL rulebook that prohibited a team from being more than two men short, so it mattered not how many penalties they took as the game wound to a close. Hull ended up winning the scoring title by virtue of having more goals: 50, to Bathgate's 28.

Besides the many honors he achieved, there were two other crowning moments of Bathgate's career in New York and both of them occurred at Madison Square Garden. The first was on November 1, 1959. It was Bathgate's shot—a brisk backhander, not a slap shot—that cut the face of Montreal's great goalie, Jacques Plante, and led to Plante returning some 20 minutes later with a face mask, the first modern-day goalie to do so.

Then, on March 14, 1962, Bathgate scored on a rare penalty shot against Detroit's Hank Bassen, propelling the Rangers into the Stanley Cup playoffs. It was one of the most dramatic games in Ranger history. According to Kenneth Rudeen of *Sports Illustrated*, "the Garden's grimy old steelwork rang with a million-decibel shout of jubilation" when the puck went in.

"I remember the goal very vividly," Bathgate said, "and I think a lot of people in New York from my old bunch remember it too. It's a once-in-a-lifetime thing. If I missed, I would have been a complete bum. But I scored, so I was a hero for years."

When Bathgate was traded to the Toronto Maple Leafs on February 22, 1964, it shocked Ranger fans to their core. Handy Andy promptly won his first and only Stanley Cup that first season with the Leafs, but more significant, it was the end of an era in New York.

Bathgate would eventually play for the Detroit Red Wings, the Pittsburgh Penguins and even had a stint as a player-coach with Ambri-Piota in Switzerland from 1971 to 1974.

He later opened a driving range in Mississauga, Ontario, and was still working there daily well into his 70s.

7 JEAN RATELLE

Games	Goals	Assists	Penalty minutes
862	336	481	192

As elegant and effective a center as the Rangers have ever had, Jean Ratelle never had a flashy nickname during a magnificent NHL career that spanned 21 seasons, 15 of which were spent in the Big Apple.

Ratelle was known simply as "Gentleman Jean," and he was certainly that, never exceeding 28 minutes in penalties for a single season. He won the Lady Byng Trophy for "clean, effective play" twice: in 1972 with the Rangers and again in 1976 with the Bruins, the latter award coming just seven months after the biggest trade in Rangers' history: the November 7, 1975, blockbuster that sent Ratelle and defenseman Brad Park north to Boston for Phil Esposito and Carol Vadnais. That event put a smashing exclamation point on the Rangers' 50th anniversary season.

It was a deal that thoroughly shocked Ranger fans, as well as Ratelle and Park themselves, Park

even admitting that the trade made him cry for the first time in his adult life. "That's how much New York, and the Rangers, meant to both of us," Ratelle said years later.

On the ice, Ratelle was graceful, "as smooth as the ice itself," Emile Francis, the club's longtime coach and general manager, said on many occasions. "You always knew what you were going to get from Jean. He was always the same. It didn't matter if it was an exhibition game, a practice, or a playoff game. He was probably the most consistent player I ever had. He was our Béliveau, our Esposito. Plus, he *never* complained about anything."

It is not at all an overstatement to compare Ratelle to a famous predecessor, Frank Boucher, or a famous successor, Wayne Gretzky. All three were superstar centers and left-handed shots.

Gentleman Jean was the glue that held together the Rangers' most famous line ever: the "G-A-G Line." The acronym stood for Goal-A-Game. They scored so much one season, 1971–72, that team

Center Jean Ratelle was a scoring threat from anywhere inside the blue line. Here, he launches at backhander towards Chicago goalie Glenn Hall.

statistician Arthur Friedman changed the nickname to "T-A-G Line" for Two-A-Game. Ratelle's wingers, more flashy by a mile, were Rod Gilbert on the right and Vic Hadfield on the left.

The high-scoring threesome finished third, fourth and fifth in the NHL scoring race in 1971–72, trailing only Boston's Phil Esposito and Bobby Orr. Ratelle, despite a broken ankle that cost him the final month of the season, had 46 goals and 63 assists for 109 points—the best season of his career. The Rangers bolted to the Stanley Cup Finals that season, and faced the Bruins. Ratelle tried a comeback from the ankle injury, but was ineffective. The Bruins won, four games to two.

Ratelle's ankle injury was really only the second serious setback of his NHL career. In 1966–67, he suffered a slipped disc, and received a spinal-fusion operation from Dr. Kazuo Yanagisawa, the Rangers' orthopedic surgeon, who performed similar surgeries on Rod Gilbert, Harry Howell, Orland Kurtenbach and Al Lebrun. Ratelle recovered completely and promptly posted back-to-back 78-point seasons and

three straight 32-goal campaigns. However, the spinal fusion did leave Gentleman Jean with a somewhat awkward skating style, stiff and upright, and made him the butt of occasional, good-natured locker room humor.

Despite the shock of the trade to Boston, Ratelle continued to display his trademark consistency, seamlessly becoming the Bruins' number-one center and scoring 105 points for the season, 90 of them with the Bruins. Even the Esposito-loving Beantowners had to respect those numbers.

Francis recalled how tough it was to trade Ratelle. "Believe me, trading Jean was every bit as hard to me as putting Eddie Giacomin on waivers [eight days earlier]," he said. "You have to remember that Ratty and I had been together for 15 years."

Less than a month later, on November 26, Ratelle was back in the Garden to face his old teammates. Surely he looked odd wearing No. 10 in Bruins white, since center Gregg Sheppard, a solid 30-goal scorer, had Boston's No. 19 safely stashed in his locker. Ratelle was greeted warmly, but not raucously, by

Jean Ratelle (19) always drew the attention of the opposition's best checking forwards. Here, California's Aut Erickson tries to stop him.

the Garden faithful, 17,250 strong, and he raised his stick at the Boston blue line in acknowledgment. He had to be somewhat nonplussed, however, when Carl Martin, the Garden public address announcer, introduced him as "Gene" Ratelle, rather than the Gallic "Jean" Martin had used when Ratelle was a Ranger. For years, Martin insisted it was merely a slip of the tongue, an announcer's gaffe. Others were not so sure.

There was delicious irony, to be sure, in that Ratelle lined up against Esposito to take the opening face-off that night, a pair of superstar centers who had just been the centerpieces in one of the biggest trades in the history of both teams.

Ratelle promptly went out and set up two Boston goals, and the Bruins won, 6–4. "A typical Ratelle performance," quipped Francis. "It didn't surprise me in the slightest."

Said Rod Gilbert, the Rangers' ace right wing and Ratelle's boyhood buddy: "Let me tell you, it was weird, the first time I had ever played against him in my career."

Boston was the immediate winner of the trade, streaking to an Adams Division championship with a remarkable 48-15-17 record. Ratelle led the team in points (90) and assists (59) while his old club, the Rangers, struggled to a 29-42-9 record, last place in the Patrick Division, and no playoffs.

Following his initial season in Boston, Ratelle still had plenty of gas in his tank. His numbers were declining, yes, but still solid: 94, 84, 72, 73 and 37 points in his final five seasons. His back began to bother him again in 1980, and he opted for retirement following the 1980–81 season, when he played in only 47 games. Trade-wise, he gave the Bruins 155 goals and 450 points in 419 games played. Esposito gave the Rangers 184 goals and 404 points in 422 games, a wash probably, especially when one factors in the leadership Esposito brought to the Blueshirts as their captain.

Ratelle continued on with the Bruins in a variety of scouting positions for quite a number of years before retiring for good. He continues to live today in suburban Boston.

1965–75

GOALTENDER

Games	Record	Shutouts	GAA
538	266-172-89	49	2.73

6 ED GIACOMIN

It's sad in a way that the defining game of Ed Giacomin's ten-year career with the Rangers should be one that he played at Madison Square Garden in the uniform of the Detroit Red Wings.

The real defining moments of Giacomin's magnificent run on Broadway should be in the numbers: 538 games played, 266 victories, a career goals-against average of 2.73 and an eye-popping 49 shutouts, the most in team history. Throw in three straight years (1966–69) in which he led the National Hockey League in victories and you have a clearer picture of just how much Giacomin meant to the Rangers of four decades ago.

In fact, until Mike Richter came along in 1989, Giacomin was the most popular goalie the Rangers have ever had—quite a statement indeed when you consider that the team's goaltending register also includes guys named Davey Kerr, Chuck Rayner, Gump Worsley and John Davidson.

That Eddie Giacomin made it in professional hockey at all might never have even happened were it not for his older brother Rollie, himself a pretty fair amateur goalie. The year was 1959.

The Washington Eagles of the Eastern Amateur Hockey League needed a goalie with four games to go in their season. They put in a call for Rollie Giacomin, but Rollie's regular job wouldn't permit him the kind of time off he needed. Rollie suggested his kid brother Eddie, then just 19 years old, and playing for Sudbury (Ont.) Bell Telephone of the Nickel Belt Hockey League, roughly the hockey equivalent of a Sunday softball league.

Eddie went to Washington, played the four games, won them all, and a storybook career had been launched. Six more seasons of minor league hockey followed, mostly with the Providence Reds of the American Hockey League. At Providence, Eddie consistently caught the eye of Johnny Gagnon, the Rangers' AHL scout who was based in Rhode Island and saw practically all of the Reds' home games.

At the same time, Emile Francis, the Rangers' new general manager, was hotly in need of a new goaltender as he launched a major rebuilding project in New York. Gagnon convinced Francis, an ex-goalie himself, to come up to Providence to watch Giacomin in action. That's all it took to convince Emile that Giacomin was the guy he needed.

Francis proposed a package of four minor-league players (Marcel Paille, Aldo Guidolin, Don McGregor and Jim Mikol) for Giacomin and presented the offer to Lou Pieri, the Reds' owner. Pieri believed that good-looking, helmetless players were good box office, so Francis brought along 8x10 glossy publicity photos of the players he was offering.

"I slid the pictures, one by one, across Pieri's desk," Francis recalled, "and I saved Mikol for last. Now, Jim was a pretty good-looking guy. Pieri smiled, and I had myself a goalkeeper."

After some rough going in his first couple of seasons in New York, Giacomin quickly blossomed, due in part to some savvy coaching by Francis. Giacomin, who grew up idolizing Turk Broda, the great Toronto goalie, was headed for greatness on hockey's brightest stage, New York.

There were six appearances in the NHL All-Star Game, and a Vezina Trophy (shared with Gilles Villemure) in 1971. More important, Giacomin's butterfly style and exciting dashes from his goal crease made him a big favorite with the fans. They called him "Goalie A-Go-Go" or "Go-Go Eddie," and even voted him the Frank Boucher Trophy, presented annually to the team's most popular player.

Until the arrival of Villemure in 1970, Giacomin was the Rangers' workhorse, playing in virtually every game, and leading the league in games played for four straight seasons from 1967 to 1971. An excellent skater and stickhandler, some called him a "third defenseman," which must have made his former Providence coach Fernie Flaman proud. Flaman played defense for over 16 years with the Bruins and Maple Leafs.

Despite his acrobatic style, Giacomin was remarkably injury-free for most of his time in New York, suffering only a broken hand in 1975–76. But, after one of the most stellar decades a Ranger has ever known, Giacomin began to show signs of age, and his play declined. The end came like a thunderclap on Halloween night, October 31, 1975. Francis, in full rebuilding mode, put Giacomin on waivers, and the Red Wings (and only the Red Wings) bit, for a paltry $2,500.

Two days later, on Sunday, November 2, as only a devilish NHL schedule maker could produce, the Rangers were to entertain the Red Wings at the Garden. It was pure irony, and Giacomin would surely be in goal.

For anyone who was there—and there were more than 17,000 witnesses—it was a surreal scene they will never forget. Eddie Giacomin, after ten seasons in Ranger red, blue and white, was looking mighty uncomfortable as he faced the Seventh Avenue end

of Madison Square Garden in the bright red uniform of the visitors from Motown. Even the number was wrong, with Giacomin wearing No. 31 for Detroit instead of his familiar New York No. 1.

The fans cheered Giacomin's first name ("EDDEE! ED-DEE!") and virtually drowned out the national anthem. Tears flowed freely down the goaltender's angular cheekbones as the stunning tribute continued for the man who had been traded away just two days earlier. Rangers fans, as loyal a group as there is in all of sports, were going to be cheering for the Red Wings that eerie night. It was one of the strangest and most emotional games ever witnessed in that arena.

The fans continued to chant Giacomin's name throughout the game. They roared some more with every save he made, and cheered lustily with each Detroit goal, of which there were six, two more than the Rangers' four. The Rangers themselves, or at least what was left of them since much of their collective psyche was at the other end of the ice, simply seemed not to have their hearts in that particular game. Giacomin surely did.

"Our players wouldn't shoot at him," Francis recalled. "They didn't want to embarrass him! And the crowd chanted his name. It was a great night for Eddie and he deserved that because he was our franchise for ten years. Then, with five minutes to go in the game, guess what they were chanting: 'Kill the Cat!' We had the best security people in MSG and when they heard that they came down at the end of the game and said, 'We need to give you protection. They're going to kill you.' And I said, 'Hey, I walked in here and I'm going to walk out. They may get me but I guarantee you I will take a couple of them with me.'"

The feisty Rangers GM, of course, made it out of the Garden that night unscathed and was surely as proud as anyone when Giacomin was elected to the Hockey Hall of Fame in 1987.

Two years later, on March 15, 1989, the Rangers and their fans saluted their popular goalie with Eddie Giacomin Night, marking only the second time in team history that a player's number was retired, with Giacomin's No. 1 joining Rod Gilbert's No. 7 in the Garden rafters.

Just how much did the Rangers really mean to Eddie Giacomin? Consider these words from the man who will always be Number One in the hearts of many Ranger fans: "I wanted to stay there [in New York] until I was 55, but they wouldn't let me. Even today, it's hard for me to sign a Detroit Red Wings hockey card. It isn't natural because I never felt like I was a Red Wing. I really loved the Rangers."

> "I wanted to stay there [in New York] until I was 55, but they wouldn't let me."

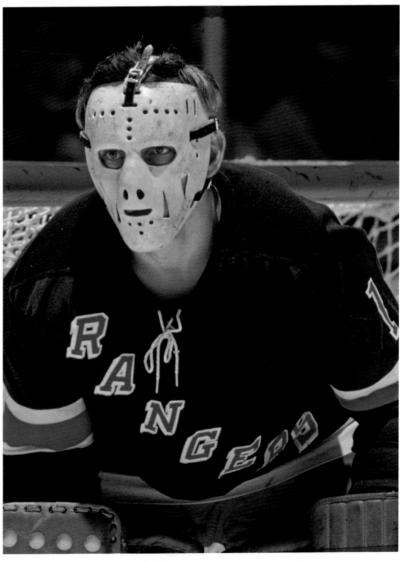

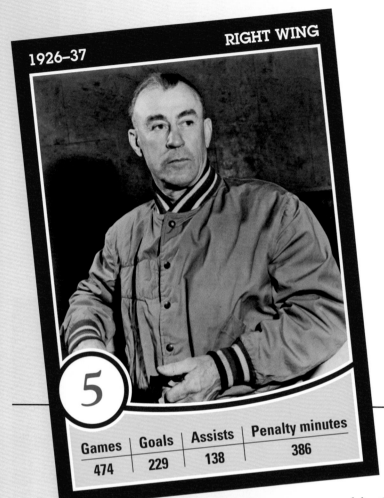

1926–37

5

Games	Goals	Assists	Penalty minutes
474	229	138	386

5
BILL COOK

That Bill Cook could start his National Hockey League career at the not-so-tender age of 30 was remarkable in itself. That he would become the NHL's premier right wing at that age was downright astounding. The Rangers—and their fans—were the beneficiaries of this remarkable athlete. They had him for 11 seasons, starting with the team's first campaign in 1926–27.

Cook was the Rangers' first captain. Wearing sweater No. 5, he scored the team's first goal, the only goal in the Rangers' first game, a 1–0 shutout of the Montreal Maroons on November 16, 1926, at Madison Square Garden. The goal came at 18:37 of the second period.

Cook, his brother Bun at left wing, and Frank Boucher at center, formed the famous "A-Line,"

named for the subway being built under the Garden, on Eighth Avenue between 49th and 50th.

The line was a perfect mix of scoring power first, but also finesse and defensive ability. Sportswriter Joe Nichols of the *New York Times* called the trio "beautifully artistic." In 1972, legendary Toronto broadcaster Foster Hewitt compared the then-emerging Soviet hockey powers to the "A-Line" of 40 years earlier. "To me," Hewitt said, "it always seemed like they had the puck on a string, and that's how the Russians play."

During his pre-Ranger days, with the Saskatoon Sheiks and the Saskatoon Crescents of the West Coast Hockey League, Cook got the nickname "Bad Bill." According to brother Bun, Bill never went looking for trouble, but he found his share anyway. "In a way, his presence on the ice took a lot of the pressure off me and Frank," Bun said. "We were finesse players

The Rangers' first great line, the "A-Line," had Frank Boucher at center between brothers Bill Cook (left) and Bun Cook (right).

primarily, and the other teams left us alone. That was fine with me."

Joe Primeau, the outstanding Toronto Maple Leafs center, played many memorable games against the Cook brothers and Boucher. He held Bill in the highest regard. "He was a terrific hockey player," Primeau recalled. "Nobody fooled around with Bill Cook because he was tough, *real* tough."

Cook's toughness undoubtedly traced to his service, starting at the age of 17, with the Canadian armed forces in World War I. He survived battles at Ypres, Vimy Ridge, the Somme and Flanders. He even saw postwar service in Russia, having been recruited to help put down the rise of Bolshevism. He had a .45 on his hip, and carried a Russian rifle. A fellow soldier described him as "one of the bravest men I had ever seen."

As captain of the Rangers, Cook was a strong, silent type. He didn't really say a lot. That was his nature. "But when he did talk, everyone listened," recalled Boucher. "Plus he had a glare about him that spoke mountains. You just knew what he was thinking, so you went out and you just did it."

Lester Patrick, the Rangers' legendary general manager and coach, recalled Bill Cook's demeanor before games. "He was a bundle of nerves, rubbing his palms against his hockey pants, just aching to get at it and break the tension. To win hockey championships, I needed Bill Cook. When it came right down to the crunch, the other players followed Bill Cook."

How good was William Osser Cook? Well, in addition to being tough as nails and commanding the respect of just about everyone on skates, he won the NHL scoring championship with 37 points (33 of

Hockey Hall of Fame

them goals) in his first season in the league, which at the time played a 44-game schedule.

Had the seasons been longer, could he have scored 50 goals? Or 60? The game has changed much since Cook roamed the ice, and speculating what he might have accomplished in the modern era is a dicey proposition, at best. But there's no denying that he was a dominant offensive force in his day.

Cook, who added another scoring crown in 1933 at the ripe age of 37, was three times a First Team All-Star selection and the first Ranger regular to be elected to the Hockey Hall of Fame in 1952. Most important, with Bad Bill as their leader, the Rangers appeared in five Stanley Cup Finals, won two Stanley Cups, and missed the playoffs only once in 11 seasons. This was the Golden Age of Ranger hockey.

When Cook's playing days were winding down, Lester Patrick tried him for a time on defense before

he retired following the 1936–37 season. He returned to coach the Blueshirts in 1951 but his coaching career was a far cry from his successes as a player.

Cook would often coach in a warm flannel shirt, and he wore rubbers behind the bench. "The players, well, we just didn't respect that," said one, anonymously. "He looked more like a farmer than an NHL coach." This was in marked contrast to two of his coaching predecessors, Patrick and Frank Boucher, who were always sartorially resplendent behind the bench.

Even if his wardrobe lacked sophistication, Cook turned out to be a taskmaster who took his mandate to toughen up the Rangers *very* seriously. When team president Gen. John Reed Kilpatrick mentioned somewhat casually that he liked to visit the dressing room between periods to give the players some encouragement, Cook snorted: "General, let's get this

Hockey Hall of Fame

straight. I allow no one in my dressing rooms between periods, and this includes you."

With a record of 35-47-23, Cook's coaching tenure was mercifully short. It was Boucher, his former linemate and then GM of the Rangers, who relieved Cook of his coaching duties in 1953.

Although his ouster as coach left him feeling bitter for a time, Cook was still a Ranger "original" who never forgot his roots. "Once a Ranger, always a Ranger" was a favorite saying of Cook's, who greatly delighted in coming back to New York and reliving his salad days. He was on hand when the Rangers gloriously closed the old Madison Square Garden on February 11, 1968.

"They brought me back because I scored the first goal in the Garden," he said. He also scored the last, ceremonially at least. Cook glided slowly toward the net at the Ninth Avenue end of the building and slid the puck in to great cheers. The organist, Gladys Gooding, played "Auld Lang Syne." One week later, on February 18, Cook helped christen the opening of the new Garden for hockey with yet another ceremonial goal. "That was quite an honor," he said.

In 1986, shortly before his death, the Rangers honored Cook again, bestowing their first New York Rangers Alumni Association Award on him. During a center ice presentation, team captain Barry Beck and broadcaster and fellow Hall-of-Famer Bill Chadwick presented Cook with a huge oil painting of the big right wing in his playing days, plus a framed No. 5 jersey. Cook, in a wheelchair, was teary-eyed.

Afterward, he delighted in meeting the Rangers of the day and regaling them with stories, particularly Beck and defenseman Mike McEwen. "So many of my memories are in these walls," he said. "I'll never forget them. We had the most wonderful times of any hockey club."

When Gordie Howe came into the NHL in 1946, one old-timer said, "There is the next Bill Cook." For a hockey player, praise doesn't come much higher than that.

1991–97, 2000–04

CENTER

11

Games	Goals	Assists	Penalty minutes
698	250	441	667

4 MARK MESSIER

When the Rangers officially removed uniform No. 11 from circulation on January 12, 2006, fans unable to attend that night's game against the Edmonton Oilers put their tickets back on the market, with front-row seats fetching upwards of $30,000.

The guest of honor for what would become the longest and most elaborate ceremony of its kind was not the first captain in Rangers history, nor would he be the last. But because he fulfilled his pledge to win the Stanley Cup in New York, Mark Douglas Messier is the captain against whom all others will be measured.

The greatest leader in professional sports earned that reputation by giving his all every night and demanding the same from his teammates. He did it with a glare that could burn a hole through lead and a smile that could warm up a room. He did it with his

stick, his elbows and the willingness to use either as a weapon. And he did it with the boundless joy of a child playing a child's game who looked as euphoric scoring NHL goal No. 694 as he had scoring his first, 25 years earlier.

A 2007 Hall of Fame inductee, Messier was as complete a player as the league had ever seen—one who could pass, shoot, skate, hit or fight his way to victory.

The five-time Stanley Cup champ was acquired from Edmonton in November 1991 for Bernie Nicholls, a pair of minor-leaguers and some cash. In hindsight, it was a small price to pay for a man charged with transforming the mindset of an entire franchise.

"He will make everybody believe that the New York Rangers can actually win," GM Neil Smith foretold, "and I'm not sure that there's ever been anybody yet in the last God knows how many years that's been able to make the Rangers believe they can win."

Expectations reached the stratosphere in 1992 after a brilliant regular season saw Messier score

107 points, win his second Hart Trophy and lead the Rangers to their first-ever Presidents' Trophy as the team with the league's best record.

It made their gut-wrenching loss to Pittsburgh in the division finals that much harder to swallow and prompted some to wonder whether this Messier character was man enough to rescue the Rangers from an eternity of "1940!" chants.

Longtime linemate Adam Graves summed it up best: "People expect him to grab the puck, fly through the air and drop the puck in the goal."

Graves was right—Messier couldn't work miracles by himself. He had to convince teammates not only that the impossible was possible, but also that it would require an unprecedented unity of purpose to succeed where so many Rangers teams had previously failed.

Such was the message delivered during the 1994 Eastern Conference Finals against the New Jersey Devils. Here, the Messier legend was born.

With the Rangers a game away from elimination, Messier earned his place among New York's sporting icons when he delivered his famous "guarantee"— the promise that his team would triumph in Game Six and extend the series to seven games.

Had Messier dabbled in clairvoyance, or was it simply his way of rallying the troops at the season's most critical juncture? When it came to motivational tactics, the big, balding centerman had a knack for knowing which buttons to push.

"Mess just kind of went along with a journalist's headline story," said Craig MacTavish, a teammate in Edmonton and New York. "I'll tell you one thing—it didn't make Mark play any harder. You knew he was going to play his rear end off in that game whether he made a guarantee or not."

Aware that failure would result in the worst kind of embarrassment, Messier backed up his bold prediction by scoring a natural hat trick in the third period, helping the Rangers erase a two-goal deficit.

Play-by-play man Mike (Doc) Emrick called Messier's signature performance "the stuff of legend," and it certainly has taken on an air of myth in the years since.

True to form, Messier also scored the Cup-winning goal in Game Seven of the finals, a series only slightly less epic than the one preceding it. The sight of him jumping for joy as the final buzzer sounded on June 14, 1994, is one no Rangers fan will soon forget (it's amazing how high a 205-pound player in full gear can leap when the weight of 54 seasons of futility is removed from his shoulders).

"New York is a tough place to play, it's a lot of pressure and a lot of focus, and he relished that," Wayne Gretzky said. "If you look at history, you look at what Babe Ruth did for the Yankees, you look at what Willis Reed did in the 70s for the Knicks, and you look at what Joe Namath did in the 60s for the Jets. That's what Mark Messier brought to the Rangers in the 1990s. He'll be forever remembered as the hockey version of those guys. Bringing a championship to the town was all that it was about."

In time, though, the ecstasy of 1994 dwindled, and it was back to business for the Rangers. Believing Messier's value would diminish in the years ahead, the team took a calculated risk in allowing their captain to reach free agency following the 1996–97 season. An offer was made to keep him in Ranger threads but it was too little, too late. Feeling slighted, Messier chose a more lucrative offer from the Vancouver Canucks.

Following a three-year exile in British Columbia, Messier celebrated his return to the Rangers at a press conference during which he and Garden president Dave Checketts symbolically buried a hatchet in a box full of topsoil. Shedding tears that have since become as much a trademark as the iconic No. 11 on his sweater, Messier vowed to restore pride in a Rangers team that had fallen on hard times in his absence.

But over the next four seasons, even he could not single-handedly drag an overpaid, underachieving collection of thirtysomethings back into the playoffs. There were no parades during Messier's second tour of duty on Broadway, or any visits to the Letterman show with the Cup in tow, but he remained an effective presence skating against players half his age.

He was the league's oldest player at 44 years, two

> People expect him to grab the puck, fly through the air and drop the puck in the goal.

months when he took his last shift on Garden ice in 2004, and officially retired a year later as the second-leading scorer in NHL history with 1,887 points (691 as a Ranger, fifth on the club's all-time list).

But Messier's Ranger legacy will never be about statistics. It's about defying bogus curses and, for a time, making an entire organization believe that nothing short of winning was important.

It was also about forming an inexorable bond with a city and its people. Sometimes, bonds can grow stronger in times of tragedy.

On September 28, 2001, mere weeks after the catastrophic attack on the World Trade Center, Messier, with the assistance of the team's lead public relations man, John Rosasco, and their beloved security guy, "Chief" Dennis Ryan, took general manager Glen Sather, Mike Richter and Eric Lindros on a visit to Ground Zero to honor the victims of 9/11 and to salute the workers laboring at the site.

"There was some apprehension going in, for sure," recalled Rosasco, "but coming out we were all thrilled, and so happy we had done it. Honestly, it's hard to put into words."

Initially, the group gathered at Police Headquarters, in the office of Commissioner Bernard

Kerik. "We brought lots of stuff: hats, T-shirts, souvenirs, anything that wasn't nailed down, basically," said Rosasco. Then it was off by van with a police escort to the site.

This was meant to be a private affair—no press and no cameras—but the attempt at anonymity didn't last long. On their way, the Rangers' contingent had to pass a staging area for the international press corps, including Canadian media, many of whom instantly recognized Messier. "Mess isn't that easy to hide," cracked Richter.

The souvenirs were distributed to the workers. "They were elated, they all came over to us, and especially to Mark," Rosasco said. "It was quite a scene."

Nine days later, the Rangers played their home opener at the Garden against the Buffalo Sabres. It was a reprise performance for Messier, who wore the heavy helmet of a missing fire chief during pregame ceremonies. "For me, personally, that was very emotional … with all the people being honored—the firefighters, the police, the volunteers and rescue workers, the entire city, our fans," Messier said. "That was a time when we started fighting back as a country."

Taking their cue from their charismatic leader, the Blueshirts went out and beat the Sabres 5–4 in overtime. They acted like New Yorkers that night, and they also acted like Rangers.

Messier's time in New York was a godsend, no doubt, unprecedented in team history. But were there warts, some speed bumps? Of course. The team

made the playoffs only five of the ten years he was on Broadway. There was the messy, not so private clash with coach Roger Neilson in the early 90s that led to Neilson having to leave. Messier's willingness to play hurt, while courageous and admirable, sometimes hurt the club as a whole. And in time, Mark's gung-ho style wore thin in the locker room with some of the players tuning him out, particularly in the later years.

But, and most important, he delivered the Stanley Cup. Enough said.

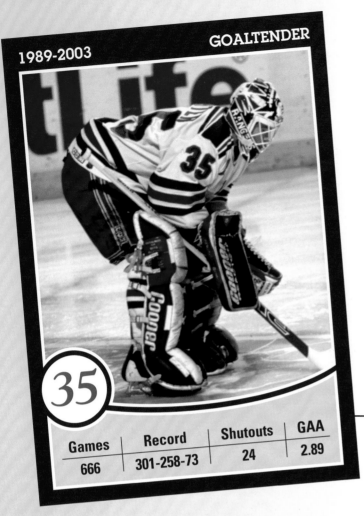

1989-2003 — GOALTENDER

Games	Record	Shutouts	GAA
666	301-258-73	24	2.89

3 MIKE RICHTER

Goalies, like pitchers, quarterbacks and Federal Reserve chairmen, always seem to be judged by numbers.

So, in the interest of full disclosure, it must be noted that the consensus greatest goalie in the history of the New York Rangers never led the league in goals-against average, save percentage or shutouts. In eight of his 14 seasons on Broadway, he had a losing record. And when his career win total is matched against those of contemporaries Patrick Roy, Martin Brodeur and Ed Belfour, 301 sounds small by comparison.

Nevertheless, Mike Richter's No. 35 banner hangs from the ceiling of Madison Square Garden because those 301 victories are the most of any Ranger goalie, because he never wore the uniform of another NHL team, because he was a man of character who consistently represented himself and the club with class and distinction, because he was one of the most focused and best prepared netminders of

his generation, and because he was the man guarding the crease when the Rangers won their fourth and most elusive Stanley Cup.

"Goaltending is the backbone of your hockey club," said Mark Messier, a man who knows a thing or two about backbone, "and there wasn't a guy who played with Mike who didn't want to follow his charge from the dressing room onto the ice and into war. He was that kind of guy—the kind you wanted to follow onto the ice. He had enthusiasm for the entire game, not just for parts of it or for the accolades. He loved all the little, casual things that come from playing hockey. That's what made him such a special teammate."

And a favorite of the ticket-buying public.

"I know New York has always been a bit of a goalie crowd and have been behind their goalie," added Brian Leetch, "but Mike stepped right into that mold with his hard work, acrobatics and big-time play. The fans supported him right from the start."

So many hockey stories begin on a frozen pond somewhere on the Canadian prairie. This one starts on a street in the suburbs north of Philadelphia, where Richter first played the game with his brothers and kids from around the neighborhood.

But starring on asphalt didn't get Mike noticed by NHL scouts. That would happen a few years later when he tended goal—on ice—at nearby Germantown Academy and then at Northwood Prep in Lake Placid. The Rangers followed his development closely and, impressed by what they saw, made Richter their second round pick in the 1985 draft.

Although he had the grades to make the Ivy League, the opportunity to play for one of the elite programs in college hockey drew Richter out west to the University of Wisconsin, where he teamed with another future Ranger, Tony Granato.

After two years at Wisconsin, he left school early to play for the U.S. National Team and then the Olympic Team. From there it was on to the Rangers' IHL affiliate in Denver. He reported to Rangers training camp in September 1988 and impressed coach Michel Bergeron, but was returned to Denver to start the season.

By April of the following year, GM Phil Esposito had deep-sixed Bergeron and was running the bench as the Rangers prepared for a first round playoff meeting with Pittsburgh. Although he had veterans John Vanbiesbrouck and Bob Froese at his disposal, Esposito summoned Richter to New York and decreed that he wouldn't hesitate to start his rookie against the Penguins.

Three consecutive Ranger losses prompted Esposito to make good on his threat, and on April 9, 1989, Michael Thomas Richter became the first goalie in club history to make his NHL debut in a Stanley Cup playoff game.

Like most of Espo's attempts at strategy, his decision to start a rookie in an elimination game drew harsh criticism—even more so after Pittsburgh swept the series. Still, the Rangers had nothing to lose and, apart from a shaky first period in which he allowed three goals on the first seven shots he faced, Richter looked pretty good ... good enough to be back in New York the following season as Vanbiesbrouck's backup.

In addition to his heroics with the Rangers, goalie Mike Richter starred often on the world stage, at the Olympics and on the United States national team.

Like his childhood idol, Flyers great Bernie Parent, Richter was a superb "angles" goalie who was rarely out of position for a shot. And when he was, he was athletic enough to make what should have been a routine stop look downright spectacular.

"You look at Mike," said Adam Graves, "and he's a great athlete. He'd come in as the best-conditioned player. If you looked at him when he walked into the locker room you'd say, 'He *can't* be a goalie.'"

If Richter's dedication to fitness was legendary, so was his ability to keep teammates (and himself) entertained. Apart from charter flights, when his nose might be buried in some thick self-help book, he was as chatty and cheerful as can be.

"Mike was the most vocal goalie I was ever around," Leetch said. "He just needs to talk even if he's saying nothing. He would say 20 one-liners in a minute. We would laugh at two of them but he would laugh at all of them. He brought such a positive energy into the locker room."

No doubt that sense of humor came in handy during the 1992 playoffs when Richter surrendered a fluky 65-footer to Penguins center Ron Francis in Game Four of the Patrick Division Finals, shifting momentum in Pittsburgh's favor. The Rangers, who had finished the regular season with the league's best record, went on to lose the game, the series and, most significantly, a very real chance to play for the Stanley Cup. Richter probably shouldered more of the blame for that defeat than he deserved.

Through it all, including a dismal, injury-shortened 1992–93 campaign and continued competition with Vanbiesbrouck that prevented either player from establishing himself as the team's undisputed No. 1 goalie, Mike remained diplomatic and upbeat, confident that he'd eventually get the chance to prove he could handle greater responsibility.

He would finally get his shot in 1993–94. With Vanbiesbrouck off to Florida and the Rangers loaded for bear in an all-or-nothing crusade for the Cup, conditions were ripe for Richter to have a huge season. He went on to lead the league (and set a

Ranger single-season record) with 42 wins, earning MVP honors at the All-Star Game at Madison Square Garden along the way.

Yes, there will always be his dazzling play throughout the 1994 playoffs (including a miraculous, groin-splitting stop on Pavel Bure's penalty-shot attempt in Game Four of the finals), not to mention his MVP-winning performance with Team USA at the 1996 World Cup. But Richter was often at his best on nights when the same could not be said for the five skaters in front of him.

He and other holdovers from the '94 squad suffered through the lean years of the late 1990s and early 2000s, when every autumn brought new hope for another Cup run but was usually extinguished by the first buds of spring. For a champion like Richter, the losing was almost unbearable.

There were more setbacks. In 2000, he tore the anterior cruciate ligament in his left knee at the All-Star skills competition, an injury that eventually required reconstructive surgery followed by months of grueling rehab. He returned, only to suffer another ACL tear in his other knee five months later.

Then, in a March 2002 game against the Thrashers, a Chris Tamer slap shot from center ice caught Richter just above his right ear. His mask, emblazoned with the Statue of Liberty head that's become as familiar a team icon as the Ranger shield, provided little protection to that part of Richter's head, and he dropped to the ice in a daze. As if the concussion wasn't bad enough, X-rays revealed he had also suffered a fractured skull.

Ever the optimist, Richter hoped to return, as he had from two knee surgeries. But the long-term risks it posed to his health were too great to ignore. He officially called it quits at an emotional press conference at the Garden on September 4, 2003.

Leaving behind a virtually unblemished record in the eyes of Rangers fans, Richter embarked on a new path that may or may not lead back to hockey. His pursuit of a degree in ethics, politics and economics at Yale hinted at a life of public service or perhaps, like former Knicks star Bill Bradley, maybe even a run for office.

Whatever he decides to do with the rest of his life, it's hard to imagine Richter not attacking any challenges with the same enthusiasm and commitment to excellence that brought him so much acclaim as a goaltender for the New York Rangers.

> " … there wasn't a guy who played with Mike who didn't want to follow his charge from the dressing room onto the ice and into war. "

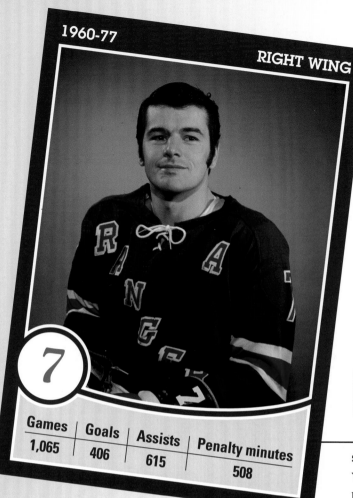

RIGHT WING

Games	Goals	Assists	Penalty minutes
1,065	406	615	508

7

2 ROD GILBERT

Many of the biggest stars in the history of hockey have worn the uniform of the New York Rangers, and their contributions to the club have ranged from the colossal to the infinitesimal. But it's safe to say that no player is more proud—or more protective—of his Ranger legacy than No. 7, Rod Gilbert.

And for good reason. The Hall of Fame right wing and holder of numerous franchise scoring records dedicated all of his 18 NHL seasons—and most of his adult life—to the Rangers, tirelessly promoting the game in a town where hockey competes with baseball, football, basketball, the theater and countless other distractions for the public's attention. In the face of that challenge, Gilbert was the ideal ambassador for hockey in New York City: he was handsome, charismatic and could score goals in buckets.

"Rocky was Mister Class," said Ted Irvine, the rugged winger who teamed with Gilbert for six seasons. "Even though he's Mister Hockey in New York, he never looks down on you. He laughs and hugs you. He had a great love for the game, respected where he came from and performed on the ice. He's a guy who fed off the New York fans and made a life out of it for himself."

Born Rodrigue Gabriel Gilbert on July 1, 1941, the blacksmith's son grew up listening to the Canadiens on the radio. Like virtually every French-Canadian kid, he dreamed that one day he'd be a big star in the NHL, too, just like his idols Bernie (Boom Boom) Geoffrion and, later, Andy Bathgate.

But as a teen, Rod was practically smuggled out of his native Montreal to the Rangers' amateur affiliate in Guelph, Ontario, before the Habs could get his signature on a contract.

"When I became a GM in the NHL," Emile Francis recalled, "the first thing that I was going to do was break up that monopoly that Montreal and Toronto had. The Montreal Canadiens boast that they had the best record in hockey and all that crap but they also had a little rule in the NHL that gave teams the territorial rights to every player in a 50-mile radius. Who the hell were we going to protect in New

York? Were we going to protect Manhattan and the Atlantic Ocean? But we had a scout in Montreal by the name of Yvan Prud'homme who spotted these kids, Gilbert and Jean Ratelle, and brought them to Guelph. The Canadiens had so many players, they overlooked them. They had *too* many."

With deceptive speed and a hard, accurate shot, Gilbert was tearing up the Ontario Hockey Association in 1960 when he received word that he was being called up to New York. Before making his NHL debut, however, disaster struck.

"I was blowing the league away with Jean," said Gilbert. "We had the best team in the OHA, I scored over 100 points and led the league in scoring. I was the MVP, too, so I won all the awards that year indicating that the Rangers had the best prospect in Canada coming to them. I had only one more game to play when I suffered an injury. One night, people threw debris on the ice. I slid, fell and couldn't get up. They had to carry me off on a stretcher and took me to the hospital. Doctors initially said, 'You have a spasm and it's gonna be okay.'"

But X-rays told a different story. Gilbert had actually broken the fifth vertebra in his back. So the Rangers put their star prospect on a 22-hour train ride to the Mayo Clinic in Minnesota, where doctors later removed bone from his leg and used it in a spinal-

fusion operation. The prospects of Gilbert walking again were excellent. Whether he'd ever play hockey again, no one could say.

But after months of arduous rehabilitation, Gilbert was back on skates and in November 1960 earned the first of several brief but encouraging appearances with the Rangers. He finally made the team outright at training camp in 1962, scoring 31 points in his rookie season.

Meanwhile, the rigors of professional hockey caused the bone graft in Gilbert's back to loosen over time. Prior to his third season, it was determined that the surgically repaired vertebrae were damaged and would require further attention.

He tried to tough it out through the 1965–66 campaign by wearing a steel, corset-like brace but it was cumbersome and affected his performance on the ice. So in January 1966, with the Rangers out of contention, Rod decided to abandon the season to undergo another back operation to save his career. What followed was a life-altering experience.

"This time," Gilbert recalled, "they took a bone from my pelvis. But seven days later, in order to prevent a staph infection, they fed me intravenously and gave me like seven pills every three hours. Since I had no food in my stomach, I couldn't digest them. I started choking at 2:00 in the afternoon. The nurse came over and said, 'We lost him. He doesn't have a pulse. He's gone.' I know I'm not gone, though, because I'm outside my body and watching.

"I could hear and see everything. Emile Francis was there and I hear him say, 'Bring him back! He's my best player!' So the doctor came in, dislodged the pills and gave me a shot that restarted my heart. That's when I had an out-of-body experience. It was only two minutes or so when I was out of body but I was very connected.

"When I came back, after thinking I had lost everything, I wanted to play and I had a new attitude. I made a deal that if He brings me back, then I was going to be an example and all that good stuff. I did fulfill a lot of promises to myself, though I still have a long way to go. But it was an honor to have had the experience of playing for the New York Rangers and producing at a high level after that awful start. When I got better, the team got better."

The prospects of Gilbert walking again were excellent. Whether he'd ever play hockey again, no one could say.

Indeed, Gilbert came through the surgery and rehabilitation well and scored 28 goals the next year when he led the Rangers into the playoffs for the first time in five years.

Sailing across the ice with elegance and determination, Gilbert soon emerged as the face of the franchise—the Rangers' very own Mickey Mantle. And like New York's *other* No. 7, Gilbert had an outgoing personality and love of the nightlife that made him a natural fit in the Big Apple, even if his coaches didn't always approve.

"The reputation was 'Rod Gilbert, Playboy' all throughout my career," he said. "If the definition of being a playboy is going out and enjoying the company of beautiful ladies, good food, traveling, dancing and enjoying life, then I'm a playboy."

It was in 1968–69 that Gilbert began playing on a line with Ratelle, his childhood pal, and the more physical Vic Hadfield. In 1971–72, the "G-A-G Line" (the "Goal-A-Game Line") made history by becoming the first line on which each player reached the 40-goal mark. As well, all three finished in the top five of the NHL's scoring race and propelled the Rangers into the Stanley Cup Finals.

It was to be Gilbert's best and last chance at a ring, for although the Rangers of the early 1970s were solid in so many areas—seasons of 49, 47 and 48 wins confirmed their regular-season dominance—the playoffs remained an annual source of frustration and disappointment.

"With Brad Park and Vic and Ratelle, we all wanted to be successful," Gilbert said. "But we were only as strong as our weakest link. I recall that the bigger the game was in the playoffs, some players didn't play hard, they didn't come up big. Some of the players didn't play to their fullest capability and it happened four or five years in a row. Yes, Ratelle broke his leg one year, but four or five years in a row we could have won the Cup. We had the better team. We *supposedly* had the better team. It didn't work out that way."

Gilbert continued to be a valuable performer well into his mid-30s, and in fact played some of his best hockey during that time. From 1973–74 to 1975–76, he had three consecutive 36-goal seasons, including a career-high 97 points in 1974–75. In 1976, 16 years after a back injury almost ended his career, the league presented Gilbert with the Bill Masterton Trophy for "perseverance, sportsmanship and dedication to hockey."

But before the start of the 1977–78 season, he found himself in tense contract negotiations with general manager John Ferguson. Following a 15-day holdout, Gilbert returned to play 19 games before being cut by the club … on Thanksgiving Day, no less. It was Ferguson's way of flushing out the last of the Francis-era Rangers, and Gilbert never forgave him for it.

Although his playing career ended somewhat unceremoniously, Gilbert has enjoyed plenty of ceremonies in his honor since taking off the uniform. In 1979, the nine-time All-Star became the first Ranger to have his number retired, and in 1982, he was inducted into the Hockey Hall of Fame alongside his former coach, Emile Francis.

Now a community relations representative for the team, Gilbert remains a valued and visible member of the Ranger family— the proudest Ranger of them all.

1
BRIAN LEETCH

DEFENSEMAN

1988–2004

2

Games	Goals	Assists	Penalty minutes
1,129	240	741	525

It was once said that for every defensive gaffe he committed that led to a goal against the Rangers, he set up or scored two goals that contributed to a Ranger victory.

While it's nearly impossible to prove or disprove the validity of that assertion—Elias Sports Bureau doesn't track conjecture—there is no doubt that this defenseman's body of work places him in an elite category among homegrown Ranger superstars.

Over 17 seasons, he rewrote the team record book and did it playing a position that traditionally affords a player fewer scoring chances. A Stanley Cup hero, nine-time All-Star and future Hall-of-Famer, Brian Leetch is also regarded in some circles as arguably the best hockey player America has yet produced.

For these reasons and more, No. 2 is our unanimous choice as the No. 1 Ranger of all time.

But don't just take our word for it.

"Brian's such an understated guy and a quiet guy but he's also very sensitive," said Mark Messier, the recipient of countless passes from Leetch in their ten seasons together in New York. "He's never wanted to be in the spotlight or to be singled out individually. That's just not his style. But he deserves to be noticed as one of the greatest Rangers ever, if not *the* greatest Ranger ever."

"Bobby Orr was very special and revolutionized the game and the position of defense," play-by-play man Sam Rosen said, "and Brian Leetch brought similar qualities to the Rangers. He brought the ability to see the ice and make plays that other players could never make, to carry the puck from end to end, to move in small spaces, to score goals, and play his own defensive position. Factor in the length of his time in New York, what he brought to the team, and what he brought as a player to the entire game, and I'd certainly have no problem with calling him the top-rated Ranger."

Admittedly, Leetch's reserved public persona doesn't lend itself to acclamation of this type, and

backers of the more dynamic Messier or the gregarious Rod Gilbert might consider either to be safer choices. But like his childhood idol, Ray Bourque, Leetch always preferred to let his play do the talking.

That's how Leetch, an Army brat born in Texas but raised in Connecticut, is remembered at the exclusive Avon Old Farms prep school.

"Although Brian always had confidence in himself, he never went out of his way to be outspoken in any sense," said John Gardner, varsity hockey coach at Avon Old Farms for over 30 years. "He was a very modest and unassuming type of guy who was a very talented and unselfish team player. I don't think he took personal glory in any of his achievements. But he had the ability to make players around him better. I tell my kids to measure greatness, it's not how good you are, but how good you make your teammates."

Leetch was New York's first pick (ninth overall) in the 1986 draft, and his ascent to all-league status was not unexpected. At Boston College, he was the first freshman finalist for the Hobey Baker Award as the top player in college hockey and in 1988 was named captain of the U.S. Olympic Team.

Scouts turned the pressure up a notch or two by touting the soft-spoken teen as the next Paul Coffey, though a more accurate subject of comparison might have been Wayne Gretzky. Leetch's offensive game flowed from his superb stickhandling skills and ability to anticipate where the puck would be next if it wasn't already at the blade of his stick. He might have ended up a center if it hadn't been for his father, Jack Leetch, a former All-American at Boston College in the 1960s. A forward by trade, Jack moved back to defense in a pinch, but it wasn't a smooth transition. Skating backwards gave him fits.

"So my dad promised himself that if he had a son," Brian said, "he would have him play defense."

Skipping his sophomore year at BC to turn pro, Leetch made his Madison Square Garden debut on February 29, 1988—Marcel Dionne Night—as the Rangers hosted St. Louis.

"I had only practiced with the Rangers twice before that game," he said. "Since I played with the U.S. National Team up until February, I remember the fans in the blue seats chanting 'U-S-A!' before the anthem. Then Chris Nilan fought Tony McKegney after the opening face-off. It was only 10 seconds into the game. I remember shaking my head and saying to myself, 'Welcome to the NHL.' I went on to play 17 games for the Rangers that year."

The following season, Leetch's 23 goals (an NHL record for rookie defensemen) and 71 points earned him the 1989 Calder Trophy as rookie of the year. Then, in 1992, he won his first Norris Trophy as the league's top defenseman after becoming just the fifth blueliner ever to crack the 100-point mark in a single season, recording 22 goals and 80 assists. But despite his offensive brilliance, Leetch had only just begun to realize his responsibilities on the defensive end.

Then Mike Keenan came to town and let it be known that in the pursuit of that elusive Stanley Cup, nobody's job was safe … not even Brian's.

"I don't know if Mike was especially tough on me," Leetch said, "though that's pretty much his calling card. He gives you the *impression* that he expects more. I heard from other players that he wanted to move me and bring in Chris Chelios. Mark Messier had a lot of influence with Mike and I know for a fact he always said positive things on my behalf. Neil Smith, the general manager, felt the same way."

In truth, it didn't take any of Keenan's head games to make Leetch realize that the fate of the Rangers was inescapably linked to his own performance. Ultimately, no one could be tougher on Leetch than he was on himself.

"Brian is a perfectionist," said Jeff Beukeboom, the former defense partner whose brute strength complemented Leetch's artistry for parts of eight seasons. "You'd see him play an unbelievable game but didn't want to mention it to him because he'd always pick out what he thought was a weakness. People don't realize how competitive he was. I'd see him go in the corner against guys who outweighed him by 20 or 30 pounds and just battle and battle. He blocked shots. He did everything. He was the ultimate team player. He was mild mannered but he was so intense internally. You could feel it. You could see it."

When the Rangers won their first championship in more than 50 years in 1994, Leetch led the way as the top scorer in the postseason with a phenomenal 34 points in 23 games and was named the Conn Smythe Trophy winner as the most valuable player of the playoffs, becoming the first American (and only Ranger) to win the award.

He added a second Norris Trophy in 1997 after the Rangers advanced to the Conference Finals.

And although he never looked fully comfortable wearing the captain's "C" after Messier's acrimonious departure to Vancouver in 1998—indeed, it sometimes seemed to weigh upon him like the albatross around the mariner's neck—Leetch dutifully accepted his role and tried to lead by example during a period marked by disappointing team performances that saw the Rangers miss the playoffs year after year.

The atmosphere of failure surrounding the organization was permeable and Leetch—hotly pursued by contending teams—wouldn't have been faulted for jumping ship. But he didn't, and as much as he is identified with the historic and joyous events of 1994, his loyalty to the city, the team and its fans during the lean years helps build an even stronger case for his position atop our list.

The Rangers, in rare rebuilding mode, may have thought they were doing Brian a favor by trading him to the playoff-bound Toronto Maple Leafs for some prospects and draft picks on March 3, 2004, his 36th birthday. But this birthday "gift," delivered without an ounce of warning, was as warmly received in the Leetch household as an IRS audit. The memory of that day still stings.

"I was led to believe I would be a Ranger for my entire career," he said, "and I wanted to be there when things turned around. I had been a part of trade rumors for years but I was hurt, disappointed, and angry. To be told you're going to be a Ranger forever and then not get any warning that you're going to be traded, I had some bitterness over that."

Also caught off-guard were the Rangers fans, who never really had a chance to say goodbye or thank you to Leetch until two years later when he came back to Madison Square Garden as a member of the Boston Bruins.

The evening began with Leetch on the Bruins blue line, soaking in waves of cheers from the crowd that followed a brief pregame scoreboard and PA welcome-back message—the kind that would have reduced his pal Messier to a blubbering mess. The defenseman raised his stick a half-dozen times in a mutual salute to the fans who gave him a two-minute standing ovation.

No one could be tougher on Leetch than he was on himself.

And it concluded with the fans chanting Leetch's name throughout his final two shifts of the Rangers' 5–2 victory, and cheering with passion whenever he touched the puck in the game's closing minutes. He raised his stick one final time as he skated off the ice to the visitors' runway.

It was the sendoff Leetch never wanted … but so richly deserved.

On January 24, 2008, Leetch had to endure one more evening in the spotlight when a banner with his name and uniform number joined those of Messier and Mike Richter, his friends and former teammates, and of Rod Gilbert and Ed Giacomin, above Garden ice.

ACKNOWLEDGEMENTS

This book was a collaborative effort in the truest sense. Not since the "G-A-G Line" has a three-man unit performed so efficiently, but we had plenty of help.

It starts with our literary agent, Laurie Hawkins, who handled three overanxious authors with aplomb and pursued every lead with vigor. She was deeply committed to this project from Day One and worked diligently to find a publisher who shared our passion for professional hockey.

Enter Karen Milner and our new friends at John Wiley & Sons, who masterfully transformed our drab-looking manuscript into the masterpiece you now hold in your hands.

The vast majority of the photos appearing in this book came from the marvelous archive of the New York Rangers, access to which was provided by the team's always-accommodating Media Relations Department. Some additional images were pulled from the authors' personal collections, while others were provided by the Hockey Hall of Fame, Vintage Hockey Photos, Steve Feldman, and Joe del Tufo of Mobius New Media.

We also offer our deepest gratitude to the players, coaches, journalists, broadcasters and others who gave of their time in interviews. This book is greatly enriched by their insights and anecdotes.

To supplement those interviews, some background material was culled from *When the Rangers Were Young* by Frank Boucher with Trent Frayne (Dodd, Mead & Company, 1973), *Hockey Scouting Report 1991–92* by Frank Brown and Sherry Ross (Douglas & McIntyre, 1991), *Messier: Hockey's Dragon Slayer* by Rick Carpiniello (McGregor, 1999), *Thunder and Lightning* by Phil Esposito and Peter Golenbock (Triumph, 2003), *Hockey Stars Speak* by Stan Fischler (Warwick Publishing, 1996), *The Complete Handbook of Pro Hockey* by Zander Hollander (Signet Books, 1981), *Pro Hockey Heroes of Today* by Bill Libby (Random House, 1974), and *Pro Hockey '72–'73* by Jim Proudfoot (Pocket Books, 1972).

We were also aided by stories filed over the years by writers for *Blueshirt Bulletin*, *The New York Post*, *New York Daily News*, *New York Newsday*, *New York Times*, *Newark Star-Ledger*, and *The Sporting News*.

Additional research material was found on the Internet Hockey Database (hockeydb.com), Hockey Draft Central (hockeydraftcentral.com), Legends of Hockey (legendsofhockey.net), and NHL.com.

I would like to thank my wife of over 20 years, Amy. Without her constant support and love of sports, my involvement with this book would not have been impossible. Thanks also to my adopted greyhounds for foregoing a few walks, and to all my friends and family for giving me the encouragement to write my first book.

Russ Cohen

Mostly, I would like to thank my dear wife Janet, whose ardent support for my projects never wavers. Plus Emile Francis, whose priceless supply of hockey stories continues to dazzle; Matt Loughran for his ongoing friendship and assistance; Rob Simpson for his droll guidance and encouragement; and Stu Hackel, Vic Hadfield, Stan Fischler, Andrew Bogusch, Kieran Blake, Mike Slattery, Phil Czochanski and the late Paul Kanow for the same.

John Halligan

Like the Rangers, I have been blessed with a loyal fan base that cheers me on through good times and bad. That's why any joy I get from this achievement is shared enthusiastically with my amazingly supportive wife Amy, as well as my mother Shelley, and my brother David.

I'm almost ashamed to admit it, but I am indebted to a New Jersey Devils fan for sparking my love of hockey. That said, Tim Blake and his Sega Genesis were also at least partially responsible for me nearly flunking out of college.

There is no shame, however, in recognizing friends and mentors June Peterson and Jack Hasson for their early encouragement and invaluable instruction, or my cousin, Elysa Gardner, a gifted writer who knows more about music than I will ever know about hockey.

Adam Raider

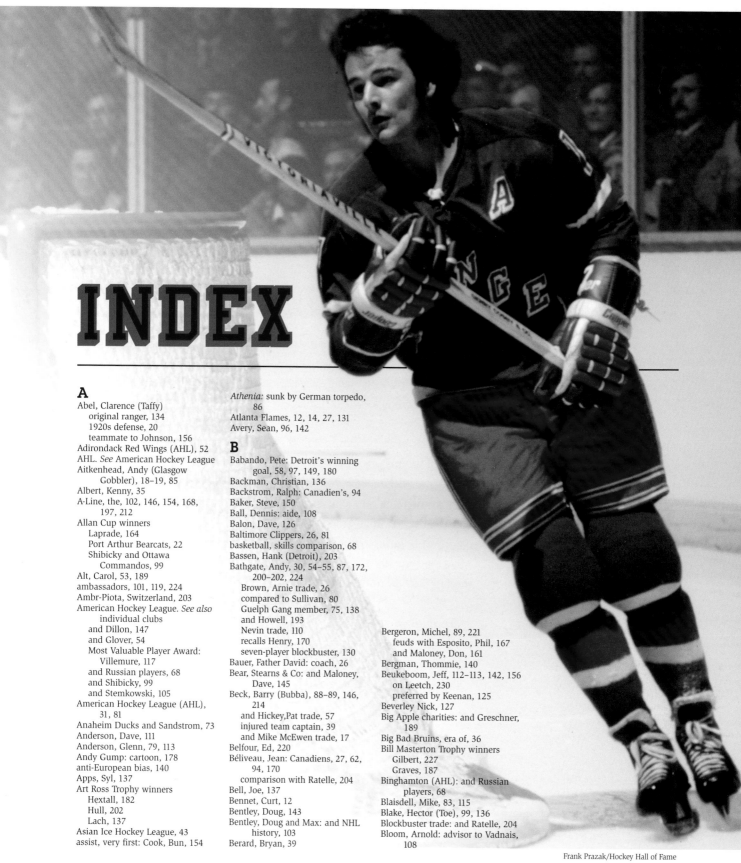

INDEX

Frank Prazak/Hockey Hall of Fame